The Bully, the Bullied, and the Not-So-Innocent Bystander

Also by
Barbara Coloroso

*kids are worth it!: Raising Resilient,
Responsible, Compassionate Kids*

*Parenting Through Crisis: Helping Kids in
Times of Loss, Grief, and Change*

*Parenting Wit and Wisdom: The Pocket Guide
to the Writings of Barbara Coloroso*

*Just Because It's Not Wrong Doesn't Make It Right:
From Toddlers to Teens, Teaching Kids to
Think and Act Ethically*

*Extraordinary Evil: A Brief History of Genocide . . .
and Why It Matters*

BARBARA COLOROSO

WITHDRAWN
The Bully, the Bullied, and the Not-So-Innocent Bystander

From Preschool to High School and Beyond:
Breaking the Cycle of Violence and Creating
More Deeply Caring Communities

wm
WILLIAM MORROW
An Imprint of HarperCollins*Publishers*

A hardcover edition of this book was published in Canada in 2002 under the title
The Bully, the Bullied and the Bystander.

FIRST COLLINS PAPERBACK EDITION PUBLISHED 2003.
SECOND COLLINS PAPERBACK EDITION PUBLISHED 2006.
FIRST WILLIAM MORROW PAPERBACK EDITION PUBLISHED 2009.
SECOND COLLINS HARDCOVER EDITION PUBLISHED 2015.
SECOND WILLIAM MORROW PAPERBACK EDITION PUBLISHED 2016.

A previous edition was catalogued by the Library of Congress as follows:

Coloroso, Barbara.
    The bully, the bullied, and the bystander: from pre-school to high school: how
parents and teachers can break the cycle of violence/Barbra Coloroso.
        p. cm.
    Includes bibliographical references (p.) and index.
    ISBN 0-06-001429-6
    1. School violence—United States—Prevention. 2. Bullying—United
States—Prevention. I. Title.
LB3013.32.C65 2002
371.7'82—dc21   2002027483

ISBN 978-0-06-257216-5 (pbk.)

    18 19 20 OV/RRD 10 9 8 7 6 5 4

To David Kent,
for asking me to write this book
and trusting that I could.
Thank you.

For my grandchildren, Adriana, Chance, and Dominic.
May you always choose to be brave-hearted.

I think we can't go around measuring our goodness by what we don't do, by what we deny ourselves, what we resist, and who we exclude. I think we've got to measure goodness by what we embrace, what we create, and who we include.

—Père Henri,
in the movie *Chocolat*

Contents

Contents

Part Two:
Breaking the Cycle of Violence and
Creating More Deeply Caring Communities

Introduction

> *I shall remember forever and will never forget*
> *Monday: my money was taken.*
> *Tuesday: names called.*
> *Wednesday: my uniform torn.*
> *Thursday: my body pouring with blood.*
> *Friday: it's ended.*
> *Saturday: freedom.*

The final diary pages of thirteen-year-old Vijay Singh. He was found hanging from the banister rail at home on Sunday.

—Neil Marr and Tim Field,
Bullycide, Death at Playtime:
An Exposé of Child Suicide
Caused by Bullying

Bullying is a life-and-death issue that we ignore at our children's peril. It can no longer be minimized and trivialized by adults, taken lightly, brushed off, or denied. Thousands of children go to school every day filled with fear and trepidation; others feign illness to avoid being taunted or attacked on the way to school or in the school yard, hallways, and bathrooms; still others manage to make themselves sick at school so as to avoid harassment in the locker room. Children who are bullied spend a lot of time thinking up ways to avoid the trauma and have little energy left for learning, or getting involved in constructive activities, or maintaining healthy relationships with their peers.

It is not only the bullied child who suffers the consequences of bullying. Some children who use physical bullying when they are young diversify and magnify their cruelty in their teen years to include dating violence, or vicious racist attacks on their peers. Many children who bully continue these learned behaviors into adulthood and are at increased risk of bullying their own children, failing at interpersonal relationships, losing jobs, and, for some, ending up in jail.

Bystanders are also affected by bullying. These onlookers may observe the bullying and turn a blind eye, walk away, jump in as accomplices, or actively intervene and help the targeted child. All of these options come at a price.

Breaking the cycle of violence involves more than merely identifying and stopping the bully or offering counseling to the targeted child. It requires that we examine why and how a child becomes a bully or the target of a bully (and sometimes both) as well as the role bystanders play in perpetuating the cycle. We must look at the cultural climate of the home, school, and community that may be cultivating the bully, reinforcing the corrupting behavior of the not-so-innocent bystanders, undermining the target of the bully, and making it difficult for brave-hearted witnesses, resisters, and defenders to stand up for the targeted child, step in, and speak out against the injustice.

A deadly combination is a bully who gets what he wants from his target; a bullied child who is afraid to tell; not-so-innocent bystanders who either watch, participate in the bullying, or look away; and adults who discount bullying as teasing, not tormenting; as a necessary part of growing up, not an impediment along the way; as "boys will be boys," not the predatory aggression that it is.

If this triad of relationships is not radically transformed, we have enough incidents in our recent past to convince us that it is not only the bully who may terrorize and haunt our community. Some victims whose cries went unheard, whose pain was ignored, whose oppression went unabated and unrelieved, have struck back with a vengeance and a rage that have racked our communities with incomprehensible horror and sorrow. Others, like Vijay Singh, who reached what they felt was an utterly hopeless and irretrievable point, have turned the violence inward and killed themselves. Feeling they had no other way out of the pain and torture heaped on them by their tormentors, no one to turn to, no way to tell, they made a tragic and final exit:

- **January 1999; Manchester, England:** Eight-year-old Marie Bentham hanged herself in her bedroom with her jump rope because she felt she could no longer face the bullies at school. Marie is thought to be Britain's youngest bullycide.
- **January 1995; Belfast, Ireland:** Maria McGovern overdosed after being bullied. The diary she left behind recorded a life of daily terror at the hands of her schoolmates.
- **April 1997; Nanaimo, British Columbia:** A grade four student pulled a knife on another student who was taunting him. According to his mother, the knife-wielding boy had been tormented by his peers for over a year. "He gave up all forms of sport, wouldn't do his homework, and would just end up leaving school—he was angry all the time. He was picked on, period. Home was the only place he could go where he wouldn't get picked on."

After the knife incident, the boy and his family were required to take an anger management course. The school took no immediate disciplinary steps against the children who had bullied him.

- **August 1997; Invercargill, New Zealand:** Fifteen-year-old Matt Ruddenklau committed suicide. The coroner's report stated, "Bullying and victimization were a significant factor in the boy's life in the months leading up to his suicide."
- **November 14, 1997; Victoria, British Columbia:** Fourteen-year-old Reena Virk died after being lured by schoolmates, attacked, and beaten unconscious. Reena's arm, neck, and back were deliberately broken before she was dumped in the Gorge Inlet. She had tried to fit in and had wanted desperately to belong to their group, but she was regularly mocked and taunted about her brown skin and her weight. Particularly startling was the fact that hundreds of students knew about the relentless taunting and even of her death before someone tipped off the police.

  Two of the girls who lured Reena to the waterway where she was mobbed and killed were sentenced to a year in custody and another year of probation. The fourteen-year-old said she was angry with Reena because she believed Reena had been spreading rumors about her. The sixteen-year-old was mad at Reena because she believed Reena had been involved with her boyfriend.
- **April 20, 1999; Littleton, Colorado:** Eric Harris and Dylan Klebold used assault weapons and homemade bombs to lay siege to their high school. The two boys killed twelve classmates and a teacher, injured eighteen other teenagers, and then killed themselves.

  Their friends said the two boys were constantly ridiculed and taunted at school. An anonymous classmate made an unfounded accusation that Eric and Dylan had brought marijuana to school, prompting a search of their property. Then there was another incident, even more humiliating than the search. "People surrounded them in the commons and squirted ketchup packets all over them, laughing at them, calling them faggots. That happened while teachers watched. They couldn't fight back. They wore the ketchup all day and went home covered with it."

In the suicide note left by Eric, it was apparent that he and Dylan felt targeted and alienated, and in their minds it was "payback time."

- **April 1999; Taber, Alberta:** A fourteen-year-old boy who was an "at home" student (he did schoolwork at home because he feared going to school) walked into the main hallway of the high school, shot and killed a seventeen-year-old student, and badly wounded another before surrendering his gun and meekly submitting to arrest. Classmates said he was "everybody's best punching bag." One student said, "He'd sometimes get body-checked into the lockers. They'd try to pick fights with him and he'd just take it. They knew he wouldn't fight back."

  The summer before the shooting, while on an outing with peers, this "new kid in town" was stuck on a rock outcropping, unable to climb up or down. His peers laughed about his predicament and taunted him instead of helping him out.

- **March 2000; Surrey, British Columbia:** Fourteen-year-old Hamed leapt to his death from the Patullo Bridge. He left a five-page note for his family describing in detail the bullying and taunting that drove him to suicide: "Mom, I was teased at school by my mates, my classmates, even my own friends laughed at me. They always called me four eyes, big nose, and geek." His mother said one of Hamed's last wishes was for people to stop bullying one another and to realize that taunting is hurtful.

Hamed's friends said they felt powerless to stop the taunting. "Everyone gets bullied. But this went too far. We stood up for him, but people couldn't get the hint that this went too far, and this pushed him." However, in his suicide note Hamed wrote that when his peers taunted him "my own friends never backed me up. They just laughed."

- **November 10, 2000; Mission, British Columbia:** Fourteen-year-old Dawn-Marie hanged herself with her dog's leash in her bedroom. She left a suicide note naming three girls at her school she said were "killing her" because of their bullying: "If I try to get help it will get worse. They are always looking for a new person to beat up and they are the toughest girls. If I ratted they would get suspended and there would be no stopping them. I love you all so much." The girls named in the note were suspended from school and later charged with uttering threats.

- **January 2001; Holyoke, Colorado:** Fourteen-year-old Miranda killed herself with a gun in her family's home. Her parents have filed a suit against local school officials for their failure to "deal seriously with the aftermath of the sexual assault" of their daughter. They accused the school district of "failing to provide their daughter with a safe and secure learning environment free of sexual harassment."

According to the suit, Miranda was a twelve-year-old student when she reported that a sixteen-year-old popular student athlete in this small rural community had raped her. The sixteen-year-old pleaded guilty to second-degree sexual assault and was sentenced to four years of probation and a deferred judgment. (He was later accused of raping and impregnating another girl. Paternity tests concluded he was the father of the child.)

Miranda's parents alleged that school officials did nothing to stop other students as well as teachers from taunting and harassing their daughter. Miranda was called a "slut" and a "whore," blamed and shamed for being a rape victim of a star student. Her parents also contend that the school took no action against the boy, against whom Miranda had obtained a restraining order. In their lawsuit, the parents said that one teacher (Miranda's basketball coach, who made it clear she supported the boy) forced the girl to stand next to her rapist in class, even though the restraining order required he not be within her sight. School officials have denied any wrongdoing.

- **March 5, 2001; Santee, California:** Andy, a fifteen-year-old high school freshman, brought a gun to school, shot and killed two schoolmates, and wounded thirteen more as well as several adults.

  Friends said he was picked on constantly. "He was so skinny that some people called him 'Anorexic Andy.'" His older brother, Michael, said Andy was used to being taunted. "He has big ears and he's real skinny. People liked to pick on him. It was like that as long as I can remember."

  "He was always getting picked on. He's scrawny, he's little," said a friend, Neil. "People think he's dumb. Recently, he had two skateboards stolen." Another teen admitted, "We abused him pretty much, I mean verbally. I called him a skinny faggot one time."

- **March 7, 2001; Williamsport, Pennsylvania:** Elizabeth, a fourteen-year-old eighth grader, brought her father's gun to school and shot and wounded a friend who allegedly turned on her and joined her tormentors.

- **November 2001; Tokyo, Japan:** A primary school boy stabbed his tormentor in an attempt to end months of *ijime* (bullying).
- **April 8, 2002; Halifax, Nova Scotia:** A popular and outgoing student, fourteen-year-old Emmet, shot and killed himself in his bedroom. He left behind a suicide note saying he could no longer take the bullying from his peers. It was reported that Emmet faced extortion, threats, and beatings from other teenagers.
- **October 2011; Otsu, Japan:** A thirteen-year-old boy jumped to his death after his classmates systematically bullied him for months. He was forced to eat paper and dead bees, tied down while his mouth was taped shut, and forced to "practice" his own suicide. Just before he died, he sent voice messages and texts to his tormentors saying, "I'm going to die." They responded, "You should die."

It has been over a decade years since I wrote the first edition of this book and, sadly, the list could go on for many more pages, detailing incidents from countries around the world. In the space of just a few months, a fourteen-year-old hanged herself, a nineteen-year-old jumped off a bridge, a thirteen-year-old shot himself, still another swallowed his father's medication to get rid of the pain and humiliation, a seventeen-year-old was found hanging from a rope outside her own bedroom window, and two eleven-year-old boys killed themselves within ten days of one another. There have been seventy-four school shootings in the United States since a young gunman killed twenty children and six teachers at Sandy Hook Elementary School in Newtown, Connecticut, on December 14, 2012. Out of the seventy-four school shootings, at least ten of the gunmen (all boys), left notes detailing humiliation and torment at the hands of their peers—no good excuses, as there are none, but part of the explanation that must be explored.

The common thread in all of these accounts is that these children were bullied relentlessly and, in most cases, the bullying went on without substantial objections, indignation, adequate intervention, or outrage. We are devastated by the final act of violence but rarely outraged by the events that led to that final act. The bottom line: These tragic outcomes need not have happened. Bullying is a learned behavior. If it can be learned, it can be examined, and it can be changed. Whether you're dealing with a long-standing or escalating problem, or whether you're concerned because your child is exhibiting some of the early warning signs—or you've seen behaviors among his or her friends that concern you—this book can help.

> *We cannot live only for ourselves. A thousand fibers connect us with our fellow men; and among those fibers, as sympathetic threads, our actions run as causes, and they come back to us as effects.*
>
> **—Herman Melville**

part one

The Bully, the Bullied, and the Not-So-Innocent Bystander

I find myself sometimes curious, often times irritated, and occasionally astonished by the whole concept of bullies, bullied, and those who are witness to the activity and remain silent. That we lack the skills of dealing with bullying in peacefully effective ways screams at us from the news headlines. And there is a line crossed all too often where the bullied becomes the bully. The idea that being excluded, shunned, ridiculed, ostracized, and physically assaulted by the bullying faction merits vengeance and violence is but one of those self-degrading ideas that we embrace, creating a cure that is worse than the disease.

—Dianne Reeves,
in a letter to the author

chapter one

Three Characters and a Tragedy

All the world's a stage,
And all the men and women merely players.
They have their exits and their entrances,
And one man in his time plays many parts. . . .

—**William Shakespeare,**
As You Like It, act 2, scene 7

Actor: Someone who behaves in a way intended to deceive or impress others.
Character Actor: Someone who specializes in playing the roles of unusual or distinctive characters.
Typecasting: To give an actor a series of parts of the same type, to the extent that the performer becomes associated with that kind of role and is overlooked for others.

The *bully, the bullied*, and *the not-so-innocent bystander* are three characters in a tragedy performed daily in our homes, schools, playgrounds, streets, and workplaces. As the examples in the introduction make clear, the play is real and the consequences can be deadly. A child who is playing "the bully" dresses, speaks, and acts the part, as do "the bullied" and "the not-so-innocent bystander." It is the posturing, the words, the actions, and the consequences of these elements combined that is the concern of this book. Young children might try out all three roles and play each one with relative ease, then abandon the bully and bullied roles to become not-so-innocent bystanders. Some children play both bully and bullied and move effortlessly between the two. A few get typecast and find it almost impossible to break out of the role they have mastered, with no opportunity to develop more constructive social skills or healthy personal relationships.

Typecasting raises the issue of language. As a former teacher, I have seen how easy, efficient, and non-productive it is to use language as a kind of shorthand to mould a diagnosis and a child into one entity and use that term as if it encapsulates that child's entire identity. A child who has diabetes is identified as a *diabetic*, a child with epilepsy is an *epileptic*, a child with asthma is an *asthmatic*, a child with a learning disability is a *learning-disabled child*. It takes a bit more effort and a few more syllables to say a *child who has epilepsy, a child who has asthma, a child who has a learning dis*ability. It is worth both more effort and more syllables to keep from defining a child by his or her illness or disability.

So why use the terms *the bully*, *the bullied*, and *the not-so-innocent bystander*? Some argue that to label the participants of a bullying episode is to typecast them and prevent them from moving out of their negative character roles. These writers prefer to focus on changing behavior and avoid labeling participants: *the person bullying, the person bullied, the person observing*. The emphasis is on providing alternatives for those taking part in or subjected to bullying.

Others use labels to intentionally typecast kids, viewing the bullying issue in black and white, as a good guy/bad guy script: "Bullies and Their Victims; the Game of Blame and Shame." In this view, it's a matter of them versus us—get rid of the bully and you get rid of the problem.

A third option is to use labels as identifiers of certain roles and the behavioral characteristics of those roles. I choose this option. When any one of these terms—the bully, the bullied, or the not-so-innocent bystander—is used in this book, it is intended to identify only a temporary role that a child is performing at that moment, in that one scene of one act in a longer play. It is not intended to define or permanently label a child's personality characteristics. The goal is to gain a clearer understanding of these roles and how the interactions involved in such role-playing, though commonplace in our culture, are not healthy, not normal, and certainly not necessary. In fact, these interactions can be devastating to children playing any of the three characters and to the community as a whole.

Once we understand these roles, we can begin to rewrite the script and create alternative, healthier roles that require no pretense and no violence. We can rechannel the governing or controlling behavior of the bully positively into leadership activities. The nonaggressive, deeply caring, sensitive behaviors of the bullied can be acknowledged and developed as strengths. The role of the not-so-innocent bystander can be transformed into that of a brave-hearted witness, resister, or defender: a person willing to stand up for a target, to speak out and act against an injustice.

Our children are not merely acting out their scripts, they are living them. They can't go home after a performance and "get real," because home is a part of their stage. But the scripts can be rewritten, new roles created, the plot changed, the stage reset, and the tragic ending scrapped. The actors can't do it alone. We adults have to get out of our seats—we cannot afford to be a passive, inattentive, bored, alarmed, or deeply saddened audience. We can't walk out, close the show, and send it somewhere else. We can't merely banish the bully and mourn the bullied child. It's the roles that must be abandoned, not our children. Our children need a new play, and we adults, along with our youth, can become active participants in a total rewrite. Before we can begin the rewrite, though, we need to analyze and understand the original tragedy.

Scenes from a Tragedy

The Bully, the Bullied, and the Not-So-Innocent Bystander is a play of many versions with the same tragic themes rendered by different actors, wearing different costumes, reading different lines.

The scene is set:

- An environment that nurtures and facilitates unquestioning obedience to authority; the routinization of cruelty, in which "mean" is the norm; and the dehumanization and denigration of individuals who are deemed less than worthy of dignity and respect.
- A culture that rewards bullies and blames targets.
- Schools that pretend to not have a bullying problem; that have a well-established hierarchy of student cliques; and that have no effective policies, procedures, or programs to address bullying.
- Parents who model and/or teach Bullying 101 at home.
- Adults who don't see—or choose not to see—the suffering or hear the cries of kids who are bullied.

Act One: Survey the Landscape

The bully surveys the playground, checks out the other characters in an attempt to identify potential targets, and looks to the audience to see if any adult is paying attention.

The potential target is playing with a ball against the schoolhouse wall, unaware or only vaguely aware that the bully is observing him.

The bystanders are throwing balls into the basketball net, laughing, enjoying one another's company and comradeship, and, without much thought, creating a deeply ingrained sense of "us versus them."

Act Two: Test Run

The bully brushes up against his target as if by accident and observes the reaction of both the bullied and the bystanders. He uses crude and hurtful names to depersonalize and denigrate the target.

The bullied target reacts with a shrug and slumps down, is uneasy, feels fear in his gut, but doesn't know what to do.

The not-so-innocent bystanders either look away or laugh, giving support and tacit approval to the bully. For some, this is a form of entertainment at the target's expense.

Act Three: Action

Viewing his target as an object of ridicule and scorn—not as a peer or an equal—the bully shoves the bullied, grabs the ball, and flings it across the playground.

The bullied blames himself for being attacked, bullies himself with words ("I'm a klutz, I'm weak, I'm a nobody"), kicks himself for being inadequate, feels powerless against the bully, tries to rationalize that the bully doesn't really mean to hurt him.

Some bystanders pretend not to see and hear what is going on; move away from the scene; and feel guilty for not stopping the bully. They feel helpless and afraid themselves, and they wonder if they will be next. Other not-so-innocent bystanders cheer the bully on or join in, verbally taunt the target, and start kicking the ball among themselves. This process of depersonalization and desensitization enables both the bully and the not-so-innocent bystanders to commit more severe acts of violence and aggression against the bullied kid.

Act Four: Emboldened

The bully finds new opportunities to taunt and torment the bullied kid. He becomes more physically aggressive and threatens more harm in order to instill terror in his target. He feels powerful when engaging the target. The results give him a sense of glee and pleasure.

The bullied spends class time figuring out ways to avoid the bully. He can't concentrate on schoolwork; gets physically sick; makes excuses to avoid the playground, bathrooms, and lunchroom; feels helpless and hopeless.

The not-so-innocent bystanders again break into two camps: One group stays clear of the bully to avoid any confrontation; the other group joins in the bullying. The first group fears the bully and the second group reveres the bully, and both groups convince themselves that they won't be next by rationalizing that the target had it coming, deserved what he got, was a wimp, was outside their limited circle of caring.

Act Five: Pinnacle of Pain

The bully continues to torment and hurt his target with increasing viciousness. He becomes typecast in the role of bully; fails to develop healthy relationships; lacks the ability to take another's perspective; is void of empathy, sympathy, or compassion; and views himself as powerful and well liked—and, indeed, by some peers and adults he is viewed as having strong leadership skills and being a "nice kid." His sense of entitlement, his intolerance toward differences, and his pleasure in excluding others are the hallmarks of his reputation.

Getting no respite from the attacks, the bullied begins to show signs of depression and may hit back at those who taget him. He is labeled as troubled or troublesome by peers and adults. Because he's been absent a lot and can't concentrate when in school, he does poorly academically—another source of pressure and shame. Not able to come up with constructive ways to regain control of his life, he spends time thinking about ways to get revenge. He might join a group of other "undesirables," who together concoct a plan for revenge, or he might withdraw further into isolation and exile in an attempt to stop the pain. He begins to resemble the dehumanized caricature the bully portrayed him to be.

The not-so-innocent bystanders do one of four things:

1. remain fearful of the bully and continue to blame the target for becoming a target of the bully;
2. join the bullying, moving up the ranks of bystanders to themselves become bullies or henchmen or active supporters; or
3. not seeing anyone else intervening, shrug their shoulders, feeling helpless to stop the bullying; or, worse yet,
4. rationalize that it is none of their concern and see no need to stop it.

Act Six: Finale

The bully grows up with a poor sense of self or an inflated sense of self, stunted social skills, and aggressive responses to provocations, slights, and perceived provocations. His bullying becomes a way of life in his personal, social, and work relationships. Seeing bullying as normal, he minimizes its damaging effects with rationalizations and excuses.

The high-status social bully is supported by the culture in the community that views his behaviors as the "norm." This support only feeds into his exaggerated sense of importance and entitlement, his feeling of superiority, and his expectations of unquestioning obedience and compliance from those around him. He often moves into a position of power in his high school, university, community, or in the business or political arena, and torments, without apparent consequence, those he sees as inferior to himself or those he sees as a threat to his own superior position.

The bullied slumps further into depression, and/or rage. He is angry with himself, with the bully, with the not-so-innocent bystanders, and with any adults who wouldn't or couldn't help him. Not trusting adults to protect or help him, and isolated from healthy peer relationships, he does whatever it takes to get rid of the pain. The pent-up rage may explode into violent aggression against the bully and all those who appeared to have helped the bully, those who stood by and did nothing, and the adults who failed to protect him. In an alternate scenario, the bullied child, with the rage imploding, kills himself to make the pain stop. In a third variant that combines the other two and is all too familiar today, he goes on a rampage that ends in multiple deaths, then kills himself or effectively ends his life by being incarcerated.

The not-so-innocent bystanders either get caught in the crossfire, feel guilt-ridden for not intervening, or become so desensitized to the violence that they minimize and normalize bullying as just part of childhood—not a big deal, just another way to toughen kids up.

The stage is set for a reprise.

Encore

No sooner does the final curtain come down on this tragedy than the bully and his accomplices begin to call for an encore. Rarely is this a flagrant justification for the ways and means of the bullies or a call for the bullying to continue, but rather it is their persistent denial that there was any bullying, and their continued shaming and blaming of the target. They declare that the target had personal problems, and that anything he did to himself or anyone else was his own fault. In the case of racial bullying, the target is often accused of being too sensitive. In the case of sexual bullying, the target is revictimized by being labeled as the wrongdoer, or accused of being complicit in the act or asking for the harm that was done.

Replace "he" with "she"; replace physical bullying with verbal bullying or shunning, rumors, and gossip; change the reason the bullied child was seen as a potential target—such as ethnicity, nationality, gender, sexual orientation, sexual identity, religion, physical attributes, mental abilities, weight, size, allergies, economic status—and you have a whole new play with the same theme, acts, and tragic ending.

This tragedy has had too long a run.

In the rest of part 1, we'll discuss what bullying is and what it isn't; statistics—the numbers behind the scene; the three main characters—their makeup, their lines, their actions; their impact on one another; and the cycle of violence they create together; as well as the dangerous myths that help perpetuate this cycle. In part 2, we'll explore how the home, school, and community can be players in setting the stage for bullying to occur and casting children into their roles. Most important, we'll look at ways for all three to come together to break the cycle of violence and create more deeply caring communities where all children can thrive.

*We have this thing about finding some simple expla-
nation which gives us the illusion that there are simple*

solutions. . . . When you look at school violence, what elevates risk is a whole bunch of things—violence in the family, violent television, bullying and being bullied, a culture that promotes violence as a successful way of getting what you want. It is most likely that the situation we're in now is an accumulation of all these factors as opposed to any one of them.

—**Dr. Howard Spivak,**
professor of pediatrics and community health at Tufts University School of Medicine and author of an editorial accompanying the first large-scale national study on bullying in schools, reported in the April 2000 issue of *Journal of the American Medical Association*

chapter two

Statistics: The Numbers Behind the Scene

*I'm doing everything I can, working with the experts, really
studying the statistics to figure out a way we can make it
cool or normal to be kind and loving.*

—**Lady Gaga**

In a study conducted by the Henry J. Kaiser Family Foundation, a U.S. health care philanthropy organization, in conjunction with the Nickelodeon TV network and Children Now, a youth advocacy group, almost three-quarters of preteens interviewed said bullying is a regular occurrence at school and that it becomes even more pervasive as kids start high school; 86 percent of children between the ages of twelve and fifteen said that they get taunted or bullied at school—making bullying more prevalent than smoking, alcohol, drugs, or sex among the same age group. More than half of children between the ages of eight and eleven said that bullying is a "big problem" at school. "It's a big concern on kids' minds. It's something they're dealing with every day," reported Lauren Asher of the Henry J. Kaiser Family Foundation.

Dr. Debra J. Pepler and her colleagues at the LaMarsh Centre for Research on Violence and Conflict Resolution at York University conducted a descriptive study on bullying at the request of the

Toronto Board of Education. Drawing on answers given by the 211 students in fourteen classes from grades four through eight, their teachers, and their parents, two other researchers, S. Zeigler and M. Rosenstein-Manner, compiled the following statistics in 1991:

- 35 percent of the kids were directly involved in bullying incidents.
- 38 percent of students identified as special education students were bullied, compared with 18 percent of other students.
- 24 percent reported that race-related bullying occurred now and then or often.
- 23 percent of the students bullied and 71 percent of the teachers reported that teachers intervened often or almost always.

This last statistic coincides with the other data collected about parents and teachers in the survey. Parents and teachers greatly underestimated the frequency of bullying when compared with student responses. This was true when Dr. Wendy M. Craig of Queen's University and Dr. Debra J. Pepler of York University did their original research and remains basically the same today.

It is both fascinating and discouraging to compare the statistics from students' responses to bullying surveys and those of school staff. In a 2007 study, "Bullying and Peer Victimization at School: Perceptual Differences Between Students and School Staff," researchers C. P. Bradshaw, A. L. Sawyer, and L. M. O'Brennan reported that 87 percent of the staff thought they had effective strategies for handling bullying; 97 percent said they would intervene if they saw bullying, yet only 21 percent of students involved in bullying said they reported it to a staff member. In the

2011 National Education Association report, "Findings from the National Education Association's Nationwide Study of Bullying: Teachers' and Educational Support Professionals' Perspectives," 5,064 NEA members—including 2,163 teachers from levels K–12 and 2,901 Educational Support Professionals (ESPs) were surveyed. According to the report, this is "the first large-scale nationwide study examining different staff members' perspectives on bullying and prevention."

Data from the survey indicated that:

- 43 percent perceived bullying to be a moderate or major problem at their school.
- 62 percent said they had witnessed bullying two or more times in the last month.
- Teachers viewed bullying as a significantly greater problem at their schools than did the ESPs.
- 45 percent of teachers and 35 percent of ESPs said students had reported bullying to them in the last month.
- 16 percent of both groups said parents had reported bullying to them in the last month.
- 66 percent working in middle schools and 65 percent working in urban areas were more likely to report that they had frequently witnessed bullying.
- 59 percent working in middle schools and 54 percent working in urban schools were more likely to perceive bullying as a serious problem.
- School staff across the board reported that verbal bullying (59 percent), social/relational bullying (50 percent), and physical bullying (39 percent) were of greater concern than cyberbullying (17 percent).

- Verbal bullying was most likely, whereas cyberbullying and sexting were the least likely to be reported to both teachers and ESPs.
- School staff reported that bullying based on weight (23 percent), gender (20 percent), perceived sexual orientation (18 percent), or disability (12 percent) were of concern in their school.
- School staff reported being least comfortable intervening in bullying related to sexual orientation and gender issues;
- 93 percent said their district had implemented a bullying prevention policy.
- Only 55 percent of the teachers and 46 percent of the ESPs reported having received training related to the policy.
- Staff in urban schools were less likely to report the existence of a district policy, and less likely to have received training on the policy (80 percent).
- 80 percent said their district's policy was adequate, and 80 percent thought it was clear and easy to implement.
- 40 percent of staff were directly involved in formal bullying prevention activities.
- 98 percent thought it was "their job" to intervene when they witnessed bullying.
- Only 58 percent reported that their school had implemented formal bullying prevention activities (47 percent in urban areas and 51 percent in high schools).
- 42 percent of teachers and 27 percent of ESPs indicated direct involvement in bullying prevention activities.
- The lowest overall staff involvement was in high schools (24 percent).

It appears that where the need is the greatest, the response is the weakest. When the majority of bullying is done not in the classroom but in the hallways, bathrooms, lunchrooms, and play yards, it should be the ESPs, as well as the teachers, who have intensive training in how to respond effectively in those settings when they witness bullying or it is reported to them.

In 2009, researchers at the University of Warwick published their findings on bullying after following 6,437 children from birth to thirteen years of age. The team found that the children's peers relentlessly targeted 13.7 percent of the children in the study over a number of years; 5.2 percent of the ten-year-old children had been severely targeted verbally, physically, and relationally by their peers. The most troubling of their findings was that children who are targeted by their peers are twice as likely to develop psychotic symptoms by the time they reach the early teen years as their peers who were never targeted. Those targeted over a period of several years are four times more likely than their non-bullied peers to develop psychotic-like symptoms by the time they reached twelve years old. The lead researcher, Professor Dieter Wolke, said: "Our research shows that being victimized can have serious effects on altering perceptions of the world, such as hallucinations, delusions or bizarre thoughts where the person's insights into why this is happening is reduced."

In "Being Bullied During Childhood and the Prospective Pathways to Self-Harm in Late Adolescence," a May 2013 study, researchers at the University of Warwick and their colleagues at the University of Bristol found that children who are targeted by their peers during the elementary school years are more likely to self-harm in their teen years than are their non-bullied peers. The study found that 16.5 percent of sixteen- and seventeen-year-olds had self-harmed in the previous year, and 26.9 percent of these did so because they felt as though they "wanted to die." Those children who were targeted relentlessly by their peers in the elementary years were four to five times more likely than their non-bullied peers to self-harm in their teen years.

Commenting on the results of the study, which were published in the *Journal of the American Academy of Child and Adolescent Psychiatry*, lead researcher Dieter Wolke explained their importance: "It is further evidence for doing away with the myth that bullying at a young age can be viewed as a harmless rite of passage. I'd like to see clinicians routinely asking children about bullying—from name-calling to more physical acts of abuse. The importance of this early intervention should not be understated."

Weight-Based Targeting: "Bodies Aren't Ugly, Bullying Is"

Frustrated and alarmed by the hateful comments online about body size, Jes Baker began the campaign "Bodies Aren't Ugly, Bullying Is" on her Militant Baker website (www.TheMilitantBaker.com), inviting people to post their own photos as a rebuke to rampant body-shaming on the Web. She writes, "I may be used to reading this kinda junk by now, but that doesn't make it any less alarming when the top searches for fat people include things like: fat people are disgusting, don't have feelings, deserve to be bullied, and should die. This immense hatred baffles me."

Despite the known serious consequences emotionally, mentally, and physically for young people targeted because of their weight, few studies have examined weight-based victimization (WBV). In one of the most comprehensive studies to date, "Weight-Based Victimization: Bullying Experiences of Weight Loss Treatment–Seeking Youth," by Rebecca M. Puhl, PhD; Jamie Lee Peterson, MA; and Joerg Luedicke, MS, of the Rudd Center for

Food Policy and Obesity, 361 teens ages fourteen to eighteen who had enrolled in two U.S. weight-loss camps were surveyed. The findings of this 2012 study indicated that:

- 64 percent reported WBV at school (the risk increased with body weight).
- 78 percent said the bullying went on for at least a year.
- 36 percent said they were bullied for five years.
- 92 percent of the perpetrators were peers.
- 70 percent of the perpetrators were supposed friends.
- 42 percent of the perpetrators were physical education teachers and sport coaches.
- 37 percent of the perpetrators were parents.
- 27 percent of the perpetrators were teachers.

As is typical in most bullying scenarios, verbal bullying was the most frequent (75 to 88 percent), relational bullying was second (74 to 82 percent), cyberbullying was third (59 to 61 percent), and the least frequent was physical bullying (33 to 61 percent).

The researchers found that WBV is a prevalent experience at home, school, and in the community for youth seeking weight loss treatment, "even when they were no longer overweight." Parents and educators need to be alert to the weight-based targeting of even those who are "currently in the healthy weight range," not just those who are already overweight or obese.

Three additional pressing concerns were mentioned in the study:

1. Overweight teens may "experience increased psychological distress (i.e., depressive symptoms, suicidal ideation, self-injury, suicide attempts) if subject to cyberbullying in addition to other forms of bullying."

2. "Of considerable concern is the high percentage of adolescents (37 percent) who reported WBV from their parents." Research has shown that the emotional and mental health problems for targeted youth are multiplied when the targeting is from multiple sources such as peers and parents. There is no safe harbor or escape for the targeted teen.

3. Teens are often targeted "because of people they were associated with, including friends (74 percent), dating partners (65 percent), and family members (32 percent). This is known as proximity bias—that is, "obesity stigma is extended to individuals closely associated with an obese person."

It is important to note that proximity bias is not unique to WBV. Children with siblings who have a disability can be taunted by their peers for attempting to stand up for their brother or sister. Teens who have a sibling or friend who has been sexually bullied are often ostracized or taunted, the stigma of sexual assault extending to anyone close to the target.

Sexual Bullying

The statistics for all types of bullying and their impact on kids who are targeted paint an ugly picture worldwide, and should be a clarion call to all of us to be active participants in early intervention. Some of the most disconcerting statistics are those that have been compiled around all forms of sexual bullying.

Comparing the results of the 1993 "Hostile Hallways" study with the latest (2001) "Hostile Hallways" study, both conducted by the American Association of University Women (AAUW) Educational Foundation, the writers noted that:

"Two findings stand out dramatically from 1993: Students today are more likely to say their schools have a sexual harassment policy or their schools distribute literature on sexual harassment. Seven in 10 students say yes, their schools have a policy on sexual harassment, while more than one third say yes, their schools distribute literature about this issue. Both findings represent substantial increases over 1993, when the plurality of students answered the same question with either no or I'm not sure."

Although the information on sexual bullying is available to most students today, the disheartening news is that the statistics for students experiencing some form of sexual bullying has not changed, i.e., "as in 1993, eight in 10 students experience some form of sexual harassment at sometime during their school lives." The finding that more boys in the 2001 study reported being sexually bullied than reported in the 1993 study could be indicative of the fact that boys are more comfortable reporting now than in 1993, or could indicate that sexual bullying is becoming an equal opportunity offense.

The 2001 questionnaire responses given by 2,064 students from grades eight to eleven offered some startling information:

- 83 percent of girls and 79 percent of boys reported having experienced sexual harassment.
- 57 percent of girls and 42 percent of boys reported being touched, grabbed, or pinched in a sexual way.
- 53 percent of girls and 43 percent of boys reported being intentionally brushed up against in a sexual way.
- 34 percent of girls and 28 percent of boys reported having their clothing pulled at in a sexual way.
- 34 percent of girls and 23 percent of boys reported being blocked or cornered in a sexual way.

- 7 percent of girls and 7 percent of boys reported being forced to kiss someone.
- 12 percent of girls and 19 percent of boys reported having someone pull their clothing off or down.
- 9 percent of girls and 12 percent of boys reported being forced to do something sexual other than kissing.

One-third of the kids surveyed reported experiencing sexual bullying in sixth grade or earlier. Boys and girls reported experiencing sexual harassment in the hallway (73 percent), in the classroom (65 percent), on the school grounds (48 percent), and in the cafeteria (34 percent). The 2001 study pointed to serious educational consequences as well as significant threats to the physical and emotional well-being of targeted kids.

The changes in the lives of those who were sexually bullied include:

1. Avoiding the person who bothered or harassed them (40 percent).
2. Not talking as much in class (24 percent).
3. Not wanting to go to school (22 percent).
4. Changing their seat in class to get farther away from someone (21 percent).
5. Finding it hard to pay attention in school (20 percent).
6. Staying away from particular places in the school or on the school grounds (18 percent).
7. Finding it hard to study (16 percent).
8. Losing their appetite or not being interested in eating (16 percent).
9. Staying home from school or cutting a class (16 percent).

Girls who mature early and boys who mature late are at a high risk for being targeted for sexual bullying. Kids of different sexual orientation, or sexual identification different from the majority, are likely to be bullied. In the article "Young, Gay, and Bullied" (*Young People Now*) researcher I. Rivers wrote about his 1996 study, in which he interviewed 140 gay and lesbian young people. He found that 80 percent of those responding had experienced taunting about their sexual orientation, and over half had been physically assaulted or ridiculed by peers or teachers. Similar results were reported in the 2012 survey "Growing Up LGBT in America—HRC Youth Survey Report Key Findings." More than ten thousand LGBT-identified youth, aged thirteen to seventeen, participated in the survey, which was conducted by the Human Rights Campaign.

- 51 percent of LGBT youth say they have been verbally bullied, compared to 25 percent of non-LGBT students.
- 17 percent report that they have been physically assaulted, kicked, or shoved at school, compared to 10 percent of their peers.
- 48 percent of LGBT youth say their peers have excluded them because they are different, compared to 26 percent of their peers.

One of the youth taking the survey expressed that: "I want to be able to go to school without being called a faggot or a dyke bitch. I don't want to hide in the shadows about my sexuality because my safety is on the line." This young person's fear is well founded. The Ashland School District in Wisconsin paid $900,000 to Jamie Nabozny, who was subjected to homophobic slurs and repeated vicious assaults by his peers and adults in the district. The administrators failed to respond to numerous complaints against his perpetrators and at times vigorously defended the bullies and blamed Jamie for the violence. The movie *Bullied: A Student, a School and a Case That Made History* documented the case.

According to the "National Transgender Discrimination Survey," a 2011 report on the nearly 6,500 transgendered and gender-nonconforming people from each state in the United States, almost 80 percent of transgendered youth said that their peers had targeted them. A staggering 41 percent said they had attempted suicide.

A Global Perspective on Gender Inequality and Violence

In an editorial in the *New York Times* entitled "Yes, All Men," Charles M. Blow talks about a discussion he had with his son while driving back to college. His son said, "I believe it's very important for everyone to be a feminist." His growing awareness of his own male privilege and the overt and covert gender inequality that is not just a problem in developing countries, but in our own, was laid out more clearly after tuning into the #YesAllWomen Twitter campaign. (The hashtag was created to raise awareness and create dialogue around the issues of violence against women after the 2014 Isla Vista killings by a man who blogged about his hatred of women.) In his editorial, Blow cites a few of the sobering statistics from the 2013 global review of available data by the United Nations Entity for Gender Equality and the Empowerment of Women:

- 35 percent of women worldwide have experienced intimate-partner violence or non-partner sexual violence.
- In some national violence studies, up to 70 percent of women have experienced violence in their lifetime from an intimate partner.

- In Australia, Canada, Israel, South Africa, and the United States, intimate-partner violence accounts for between 40 to 70 percent of sexual violence reported.
- Aproximately 140 million girls and women in the world have suffered female genital mutilation/cutting.
- In the United States, 83 percent of girls ages twelve to sixteen have experienced some form of sexual harassment in public schools.

Noting that the underlying problems are female objectification and discrimination (the same underlying problems that young girls face in the hostile hallways of our schools), Blow writes that "fighting sexism and misogyny isn't just women's work . . . it must also be the pursuit of men. Only when men learn to recognize misogyny will we be able to rid the world of it. Not all men are part of the problem, but, yes, all men must be part of the solution."

Cyberbullying

The most significant finding of the 2014 "Teens and the Screen Study: Exploring Online Privacy, Social Networking and Cyberbullying," conducted by McAfee, a subsidiary of Intel Security, was the startling statistic that of 1,502 youth aged ten to eighteen in the United States, 87 percent had witnessed cruel behavior online versus 2013's figure of only 27 percent.

Other statistics that should cause us all to reflect on the impact such cruelty online has on our youth offline:

- 72 percent said they were targeted because of their appearance.
- 26 percent said they were targeted because of their ethnicity or race.

- 23 percent said they were targeted because of their sexuality or perceived sexual orientation.
- 53 percent who witnessed the cyber attacks said the target became defensive or angry.
- 47 percent observed that the cyber-attack targets deleted their social media accounts.
- 24 percent of all of those surveyed said they did not know what to do if they were targeted online.
- 50 percent said they had been involved in an argument because of something posted on social media (the study in 2013 found only 33 percent had been involved).
- 4 percent said the online bullying had led to on offline physical altercation.
- 61 percent said they had enabled the privacy settings on their online profiles to protect their privacy and their contents.
- 52 percent do not turn off their GPS services or location services—making them accessible to strangers.
- 59 percent have interacted with strangers online.
- 9 percent met the online stranger offline.
- 14 percent had posted their home addresses online.
- 97 percent frequent YouTube on a weekly basis.
- 92 percent frequent Instagram on a weekly basis.
- 90 percent thought their parents trusted them to do what was right online.
- 45 percent would change their online behavior if they knew their parents were watching.
- 53 percent clear their online history and close or minimize their Web browser if a parent enters the room.
- 79 percent have not used the Internet or social media to reinvent themselves.
- 33 percent said they feel more accepted on social media sites than they do offline.

- 25 percent are afraid their privacy will be compromised online.
- 25 percent are afraid of being hacked.
- 16 percent are afraid of being unpopular online.
- 12 percent are afraid they might be cyberbullied.
- 77 percent know that what is posted online is permanent and public.
- 49 percent have regretted something they posted online.

The study's report listed its top five recommendations for parents to help educate their kids:

1. **Connect with your kids.** Casually talk to them about the risks of all online connections and make sure the communication lines are open.
2. **Gain access.** Parents should have passwords for their children's social media accounts and passcodes to their children's devices to have full access at any given moment.
3. **Learn their technology.** Stay one step ahead and take the time to research the various devices your kids use. You want to know more about their devices than they do.
4. **Get social.** Stay knowledgeable about the newest and latest social networks. [And I would add apps to the list.] You don't have to create an account but it is important to understand how they work and if your kids are on them.
5. **Reputation management.** Make sure your kids are aware anything they post online does not have an expiration date.

None of us can stand by idly as so many of our boys and girls throughout the world are being targeted in their homes, schools, and communities. The statistics are the bare bones of the problem. In order to begin to flesh out the solutions, we need to have a better understanding of the conditions that allow such cruelty to flourish and that weaken our moral inhibitions against such violence. We need to believe that we can create conditions that will strengthen our inhibitions against violence and nurture the bonds that connect us to one another. To do this we must understand what bullying is and what it isn't.

> *When the dignity and safety of an individual is assaulted,*
> *the dignity and fabric of the group as a whole is diminished.*

—William M. Bukowski and Lorrie K. Sippola,
"Groups, Individuals, and Victimization: A View of the
Peer System" (*Peer Harassment in School*)

chapter three

Bullying: What It Is and What It Isn't

> *Not surprisingly, there has been no absolute consensus on*
> *how bullying should be defined. And yet its definition is a*
> *very important matter. Unless there is a reasonable level*
> *of agreement about what bullying is we cannot usefully*
> *discuss it and we cannot collaborate in countering it.*
>
>   *In the most general sense, I suggest that bullying is "the*
> *systematic abuse of power in interpersonal relationships."*
>
>   **—Ken Rigby,**
>   *Children and Bullying*

As the statistics show, young people are confronting bullying more than many of us realize or are willing to admit. According to the National Association of School Psychologists, about one in seven schoolchildren has been either a bully or the target of a bully. Kids, parents, and educators need to feel more comfortable talking together about what's really going on in kids' lives. Before we can begin such a constructive conversation, two obstacles must be overcome: ignorance and apathy. First, not *knowing* what bullying is, what roles people play in this tragedy, and how to break the cycle of violence means not being able to address these issues effectively and allowing a culture of mean to flourish. Second, not *caring* about the person who is targeted by the bully, or not caring that bullying is happening in the home, school, community, or workplace is an even greater impediment than not knowing. Ignorance can be remedied through thoughtful and effective instruction. Not caring is harder to fix.

Empathy, Sympathy, and Compassion

Kindness is in our power, even when fondness is not.

—Samuel Johnson

In our encounters with one another, it is not always necessary to "like" the other person, but we must honor their humanity and treat them with dignity and regard. Martin Buber called such encounters "meeting one another as an I and a Thou." To see the other as a "Thou" is to honor their uniqueness and individuality, and at the same time to recognize our common bond, our solidarity, our interdependence, and our interconnectedness. What seems a paradox is actually two necessary parts of the whole: individuality and commonality. We are both an "I and Thou" and a "We."

Compassion is the sympathetic consciousness of another's sorrow, pain, or misery, together with the passion and desire to alleviate it. This passion is more than a sentiment or a thought. It is knowing, feeling, and being compelled to do something to alleviate another's misery or hurt. Theologian and writer Matthew Fox said, "Compassion is not sentiment but is making justice and doing works of mercy." Without actions of "making justice and doing works of mercy" we remain merely agitated, sorrowful, or concerned. There is no compassion without action.

The driving forces behind compassion are empathy and sympathy. Empathy and sympathy are often mistakenly referred to as if they are one and the same. They are not. When we empathize we *resonate* with another, we echo or amplify that person's feelings. When we sympathize we *respond* to another, and our feelings are in harmony with the other's but are not the same. Both empathy and sympathy are critical to human bonding. For children, feeling empathy—echoing or resonating with another person's feelings— is the beginning of their knowledge that we are all made of the same delicate fabric. Sympathy is sorrow or concern in response to someone else's distress or misery. Empathy helps create the sense of "We" through feelings in common; sympathy helps create the sense of "I and Thou" through two unique feelings, each bound to the other by the "and." The more children can do both—respond and resonate—the better able they will be to act compassionately when one of their peers is targeted.

Empathy can be corrupted, perverted, or negated. Children who bully often have empathy in the sense that they are able to vicariously experience the targeted child's feelings, but instead of resonating with these feelings, they take great glee in causing further distress to the targeted child.

Sympathy can be just as easily corrupted. Sympathy is not merely feeling sorry or upset about someone else's plight. It is a much greater regard, a deep sorrow and concern for the weal and woe of the other. Often labeled as sappy, sentimental, or patronizing, sympathy is none of these when it is a sincere response to another's pain. Perverted or corrupted, it can be all three. When a person wants to *appear* sympathetic but is not really open to taking in the other person's distress, his reaction—not *response*—will tend to be artificial, sappy, sentimental, and/or patronizing. With flowery words and a condescending tone, the imposter talks a good talk but has no intention of relieving the other person's pain. Such a show of sympathy is merely an act of self-indulgence. An administrator who gives a condolence speech after a student in the school has committed bullycide but who did little or nothing effective to relieve that child's suffering before the suicide and then does little or nothing to make sure it doesn't happen again is the embodiment of sympathy corrupted. Bullies crying and offering a meaningless apology to the peer they targeted ("I'm sorry if you were offended." "We didn't mean to hurt you.") are usually crying and offering the apology only because they got caught and they care about what could happen to them, not because they care about their peer.

Empathy and sympathy can be negated by rationalizing that the targeted children brought their problems on themselves, or that they somehow deserved the misery, or that they are "not like us." Empathy and sympathy can be overwhelmed, especially when the tragedy, such as a school shooting, is so devastating that the one who feels the empathy or sympathy begins to feel helpless and hopeless. Both emotions can be overwhelmed by anger. When a bullied teen finally strikes back, sympathy for him can be overwhelmed by the frustration and anger we feel because of the act and the hurt inflicted, often on innocent parties as well as on those who targeted him. Both empathy and sympathy can be drowned by a clamor for revenge, and totally deadened by hatred.

Contempt Is the Key

Bullying is not about anger. It's not about conflict. It's about contempt—a powerful feeling of dislike or disdain toward somebody considered to be worthless, inferior, or undeserving of respect. Just as bullying can range from mild to moderate to severe, so contempt can range from disregard to scorn to hate. The biases at the foundation of this contempt are often deeply rooted attitudes found in our homes, our schools, and our society. Any bias or prejudice can and will be used by a bully to validate and justify contempt for an individual child or a group of children.

Once someone has contempt for another person, it becomes

possible to do anything to the targeted person and not feel any empathy, sympathy, compassion, or shame. In the mind of the bully, the target, no longer a "Thou," has become an "it"—less than human, not worthy of care and concern, but certainly good for some laughs, and a great target to humiliate and torment.

In Laramie, Wyoming, two young men took Matthew Shepard, beat him up, and hung him on a fence post and left him to die. Their excuse: "He was gay."

In Jasper, Texas, three young men, "for sport," dragged James Byrd Jr. behind a pickup until he was dead. One of the young men casually commented, "Yeah, but he was black."

In Littleton, Colorado, a third grader was thrown to the ground and covered with mud by her peers. As they were being reprimanded by the teacher, the leader of the mean girls giggled and said, "But she's already brown and ugly; we were just making her browner and uglier."

In each one of these cases, the bullying did not begin with the physical attack; it began with the dehumanization of the targeted person—gay, black, and brown and ugly. In the mind's eye of the bullies, the targeted person became an "it," undeserving of any kind of respect, concern, and kindness.

Such contempt comes packaged with three *apparent* psychological advantages that allow kids to harm another human being and get pleasure from the pain they inflict on their target. If any of these exist in your home, school, or community, there is fertile soil for bullying:

1. **A sense of entitlement**—the privilege and right to control, dominate, subjugate, and otherwise abuse another human being. Is there any one group that feels, acts, and is treated as superior to other groups in the community? Are there rituals and traditions that reinforce the notion that some people have more worth or value—and thus more dignity?

2. **An intolerance toward differences**—different equals inferior and thus not worthy of respect. The opposite of intolerance is not tolerance. Asking people to merely tolerate those they play and work with at home, at school, or in the community feeds into bigotry and contempt. The opposite of intolerance is to care deeply about others. This caring implies a *must* to relieve someone else's suffering, and wishing them well. It does not mean that you especially like them or want them as a friend, but if you saw them being hurt you would care deeply enough about them as human beings to want to relieve their suffering, to speak up, to step in to stop the cruelty.

3. **A liberty to exclude**—to bar, isolate, and segregate a person deemed not worthy of respect or care. Does your school or community have cliques and groups that revel in their exclusiveness and regularly exclude others? Do they treat those outside the clique as "less than"?

Bullying is *arrogance* in action. Kids who bully have an air of superiority that is sometimes a mask to cover up deep hurt and a feeling of inadequacy. They rationalize that their supposed superiority entitles them to hurt someone they hold in contempt, when in reality it is often an excuse to put someone down so they can feel "up." For others, this air of superiority is not masking or covering up a deep hurt; these kids have been taught that they *are* superior and that those whom they target are not worthy of respect or concern. They inflate their own ego by deflating someone else's.

In his profoundly moving book, *Convicted in the Womb: One Man's Journey from Prisoner to Peacemaker*, Carl Upchurch, an elementary school dropout, former gang member, and ex-convict, who became an author and respected community leader in the civil rights movement, wrote about "institutionalized racism" and its impact on him as a young child.

> The contempt for my people—every assumption, insult, and slur—was trimmed and tailored for my infant shoulders before I was born. . . . It took me more than thirty years to learn that, unlike being male or being black, being nigger wasn't coded into my DNA. . . . I grew up believing that I deserved society's contempt just because I was black. . . . I was governed by a careless, heartless ruthlessness fostered by a pervasive sense of inferiority.

By his own admission, Carl was a bullied bully. The careless, heartless ruthlessness was the hard shell he wrapped himself in to protect the quiet, gentle, sensitive child that he was from the disregard, scorn, and hate he was subjected to regularly.

When we have contempt for another person and act on that contempt, we violate, denigrate, and diminish not only the "I and Thou" but also the "We." Explaining the African concept of ubuntu, Archbishop Desmond Tutu noted that it means "I am me only because you are you; my humanity is caught up in your humanity. If I dehumanize you, I am inexorably dehumanized. . . . Concern for others is the best form of self-interest." Each one of us depends on the well-being of the whole; if the "We" is diminished, each one of us is less.

A simple and powerful storybook for younger kids to start a dialogue about being accepting of differences and celebrating our uniqueness and our interdependence is Danielle Dail's *Shoo Fly Shoo*. Buzz is trying to find a friend in his neighborhood who will play with him, but nobody wants to play with an annoying fly. All of the animals shoo him away. When he finally leaves, the animals realize what an important role he plays in all of their lives and in the environment—Buzz matters.

Bullying: A Definition

As Ken Rigby noted, in order to start the conversation, we need a common language and an understanding of the dynamics of bullying. There are numerous definitions of bullying—some far too narrow and some far too encompassing. Some define it and its solution as a conflict needing resolution. Others limit it to a continual and repeated behavior. The definition I use has been developed through my experience in dealing with the topic over the past forty years, watching the evolution of the ways and means of bullying, the programs that have been created to combat it, and the research delving into it.

For me, bullying is a conscious, willful, deliberate, offensive, malicious, or insulting activity that is intended to humiliate and harm the target while providing the perpetrator(s) pleasure in the targeted person's pain or misery. It often induces fear through threats of further aggression and can create terror. It can be verbal, physical, and/or relational; it can have as its overlay race, ethnicity, religion, gender, sexuality, sexual identity, sexual orientation, physical or mental ability, weight, allergies, or economic status. (These overlays often increase the cruelty and its impact on the target.) It can be, and often is, persistent, continual, and repeated over time, but it does not have to be. Once is enough to constitute bullying.

If it is persistent and directed at a protected-status group, it could be a form of bullying commonly called harassment, and if severe enough, could constitute a hate crime. It includes all forms of hazing and cyberbullying. In other words, this "systematic abuse of power in interpersonal relationships" is about mean, is about cruel, is about getting pleasure from someone else's pain and distress.

Four Markers of Bullying

Whether it is premeditated or seems to come out of the blue, is obvious or subtle, "in your face" or behind your back, easy to identify or cloaked in the garb of apparent friendship, done by one kid or a group of kids, bullying will always include these three markers:

1. **Imbalance of power:** The bully can be older, bigger, stronger, more verbally adept, higher up on the social ladder, of a different ethnicity, or of the opposite sex (more on this one later). The bully has more power and influence than the bullied. Sheer numbers of kids banded together to bully can create this imbalance. Bullying is not sibling rivalry, nor is it fighting that involves two equally matched kids who have a conflict.

2. **Intent to harm:** The bully means to inflict emotional and/or physical pain, expects the action to hurt, and takes pleasure in causing and witnessing the hurt. This is no accident or mistake, no slip of the tongue, no playful teasing, no misplaced foot, no inadvertent exclusion, no "Oops, I didn't mean it." The bully means to exclude, means to taunt, means to humiliate.

3. **Threat of further aggression:** Both the bully and the bullied know that the bullying can and probably will recur. This is not meant to be a one-time event, especially if the target appears vulnerable. Often it begins with verbal bullying (insults, racial slurs, derogatory sexual terms, demeaning comments about the physical or mental abilities of

the target) then escalates to relational bullying (shunning, rumor, gossip, and exclusion), and then, if the climate and culture of the school allow, the bully freely and with abandon escalates the abuse to the physical (slapping, kicking, tripping, caging [locking the target in a cage], hazing, requiring demeaning or impossible physical activities of the target, and/or depriving the target of necessary physical accommodations and comfort) knowing no one will intervene to stop the cruelty.

When bullying escalates unabated, a fourth element is added:

4.   **Terror:** Bullying is systematic violence used to intimidate and maintain dominance. Terror struck in the heart of the child targeted is not only a means to an end, it is an end in itself. Once terror is created, the bully can act without fear of recrimination or retaliation. The bullied child is rendered so powerless that he is unlikely to fight back or tell anyone about the bullying. The bully counts on bystanders becoming involved or at least doing nothing to stop the bullying. Thus the cycle of violence continues.

The Ways and Means of Bullying

There are four ways and three means of bullying. For far too long, the act of physical bullying has taken center stage in research, surveys, and in the minds of adults and kids alike. Less thought and attention have been given to the gravity of and the damage caused by the other means of bullying. For almost as long, the accepted definition of bullying has specified that, to qualify, a behavior must be continual and repeated over time. Both the emphasis on physical harm and the insistence that cruel acts be continual and repeated in order to be defined as bullying have hindered our ability to break this cycle of violence.

The four ways of bullying include:

1. a one-time malicious act;
2. continual and repeated acts of malice directed toward the target;
3. hazing; and
4. digital (or cyber) attack (aka technology-assisted bullying).

One-Time Malicious Acts

Being dunked into a toilet ("swirling") once counts; being called an Irish slut once matters; being intentionally locked out of a chat room once hurts. All of these are acts intended to harm the target, and the perpetrators get pleasure from the targeted child's pain and humiliation. "Just joking," "just fooling around," "just having fun" are the lame excuses bullies use in an attempt to reframe the acts as normal kid stuff. But in all three acts, the "just joking," the "just fooling around," the "just having fun" are *at the expense of the child who is being targeted.* "Normal kid stuff" involves laughing *with*, not *at*, another person. If these one-time malicious acts are recognized as bullying and dealt with effectively, there is less likelihood that they will be repeated, or become the first in a series of attacks on the targeted child.

If these individual acts are written off as unimportant, as something the targeted child should not be bothered by, or as "girl drama," the stage is set for a "culture of mean" to flourish, and for the targeted child to begin feeling the sting of humiliation, rejection, and isolation. In his book *The Ethics of Memory*, Avishai

Margalit explains the difference between "the memory of insult and the memory of injury (that is, the physical pain)."

> In remembering torture, the victim dwells on the humiliation, whereas in experiencing torture he dwells on the pain . . . we remember insults better than the pains in the sense of reliving them. The wounds of insult and humiliation keep bleeding long after the painful physical injuries have crusted over.

A targeted child will probably not *forget* the one act of physical cruelty, but the *memory* of the physical pain experienced during the act will likely fade. However, if that act of cruelty is not adequately addressed, the targeted child is likely to relive and dwell on the humiliation, rejection, and isolation she felt when the physical pain was inflicted, as well as the aftermath, when the not-so-innocent bystanders snicker and sneer, or taunt, or further isolate her—seeing her as an ever-weakening target.

And it is not just physical pain that begins the painful "memory of insult." Using fMRIs, researchers have demonstrated that when a child is intentionally excluded from his or peer group or verbally taunted, the brain's pain response is similar to the pain response to a physical assault. Thus, a child who is verbally or relationally bullied also experiences the "wounds of insult and humiliation (that) keep bleeding." Targeted children who are shunned and isolated by their peers will often express the wish that the bully had just hit them—it would have been less painful.

Continual and Repeated Acts of Malice

If a bully becomes emboldened by the complicity and apparent approval of the not-so-innocent bystanders as well as by the lack of consequences for his or her cruelty, the bullying will most likely continue and escalate. The most common way of bullying is continual, repeated acts of malice. (See "Scenes from a Tragedy," page 16.) And it is these continual acts of malice that can have devastating effects on the physical, mental, and emotional well-being of the targeted child.

Tina Long wrote that her seventeen-year-old son, Tyler, "committed peer-abuse driven bullycide on October 17, 2009. . . . Tyler was a bright, sweet child with autism; he was a month from earning his black belt in karate." Tyler was targeted for years by his peers in the Murray County, Georgia, school system. Peers mocked him and laughed at him. They threw him down a flight of stairs and pushed him down a set of bleachers. Tyler's dad, David Long, who found Tyler hanging by his belt, said that the bullies "took his pride from him," that he went from a fun-loving child to "just a shell of the boy we once knew. . . . He was a hollow person. . . . They would take things from him, spit in his food, call him 'gay, faggot.' One day to the next, it was continual harassment from other kids in the classroom. . . . Even after his death, some of the bullies wore leather belts on their necks to mock Tyler's death." (The Longs sued the school system and lost their case. However, the federal judge's comment in their case reaffirmed that the continual and repeated acts of cruelty by the perpetrators had real and deadly consequences. "Under those circumstances, the Court finds that the harassment was severe and pervasive. Plaintiffs provide evidence that years of harassment ultimately caused Tyler to commit suicide—necessarily barring Tyler from educational opportunities.") Had the first acts of cruelty been dealt with swiftly and effectively, Tyler would not have changed from a fun-loving child to "just a shell of the boy we once knew."

Hazing: "It's Part of the Game"

The National Federation of State High School Associations, on its website, www.NFHS.org, defines hazing as "any humiliating or dangerous activity expected of a student to belong to a group, regardless of their willingness to participate."

Hazing is more than horseplay. It is abusive and degrading, creates a climate of fear, and breeds mistrust and apathy. Often written off as a harmless initiation rite, hazing has all of the markers of bullying:

1. imbalance of power (including the target of the hazing being outnumbered by or lower on the social ladder than those doing the hazing);
2. intent to harm (being forced to drink or exercise until passing out; to eat disgusting things; to be tattooed, pierced, or shaved; being beaten or made to beat someone else; being forced to wear embarrassing or humiliating attire for the enjoyment of those who get pleasure from someone else's pain or humiliation);
3. threat of further aggression (either stated or implied— "do it or else" is the message received by the target of the hazing); and
4. terror (not knowing what will happen next or when the hazing will stop is a recipe for terror. "I was afraid of what else they might do to me").

In 1993, Brian, a teenage football player, was dragged out of the locker-room shower and taped naked to the horizontal towel rack by five of his teammates. His hands, feet, chest, and genitals were bound with athletic tape. Then the five boys brought a girl Brian had once dated into the locker room to see him hanging from the towel rack. When the incident was reported to the administration, the team was banned from the high school regional playoffs. The season was over for the boys, but the bullying for Brian was not. Players, other students, parents, and community members felt the penalty was too severe; they argued that the humiliation Brian suffered was "part of the game." "It happens all the time." "It's been going on since we were sophomores . . . nobody told us not to do it." "It was just a joke." Brian was called abusive names, shunned, and shoved by classmates. He, not his five teammates, was blamed for the cancellation of the rest of the season. He was kicked off the football squad apparently for not apologizing to the team for "ratting on them."

Although Brian's parents supported him through the whole episode, peer backlash, community outrage, and the lack of administrative support compounded the humiliation and pain of the original incident.

In 2011, drum major Robert Champion died after he was beaten by his fellow band members at Florida A&M University in a hazing ritual. Some band members protested that Champion willingly subjected himself to the beating. Several band members were charged with manslaughter and several others with felony hazing.

In 2013, nine students from Garfield High School in Seattle, Washington, were disciplined for hazing that involved paddling, egging, and forcing younger students to wear diapers. When the principal intervened, racial slurs were thrown at him. In a radio interview, one girl defended the practice of "froshing"— i.e., hazing freshman—as fun and a good way to bond; another girl described her part in the froshing activities and admitted, after the fact, that she did not feel good about having participated and wished this humiliating ritual would go away.

It is important for all of us to feel that we belong. It can be such a powerful force for young people that they often will do unspeakably cruel things to themselves and others in order to be accepted into a group. When someone complains or is hurt—or in the case of the Florida drum major, is killed in the hazing episode—people protest that the targeted person consented to the hazing.

Target consent can no longer be used as a criminal defense in jurisdictions that have laws concerning hazing or bullying. Taking into account the pressure students face when the offender is an older peer or a group of peers who could easily make things even more hostile for the one who does not "consent" to the hazing, the law recognizes that such consent may not be *actual consent*.

Fear of being ostracized, further hazed, or removed from a club or team does not make it easy for someone to object. The question should not be "Did he or she consent?" but rather "Is the activity that is required demeaning, humiliating, abusive, and/or degrading?" A second question that can affirm that the activity is hazing is "Who is having fun and at whose expense?" If the perpetrators are laughing at the target's humiliation, pain, or degradation it is a sure sign that the activity is not merely horseplay or a practical joke; it is hazing.

In an article about hazing in *USA Today*, Tamara Henry cited an April 2000 study by Alfred University concerning the "risk of initiations that include being humiliated or forced to engage in illegal or dangerous activities" when high school kids join sports teams; music, art, and theater groups; scholastic or intellectual clubs; and church groups. Of the 1,541 high school students who responded to the random survey, 48 percent said they were subjected to hazing. The statistics are disturbing: 43 percent reported being subjected to humiliating activities, 23 percent were involved in substance abuse, and 29 percent told of performing potentially illegal acts.

One of the researchers, anthropology professor Robert Meyers, commented, "Our culture views hazing as 'fun and exciting.' America's obsession with 'fun' apparently gives us license to justify almost any type of behavior, no matter how abusive." The principal investigator, Nadine Hoover, noted, "We anticipated that we would find some level of hazing. What we found distressing was the prevalence." This study was done after several students died in hazing "rituals" at Alfred. (According to data compiled by Bloomberg news, there have been more than sixty fraternity-related deaths since 2005).

In 2014 the *New York Times* reported that after six pledges drowned in a hazing *praxes* (a Portuguese term for university initiation rituals) at a prominent Portuguese university, students, faculty, and the broader community debated the value of *praxes*. Some argued that it helps to build esprit de corps while others pointed to the deaths, saying the ritual has grown increasing dangerous. One student from another Portuguese university trying to get *praxes* banned said that not joining in the degrading rituals "makes you an outcast." As the debate continues to rage, the parents of one of the dead students said that they wanted only to find out who was legally responsible for the death of their son. "We want to find out the truth, but not eliminate the *praxes*, because they've also made many students happy, including our son Pedro."

We have to wonder why it is considered "fun and exciting" to demean another human being. We speak out of both sides of our mouth when we tell children not to bully one another on the playground, then encourage or condone hazing in our schools, calling it "character building," "practical jokes," "horseplay," or "just part of the game." And even worse is for us, as adults, to model it by doing the same things and making the same lame excuses in our workplaces.

In a March 9, 2010, report on hazing in the Mississauga, Ontario, Transportation and Works Department, the following were some of the incidents detailed:

- Two male employees were bound face-to-face with duct tape on top of a large table in the sign workshop. Other employees threw water balloons at them.
- An employee was wrapped up with duct tape, thrown in the back of a truck, and driven through a car wash.
- On his birthday, an employee was told to lean over a table; other workers were instructed in turn to hit him, allegedly to "hit hard and kick or punch in the face, ribs or groin area." If the blows were not hard enough, the workers were told to hit harder.

The city was notified about the hazing in November of 2009 and ordered an investigation resulting in "changes to workplace harassment policies," but no one was suspended then. Even after a "full investigation" the city manager stated that "the behavior was in the nature of horseplay . . . locker-room behavior." After the investigation by the city's human resources department, the Ontario Ministry of Labour reviewed the case, but still no disciplinary action was taken against the perpetrators. The Peel Regional Police investigated and reported that they could not file charges, as "eyewitnesses said that the employees involved in the hazing incidents consented to the activity."

However, once cell phone–video footage of one of the hazing incidents was made public, a further investigation resulted in two supervisors being suspended without pay and required to submit written apologies to residents of Mississauga, department staff, and the city council. The same city manager who had called the incidents "horseplay" and "locker-room behavior" was now saying that she was "disgusted and appalled" by the video and "in no way do we condone this type of behavior." Then-mayor Hazel McCallion said, "As you can appreciate, it's completely unacceptable. It is contrary to the code of conduct of the employees of the city of Mississauga, and the necessary disciplinary action has been taken. The employees have been warned and if any action near this were to happen again, they would be terminated by the city. Such actions should not happen on city property and on taxpayers' money." The employee who provided the cell phone–video footage and filed the complaint with the Ministry of Labour against the Mississauga Transportation and Works Department was quoted in the *Toronto Star* on June 3, 2010: "I can assure you it's more than horseplay. It's oppression. We live in fear. I've complained repeatedly to no avail. People are afraid of coming forward to report the abuse and it is fear that compelled people to take part in hazing. . . . It's so serious, we fear for more than just our jobs. (We) fear for our safety, safety of the people I love."

He and other workers confirmed that some employees had been beaten and abused by other workers for about five years. Most said they went along with the hazing for fear of reprisal or being fired. An employee asking the question "Why didn't these (targets) fight back?" answered his own question with "I guess they had no choice. They were overpowered." Yet, some other employees said it was just "practical jokes," and was "appreciated, good-natured, and voluntary." In a blog attached to the *Toronto Star* story a blogger commented that "these guys are only trying to make their work environment a little more fun and now [the whistle-blower] has taken all of the fun out of the job."

As is typical in so many workplace (and school) hazing incidents, in the Mississauga case, the person who reported the hazing received some support and affirmation of the abusive antics from coworkers who had been targeted themselves, while others wrote it off as a practical joke—noting that a supervisor had participated in the hazing—and concluded that no harm was done. The lack of support by the supervisor, the dismissal of the complaint by the city manager, and coworker backlash against the whistle-blower compounded the humiliation and pain of the original incident.

In a 2008 survey of university students in the U.S., "Hazing in View: College Students At Risk" by Elizabeth J. Allen and Mary Madden, 95 percent who had endured hazing said that they did not report the incidences to campus authorities because:

- 37 percent did not want to get the responsible team or group in trouble.
- 20 percent were afraid of negative consequences to themselves personally from other team or group members.
- 14 percent were afraid they would be cast out if other members of the team or group found out they had reported it.
- 8 percent felt they might be hurt by the team or group if those members learned they had reported it.
- 54 percent did not report for other various reasons.

Those are legitimate fears. After a nineteen-year-old pledge reported the severe hazing rituals he and other pledges were required to undergo in order to join the fraternity Sigma Alpha Epsilon (SAE), Salisbury University in Maryland suspended the chapter from November 2012 through the spring of 2014. According to a 2013 Bloomberg news report, SAE members beat the pledges "with a paddle, forced pledges to drink until they almost passed out and dressed them in women's clothing and diapers. . . . Fraternity members confined recruits for as long as nine hours in a dark basement without food, water, or a bathroom, while blasting the same German rock song at ear-splitting volume." The pledge endured weeks of the hazing, afraid that if he quit he would be shunned. "You feel like you have so much to lose—it's worth staying. I thought it would pay off in the end." He did quit after an especially horrific hazing night and decided that "his desire to protect pledges from harm far outweighed his fear of retaliation." His grades dropped, he had trouble sleeping, and he worried about his own safety on campus.

Former and active SAE members denied his and another pledge's allegations. Even some of his fellow pledges who had gone through the same hazing denied it had ever happened (code of silence?). After the name of the pledge who broke the code of silence was leaked during the university's investigation, retribution quickly followed. His father reported that "he essentially had been blackballed from any social life, eats his meals alone and is miserable." He finally moved to another school to complete his degree. Yet he still has nightmares of his time in the basement.

Even Salisbury University was affected by the suspension of the fraternity. The founder of the SAE chapter cancelled a planned $2-million dollar pledge for the university stadium, saying spitefully, "If they decide that's the hill they want to die on, then let them." Apparently, the university taking a stand was more offensive to this alumnus than the fact that the fraternity he so cherished had the most reported fraternity-related deaths in the U.S. Since 2006 there have been more than sixty deaths related to American fraternities, nine of which occurred in SAE-related events.

One problem of our modern culture is that we have not developed healthy, appropriately rigorous rites and rituals to mark the passage from childhood into adulthood, or to mark the acceptance of an individual into a group. The Alfred University hazing study involved school- and church-sanctioned youth groups—groups that could be, and should be, places to foster more healthy initiation rites. Rites of initiation can be powerful and meaningful—and fun. They do not have to be humiliating or demeaning. Celebrations with teammates or club mates can be exciting and creative. They do not have to be cruel or sadistic. A school climate can be lightened with humor. The laughter just needs to be shared levity, not laughter at the expense of a peer.

Digital (or Cyber) Attack (aka Technology-Assisted Bullying)

The fourth way of bullying is the use of technology to intimidate, threaten, stalk, ridicule, humiliate, taunt, and spread rumors about the targeted person. Our children are venturing into the global neighborhood via the Internet, the cell phone, personal assistance devices (PADs), iPads, and tablets. In such a media-saturated world, the fundamental nature of childhood is changing. So, too, is the nature of bullying. Bullies have long tormented, intimidated, threatened, stalked, ridiculed, humiliated, taunted, and spread rumors about their targeted peers with low-tech verbal, physical, and relational tools; now they are using high-tech tools to do the same.

The last thing fourteen-year-old Dawn-Marie heard before she killed herself was the voice of one of her tormentors. The cell phone message said, "You're dead."

Bullies attacked a fourteen-year-old boy in Erskine, England, more than a hundred times in five months in 2005. On one occasion he was subjected to a "happy slapping" attack—an assault recorded by not-so-innocent bystanders using cell phone cameras. When his parents began complaining to the school, the boy admitted that he had cut his wrist in the past "to get rid of the pain" and had considered suicide.

After posting the name and address of a sixteen-year-old boy on a website devoted to soliciting sex partners for men, a teenaged bully in Massachusetts watched in amusement from across the street as men started showing up at the boy's home, expecting the date he had supposedly sought online. (It is easy to disguise your identity and/or pose as someone else. Anyone can get a Web-based e-mail account with an ISP, make up a screen name, and post comments without much fear of being caught, unless the police become involved and even then, it may take a long time for the perpetrator to be tracked down.)

In 2002, someone—probably another student in Burlington, Ontario—set up a website that made fun of a high school peer. Soon there were pages of hateful and lewd comments directed at the teenager, who had been taunted and punched for years. The humiliation he suffered from cyberbullying was the worst of all. The target explained, "Rather than just some people, say thirty in the cafeteria, hearing them yell insults at you, it's up there [on the Internet] for six billion people to see. Anyone with a computer can see it. And you can't get away from it. It doesn't go away when you come home from school. It made me feel even more trapped." He finished his final year of studies at home.

In April 2003, Ghyslain Raza, a fifteen-year-old from Trois-Rivières, Quebec, made a video of himself re-enacting a Star Wars fight scene. One schoolmate found the video and shared it with another, who digitized it on a school computer "to pull a joke" on Raza. As the video was being e-mailed among schoolmates, a third student created a website and posted the video online. One month later a blogger who had posted the video reported that the two-minute clip had been downloaded 1.1 million times. Eventually becoming an Internet meme, the video was estimated to have had over a billion hits. Raza became an international object of ridicule, and life at his own school became unbearable. Schoolmates regularly mocked and taunted him both on- and offline. Strangers online suggested he kill himself. He said the bullying left him depressed and unable to attend that school. "It was simply unbearable, totally." His parents sued the families of the three schoolmates, and in 2006, they reached an out-of-court settlement.

Ten years later, now a graduate of McGill University's law school, Ghyslain Raza spoke out about the dangers of cyberbullying in the hopes of helping others who have been cyberbullied. Raza told journalist Jonathan Trudel of the French-Canadian magazine *L'actualité* (an English translation of Raza's story appeared in *Maclean's* magazine in May 2013) that he lost his few remaining friends and had to change schools. "It was a very dark period," he said. "No matter how hard I tried to ignore people telling me to commit suicide, I couldn't help but feel worthless, like my life wasn't worth living." Raza said he hopes talking about his experience will help others deal with cyberbullying and urged other young victims to "overcome (their) shame" and seek help. "You'll survive. You'll get through it. . . . And you are not alone. You are surrounded by people who love you."

In October 2003, a thirteen-year-old boy from Essex Junction, Vermont, killed himself. His peers had targeted him since grade five. In grade seven, his peers spread ugly sexual rumors about him via the Internet, his grades dropped, and he began to spend hours on the computer. After their son's death, his parents learned he had been instant messaging (IM'ing) with a teen who was encouraging him to commit suicide. (Targeted youth are at risk for joining online communities of youth or adults who normalize, encourage, and reinforce unhealthy, harmful, or antisocial activities.)

In a chat room, Jeffrey wrote: "I'm a retarded [expletive] for ever believing that things would change. I'm starting to regret sticking around; I should have taken the razor blade express last time around"; "It takes courage to turn the gun on your own self, takes courage to face death. Knowing you're going to die actually following through takes heart, I don't care who you are"; "... kind of rocky right now so I might disappear unexpectedly." Shortly after the last entry, in April 2005, Jeffrey laid siege to his high school in Red Lake, Minnesota, and then killed himself.

On June 29, 2005, a fifteen-year-old in Cape Coral, Florida, hanged himself after being repeatedly taunted online for two years by his classmates. Those students referred to him as a "stalker of many sorts," labeled him with profane and derogatory sexual terms, and said, "He needs to die." The night before he died he e-mailed an online gaming friend from Canada and wrote, "I'll never get over eighth grade."

In April 2006, on MySpace.com, a student in Palm Springs, California, posted pornographic images and lewd comments near a fifteen-year-old girl's picture. The girl was quoted as saying, "It's not fair to me. I can't even go to school and have a regular life." This type of cyberbullying is known as revenge porn, described at www. EndRevengePorn.org as "a form of sexual abuse that involves the distribution of nude/sexually explicit photos and/or videos of an individual without their consent."

The characteristics of bullying—an imbalance of power, the intent to harm, the threat of further aggression, and the creation of terror—are magnified with the use of electronic technologies. Faceless and sometimes nameless electronic transmissions make it easy for bullies to torment their targets anywhere and at any time, with apparent anonymity and few, if any, consequences.

Cyberbullying is almost always combined with or is an entrée to other ways of bullying to create terror for the targeted child. Using cell phones or PADs, instant messaging (IM), e-mail, blogs (online journals), defamatory personal websites, diary sites, online profiles, online personal polling websites, or interactive games (online gaming), bullies are emboldened by the apparent anonymity and the ability to be an alter-self afforded them in cyberspace. They are removed from the immediate reaction of the target, and are far too often not held accountable for their actions. They can easily send messages to the target using an unknown e-mail address, a third-party website, a school or public-library computer, or a throwaway cell phone. Cyberbullies use all of these technology tools to torment their targets by:

- **Bash boarding**—using online message boards that encourage bullies to make malicious postings about the targeted peer.
- **Coding**—sending malicious code to damage the targeted peer's computer, or to steal private and personal information from the target, or to spy on the target.
- **Dissing**—sending gossip, rumors, or misinformation about the targeted peer in order to damage his or her reputation or destroy friendships.
- **Flaming**—sending an electronic message about the targeted peer that is insulting, hostile, cruel, or vulgar.
- **Impersonation**—pretending to be the targeted peer in order to get them in trouble, harm their reputation, or destroy their friendships.
- **Polling**—asking and answering hurtful or mean questions about the targeted peer.

CELL-PHONE BULLYING

Most models of today's cell phones are actually powerful, minia-ture, handheld multimedia computers that kids can use to talk to one another, chat via IM, send text and multimedia messages with still and video images, chat online, surf the Internet, download songs, watch TV, and "geolocate" one another. They make a great portable tool for cyberbullying any time, any place.

Children as young as five have reported being cyberbullied via cell phone or have themselves cyberbullied a peer or a sibling. For elementary school children, the cell phone is the electronic tool of choice for bullying. Often parents and educators closely supervise young children's time on the computer but are not as vigilant about cell phone use. Older kids often use cell phones in combination with the Internet to target their peers. Here are a few of the methods they may use:

- Abusive, insulting, or threatening voice messages.
- Abusive, insulting, or threatening text messages.
- Silent calls.
- Stolen identity (impersonation)—sending a text message to schoolmates or adults through a website using the name and phone number of the target in order to get the target into trouble, spread a rumor, or tempt others into retaliating against the unsuspecting target.
- Numerous calls or text messages (text attacks) to a cell phone in order to run up a large phone bill for the target.
- Photo bullying—using cell phones or PADs to take compromising or humiliating pictures or videos of the target, sending those pictures or videos to everyone in the bully's and/or the target's address book, and posting the pictures for perpetuity on a file-sharing service for anyone to download or view.

Teaching young people basic cell phone etiquette is a start, but parents and educators need to be aware of the ways a cell phone can be used to bully, and talk with kids about the privileges and responsibilities that come with using one. Misuse of a cell phone or any other electronic device should result in the loss of certain privileges related to that device—or removal of the device, with specific conditions for getting it back.

Messaging-App Bullying

Lest you think that cyberbullying has reached its zenith with sites like YouTube, Facebook, Twitter, and Instagram, check out your teen's phone for the latest in messaging apps. New apps are being released regularly, each with their own spin on anonymous connections and "truth-telling," which can easily morph into cyberbullying. Not intended to be used for cyberbullying, apps such as Yik Yak, Snapchat, Ask.fm, Kik, Rumr, Lulu, Whisper, and Truth have all been used to target young people who unwittingly posted texts, photos, or videos that were later used against them, or who found themselves on the receiving end of the anonymous answers to ugly questions. Three popular apps are:

1. **Yik Yak**, a text and photo messaging app that is location-enabled and allows—invites—people to say and show anything, supposedly anonymously, to anyone in a 1.5 mile radius. There are no profiles and no passwords. Teens are emboldened by the idea that whatever they say or show is anonymous and can't be connected to them. Neither is totally true. After posting a message on Yik Yak that there would be shootings at two local high schools, a teen in California was charged with three felony accounts of making a terrorist threat—serious charges for something he thought was "funny and untraceable."

2. **Snapchat**, a photo-messaging app that ostensibly allows users to send a picture or video to one or more people for a limited time, after which the photo or video supposedly disappears. In reality, it does not disappear. It can be retrieved

from a user's phone or the company's server, or can be captured in a screenshot. The once-private photo or video can become very public and may end up all over the Internet, forever—no delete button here. Those trolling the app can get live feeds of what their peers are doing.

3.   **Truth**, a messaging app that allows someone to text an anonymous message to anyone who is on their contacts list. If a teen receives a "truth" from an anonymous person, unless she has the app on her phone, she will see only an enticing part of the message and an invitation to download the app so the full message can be revealed. What is revealed can be a "truth" about something good—but then, why not say it openly or face-to-face? Canadian journalist Richard J. Needham's quote sums up what can be so wrong with anonymous truth-telling: "People who are brutally honest get more satisfaction out of the brutality than the honesty."

The biggest problem isn't the apps themselves. Good things have happened through the use of these apps. The problem is that the anonymity the apps afford allows cyberbullies to freely engage in hate speech, make indecent and obscene comments, and demean or threaten their targets. Getting ganged up on by nameless, faceless people is never fun for anyone but the bullies and their henchmen. In reviewing Rumr when it first came out, Michael Carney, the West Coast editor at PandoDaily wrote, "Rumr appears more like a digital sniper's rifle that in the wrong hands could be wielded to cause acute pain and suffering. . . . We've seen enough of the Web to know that when people can be anonymous, hate follows. Maybe it's not all hate, but there's never been a case where hate or bullying didn't follow."

INTERNET GAMING BULLYING

Games played on a gaming device like the Xbox 360, Sony Play-Station, and Wii U, or on cell phones, computers, and PADs allow players of all ages from around the world to play together or in competition with one another. The features of a game can influence the chances of a child being bullied or participating in the targeting of another player. Games that enable chatting and private messages increase the risks. The chat-box feature in most online games can allow a cyberbully to post links and codes that can damage or disable the targeted player's computer. Cyberbullies who frequent gaming communities (griefers) use the games as platforms for their bullying (griefing), where they taunt, threaten, lock their target out of the game, or hack his account. They can do all of this via text, voice, or video message. A group of players can work together to plan and execute attacks on a player they deem weak or poor at playing the game—or a player who is very good at the game—and drive the targeted player out of the game.

Not all Internet games are violent, but those that are can greatly impact the bully, the bullied, and the not-so-innocent bystander. Not only can these games normalize violence and make it routine, they set up other people as adversaries, prey, or targets. They may even help create neural pathways that connect violence with pleasure and rewards rather than with fear, sadness, or sympathy.

Some games tend to cultivate a sense of danger, mistrust, alienation, and gloom. The makers of the *Grand Theft Auto* video games—Rockstar Games, owned by Take-Two Interactive—created a malevolence-filled computer game called *Bully* in 2006 and an updated star edition, subtitled *Scholarship Edition*, in 2008. The game is set in a virtual school in which players rehearse turning the tables on school bullies and teachers, bludgeoning them with bats, shooting them with slingshots, dunking their heads into toilets, and punching, kicking, and body slamming them, all to "settle scores."

The Simon Wiesenthal Center, which keeps track of hate websites, released a report in April 2004 that noted a surge in the number of online games in which gamers can "shoot . . . illegal immigrants, Jews, and blacks." If a young gamer playing a video game routinely brutalizes or kills his on-screen opponents, and feels excitement or thrills at doing so, rather than sadness, sympathy, or fright, then when he sees a real peer being hurt or bullied he is more likely to join in the "fun" than to come to the targeted child's rescue. Throw in being rewarded in the game for maiming and killing, and you get a child more willing to participate in violent activities if he is promised some of the bounty, or is awarded higher status in a group of his peers.

CYBER SEXUAL BULLYING

Just as low-tech peer-to-peer sexual bullying is one of the most widespread forms of violence today, high-tech sexual bullying is one of the most widespread forms of violence experienced by both teenage girls and boys in the cyber world. In a 2002 study by the Girls Scouts of the United States of America, "The Net Effect: Girls and the New Media," Whitney Roban, PhD, reported that of one thousand girls aged thirteen to eighteen, 30 percent said that they had been sexually bullied in a chat room, including being subjected to pictures of naked men, demands for personal details such as bra size, and requests for cybersex. Only 7 percent of those targeted reported telling their parents, and 30 percent said they didn't tell anyone. Because our sexuality is an integral part of who we are, sexual bullying cuts to the core of our being and can have devastating consequences. Sexual bullying in cyberspace can multiply the humiliation and magnify the damage.

Feeling neither compassion for their targeted peer nor shame over what was done, cyberbullies can destroy a peer's reputation with a few keystrokes, or terrorize the target with threats, or humiliating and degrading pictures, and get great pleasure from the pain inflicted. The ability to inflict pain anonymously, and with such a wide audience to reinforce the humiliation, often emboldens the cyberbully to inflict far greater damage on the target than would have been imaginable in a face-to-face encounter. (See chapter 12, "Keeping Young People Involved, Connected, and Safe in the Net Neighborhood.")

The Three Means of Bullying

All four of these ways of bullying—one-time, continual and repeated, hazing, and cyber—can be vertical (i.e., bullying someone in your care or above you) or horizontal, (i.e., bullying a peer). A teacher or parent or older sibling who torments a child is engaging in vertical bullying. A group of teens who haze a peer are engaging in horizontal bullying. A teacher and students ganging up on another student are engaging in vertical and horizontal bullying combined—a devastating combination for the target.

There are three means of engaging in these four ways of bullying: verbal, physical, and relational (or social). Each one alone can pack a tremendous wallop, but they are often combined to create a more powerful attack. Boys and girls use verbal bullying equally. Boys tend to use physical bullying more often than girls do, and girls use relational bullying more often than boys. This difference has more to do with the socialization of males and females in our culture than with physical prowess or size. Boys tend to play in large, loosely defined groups, held together by common interests. They establish a pecking order that is clearly delineated and honored. There is jockeying for a dominant position. Physical prowess is often honored above intellectual ability. Thus we see boys shoving smaller, weaker, often smarter boys into lockers, calling them "wimp," "nerd," "sissy" (the latter word both an allusion to the inferior emotional makeup of the bullied boy and reflecting the attitude that girls are on the lowest rung of the ladder of power and respect).

Physical bullying is not exclusive to boys. Bigger girls are known to trip, shove, and poke smaller girls or smaller boys. Girls just have a more powerful tool in their social arsenal to use against other girls—relational (or social) bullying. Compared with boys, girls tend to play in small, more intimate circles with clearly defined boundaries, making it easier to harm a girl merely by excluding her from a social circle.

Verbal Bullying

"Sticks and stones may break my bones, but words will never hurt me" is a lie. Words are powerful tools and can break the spirit of a child who is on the receiving end. Verbal abuse is the most common form of bullying used by both boys and girls. The bully often rationalizes or defends this behavior by saying "I was just kidding" or "I didn't mean any harm." It accounts for 70 percent of reported bullying. It is easy to get away with and can be whispered in the presence of adults and peers without detection. It can be yelled out on the playground and blend into the din heard by the playground supervisor, written off as crass dialogue among peers. It is quick and painless for the bully and can be extremely harmful to the target. Younger children who haven't yet developed a strong sense of self are the most susceptible to it, although repeated attacks will eventually wear down even those who have a healthy sense of self and a strong support system.

The list of the verbal taunts to Hamed, the fourteen-year-old who leapt to his death in Surrey, British Columbia, filled four of the five pages of his suicide note. The most common directed at him were "four eyes," "big nose," "geek," "queer," and "fag." Elizabeth, the fourteen-year-old who shot and wounded a friend who had allegedly turned on her and joined in with her tormentors, said that they called her "idiot, stupid, fat, and ugly."

Fourteen-year-old Jamey of Buffalo, New York, was verbally bullied on- and offline from grade school through his first year of high school with comments like "faggot" and "I wouldn't care if you died. No one would, so just do it :) It would make everyone WAY more happier." As a result, he committed suicide. Posting an "It Gets Better," video shortly before his death gave his bullies another excuse to ramp up their bullying. Even in death he was taunted. After Jamey's wake, his sister attended a school dance and was subjected to chants of "We're glad you're dead" from her brother's tormentors.

If verbal bullying is allowed or condoned, it becomes normalized and the target dehumanized. Once a child has been dehumanized, it becomes easier to attack that child without eliciting the normal compassion from those who are within earshot. When a child becomes the regular butt of jokes, he or she is often excluded from other more prosocial activities, the last to be chosen, the first to be eliminated. Who wants to have a loser on their side?

Verbal bullying can take the form of name-calling, taunting, belittling, cruel criticism, personal defamation, racist slurs, and sexually suggestive or sexually abusive remarks. It can involve extortion of lunch money or possessions, abusive phone calls, intimidating e-mails, gross text messages, suggestive Twitter comments, anonymous notes containing threats of violence, untruthful accusations, false and malicious rumors, and gossip—yes, gossip can be a form of bullying. Hesiod, an eighth-century B.C. poet, called gossip "mischievous, light, and easy to raise, but grievous to bear and hard to get rid of." Gossip cheapens human relationships and sensationalizes a bullied child's problems, mistakes, and interactions: "Did you hear what she did?"

Physical Bullying

Although it is the most visible, and therefore the most readily identifiable, means of bullying, physical bullying accounts for less than one-third of the bullying incidents reported by youth. It is rarely the first means employed by bullies. Usually they will verbally and/or relationally bully the targeted child and, seeing that they can get away with such abuse, then move on to physical attacks, where the signs of distress are more visceral and the results more obvious. The older and stronger the bully, the more dangerous this kind of attack becomes, even if *serious* harm is not intended: "I only meant to scare him. I didn't mean to break his arm."

Physical bullying can include, but is not limited to, slapping, hitting, choking, poking, punching, kicking, biting, pinching, scratching, twisting limbs into painful positions, spitting, forceful confinement, and damaging or destroying clothes and property belonging to the bullied child. It can include weapons or objects used against the target.

In 2012, CNN reported that in Daegu, South Korea, thirteen-year-old Lim Seung-min jumped out of a window in his apartment building and fell seven stories to his death. He left a suicide note detailing "being beaten with sticks and boxing gloves, robbed, and burned with cigarette lighters and having electrical wire tied around his neck as a leash" by his classmates. He wrote of the years of verbal abuse, extortion, and humiliation that had preceded the physical assaults.

In the Korean language, the most common terms for this kind of cruelty are *hakkyo-pokryuk* (forcing a peer to do something he or she does not want to do, extorting, threatening, insulting); *gipdan ttadolim* (shunning and isolating); and *wang-ta*, (physical or sexual abuse). Lim Seung-min was subjected to all three. Note that he wrote of years of verbal abuse, extortion, and humiliation before the bullies moved on to the horrific physical bullying. This is a common path—verbal bullying to relational bullying to physical bullying. If you have a child who has been physically bullied, you can almost always be sure that he or she has experienced verbal and/or relational bullying in advance of the attack.

The young people who employ physical violence to bully their peers are often the most troubled and troubling of all of the bullies and most likely to move on to more violent criminal offenses.

BEYOND THE SCHOOLYARD

There are two professions in which there has been a decrease in an already low rate of horizontal physical violence (violence against one worker by another), and a significant increase in vertical physical violence (violence by someone under the targeted person's care): education and nursing. Members of both groups do experience horizontal and vertical verbal and relational bullying, but the biggest concerns they have expressed—and the most wearing—have been about the physical attacks by people they are trying to help—patients and students.

The same day that a group of young girls from Carson City, Nevada, were arrested for inviting, through Facebook, other middle school students to join them in "Attack a Teacher Day," a seventeen-year-old boy in Omaha, Nebraska, shot and killed his assistant principal and seriously wounded his vice principal before killing himself. The girls were considered good students, who had good grades, and some held leadership positions in their middle school. In other words, they were high-status social bullies. The boy had been recently suspended from high school.

In her 2010 article "Violence: Not in My Job Description," Laura A. Stokowski, RN, MS, discusses the prevalence of violence against nurses in the workplace (48 percent of all non-fatal injuries from occupational assaults and violence occurred in health care and social service settings) and the reasons nurses often do not report the abuse:

> Nurses may fear reporting violence will affect patient satisfaction scores, or that hospital administrators will retaliate. Some don't know the hospital's reporting policy or believe that they can only report visible physical injuries. Other nurses avoid reporting violence because they believe that supervisors will question their competence, suspect that they somehow provoked the incident, or label them as troublemakers if they have no obvious physical injury. When nurses do report incidences of abuse, more than 85 percent do so only verbally.

Students who are targeted and afraid to tell express similar fears. Although today most schools have a confidential and safe reporting system in place for students, they are just as likely as nurses to report the bullying only verbally and rarely at first to school personnel.

Relational (or Social) Bullying

The most difficult to detect from the outside, relational bullying is the systematic diminishment of a bullied child's sense of self through ignoring, isolating, excluding, or shunning. Shunning, an act of omission, joined with rumor, an act of commission, is a forceful bullying tool. Both are unseen and hard to detect. The child being talked about may not even hear the rumor but will still suffer from its effects. ("Stay away from him, he has cooties." "Don't hang with her; she's slept with half the boys on the baseball team. People will think you're just as easy.")

The eighteenth-century British philosopher and essayist William Hazlitt wrote that "Calumny requires no proof. The throwing out of malicious imputations against any character leaves a stain that no after-refutation can wipe out. To create an unfavorable impression, it is not necessary that certain things should be true, but that they have been said." With cyberbullying, the rumor that is spread is public, permanent, and pernicious (causing great harm or damage, often in a way that is not easily seen or noticed). No amount of apology after the fact can remove the rumor from cyberspace, nor can it remove the "unfavorable impression" that has been created.

Relational bullying can be used to alienate and reject a peer or to purposefully ruin friendships. It can involve subtle gestures such as aggressive stares, rolling of eyes, sighs, frowns, sneers, snickers, and hostile body language.

Relational bullying is at its most powerful in the middle school years, with the onset of adolescence and the accompanying physical, mental, emotional, and sexual changes. It is a time when young teens are trying to figure out who they are and trying to fit in with their peers. Intentionally excluding a child from sleepovers, birthday parties, and playground games is often overlooked as a form of bullying because it is not as readily identifiable as name-calling or a fist in the face; the results are not as obvious as a black eye or a torn jacket; and the pain it causes is usually hidden or, when expressed, dismissed. ("You wouldn't want to go to their party anyway.")

In 1992, Vivian Gussin Paley, a kindergarten teacher at the University of Chicago demonstration school, saw that even as she had rules about not hitting or calling others cruel names, some of her students controlled the social order in the classroom by purposefully excluding some of their peers. To address the problem, she instituted a rule: "you can't say 'you can't play,'" which became the title of a book she had published by the Harvard University Press. Some have criticized her rule, concerned that one child who was mean to another and then invoked "you can't say 'you can't play'" would essentially be forcing the targeted child to play with her tormentor. One educator suggested that the rule be more positively stated: "Find a way for everyone to play."

I would say we need a bit of both rules. Paley's rule has added a necessary component to breaking the cycle of violence and creating more deeply caring communities. It is important for children to learn that it is not kind to purposely exclude a peer. They need to learn to play with one another, to respect differences, and to celebrate diversity. It is just as important that children learn to assert themselves and take care of their own needs and safety without trampling the basic human rights and dignity of another child. ("You can join us at our lunch table if you don't say mean things about the new girl." "I want you to play with us, but you can't keep taking the ball away from Jamie. He is a part of our team, too.")

The Masquerade of Deception

Individual incidents of verbal, physical, or relational bullying can appear trivial or insignificant. They may seem like nothing to be overly concerned about, just part of the school culture. But it is the imbalance of power, the intent to harm, the threat of further aggression, and the creation of an atmosphere of terror and fear that should raise red flags and signal a need for intervention. Sadly, even when the four markers of bullying are clearly in evidence, adults have been known to incorrectly label, minimize, or dismiss the bullying, underestimate its seriousness, blame the bullied child, and/or heap on additional insult to injury simply by failing to properly identify what is really going on.

Taunting is not teasing no matter how much those doing the taunting protest that they were "just joking." Sexual bullying is not even related to flirting, and no matter what form it takes—verbal, relational, or physical—it is an act of contempt-fuelled aggression, not passion. Racial bullying can never be "just having fun." Hazing by its nature is mean and cruel; it is not a healthy way to celebrate anything—let alone an important rite of passage or a milestone. These four—taunting, sexual bullying, racial bullying, and hazing—are often cloaked in the garb of locker-room humor, innocuous behavior, innocent banter, harmless antics. They are none of these.

Power Plays in the Schoolyard: Corrupting, Colluding, and a Con Job

Eight-year-old Meghan was suspended from school for pulling her pants down on the playground in front of a group of boys while a group of girls watched. One child reported the incident to the supervising teacher. When the teacher arrived on the scene, most of the boys and girls were laughing at Meghan. The teacher grabbed Meghan's arm and marched her into the principal's office, all the while telling her how ashamed she should be of her outrageous behavior. The principal couldn't get Meghan to tell her why she would do such a thing. Meghan just sat in the chair in front of the principal's desk, shrugged her shoulders, and stared off into the distance.

When her father arrived, he found Meghan curled up in the office chair, sobbing. The principal suggested that the father get some help for his daughter, who was corrupting others on the playground by "exposing" herself. The father brought Meghan home and tried to comfort her and find out what had really happened.

Having no luck, he called a family friend who was a social worker. The friend took Meghan to lunch and got the facts from this distraught second grader.

Behind in reading since first grade, called "stupid" and "dumb," often excluded from her peers' play circles and parties, Meghan was desperate to belong to the popular group. The leader told her she could join the group if she would pull her pants down in front of the boys; if she didn't, the bigger girl would make sure nobody else played with her. Corruption, yes, but the wrong player had been accused.

When confronted with the facts, Meridith (the bully) denied ever telling Meghan (the bullied) to do such a thing. Then she got the other girls (the not-so innocent bystanders) to go along with her by threatening to hurt them if they told anybody the truth. Finally, one girl, Julie (a bystander turned witness), was so upset by the whole ordeal that she told her mom what had really happened and what was still going on at recess. In taking that risk, knowing that her mom would probably believe her, Julie started a chain of events at school that would make a world of difference for Meghan, Meridith, and their classmates—a difference that Meghan's suspension never could make. Meghan was fortunate to have a girl in her class who was willing to stand up, speak out, and support her. Other kids are not as fortunate.

Cliques and the School Social Ladder

To gain acceptance and security during the preteen years and throughout their teens, kids not only join groups, they form groups called cliques, which have a commonality of interests, values, abilities, and tastes. This is good. There is also exclusivity and exclusion. This is not good. School cultures that nurture cliques and elevate some groups above others also nurture discrimination and bullying.

The comments made to the police by the student body president of Columbine High School demonstrated how such a school culture can reinforce a sense of community by erecting strong walls to comfort and protect those on the inside. For those cast outside those exclusive walls, such a culture can mean systematic abuse, denial of equal protection, and an everyday life that is frightening and/or unbearable. Kids who don't fit into the honored and revered cliques are often subjected to cruel and persistent bullying by members of these groups. The student body president was quoted as saying that "all the 'sports type' kids referred to Dylan and Eric as the 'no sports.'" He knew these kids got picked on all the time and that it was some members of the football team who relentlessly targeted them.

Having been taunted, shunned, and physically bullied, "outsiders" often turn to other groups that will accept them. Tensions can rise between two cliques that are at the opposite ends of the social ladder. Administrations in such settings turn a blind eye to the abuse heaped on the lower group by the upper echelon, reinforce it, or contribute to it by denying the problem. When asked about the apparent "jock culture" at the school, an administrator was quoted in the local newspaper as saying, "The only jock culture at Columbine are staph infections" (aka "jock itch").

After the videotapes shot by Dylan and Eric were made public well over a year after the shootings, there was still a sense of entitlement and superiority expressed by at least one member of the Columbine football team. In his mind, he had a right to taunt and torment anyone who was "different," anyone for whom he had contempt: "Columbine is a good, clean place except for those rejects. Most kids don't want them here. They were into witchcraft. They were into voodoo. Sure we teased them. But what do you expect with kids who come to school with weird hairdos and horns on their hats? It's not just jocks; the whole school's disgusted with them. They're a bunch of homos. . . . If you want to get rid of someone, usually you tease 'em. So the whole school would call them homos. . . ."

In a column in the *Denver Post* shortly after the Columbine shootings, Chuck Green wrote, "Even as the shots were being fired, Columbine killers Eric Harris and Dylan Klebold were making one of their motives very, very clear: They resented the caste system at the high school, where popular athletes were provided star status. 'Jocks,' as the athletes are commonly called, were at the top of the social order at Columbine, worshiped as the dukes of their campus fiefdom. In the first few days after the shootings, other students voiced similar concerns—that there was a class structure at Columbine, perpetuated by students and tolerated by administrators, that favored major-sport athletes over common students."

The jock culture problem obviously extended beyond "jock itch." Green went on to expose a case involving one of the most popular student athletes. Courted by the likes of Stanford, Harvard, and Colorado University, this student was also an accused stalker and prowler. He had been under a restraining order to stay away from his ex-girlfriend, also a student at Columbine. The student declined violence counseling and planned to fight the criminal charges.

Rather than focus on keeping the athlete—and alleged stalker—away from the girl, the administrators at Columbine proposed another solution: "The girl could leave school now—three weeks before graduation—with no penalty, to avoid contact with the football star. It would leave no mark on her record." No penalty and no mark on *her* record for being told to stay home? It is a strange, though all too common, way to treat the target of a bully.

Chuck Green's column did make a difference. After reading the column, administrators from the school district's central office asked for an inquiry and a detailed report. School board members demanded a full explanation of the facts in the case and reasserted the need for school administrators to pay more attention to intimidation and harassment of students and gender equity issues.

In a letter to the superintendent of schools, board member David DiGiacomo wrote, "This isn't the first time issues like this have come up, and we need to be more attentive to them. The problem isn't limited to Columbine. I'm convinced it is a systematic problem in most school districts."

Cindy Key, a parent of elementary-age children, voiced the concern of many parents in the district: "Our main issue is that respect and tolerance need to be taught in our schools, and it should begin in grade school. We are concerned about bullying and teasing, and taunting. We can spend all the money in the world on security *around* the school, but it won't do much good if students don't feel safe *inside* the school."

Comedy Is Not a Prelude to a Tragedy—Teasing Is Not Taunting

In many of the stories in the introduction, kids were tormented with words, taunted about their race, ethnicity, religion, gender, sexual orientation, physical attributes, or mental abilities. Often when confronted, the bullies would protest, "I was just kidding," "I was just joking." It's difficult to teach children that teasing is a normal part of healthy human relationships and at the same time tell them that if they tease someone else, they could be called to account for bullying. It's even more difficult to teach children to stop teasing when it becomes harmful, hurtful, and no longer fun. It is more helpful to give kids two different words to describe two different activities. When kids understand that one is a part of having fun with friends and the other is outright bullying, we can reduce the excuses.

Teasing is not taunting, and there is no slippery slope on which teasing slides into taunting. They are very different from the start—and at the finish. By learning the unique characteristics of teasing and taunting, and giving each its own name, kids will be able to label what they are doing and understand more clearly why one is acceptable and the other is not.

Teasing is a fun thing you do with friends—with people you care about. It is about laughing *with* someone. Taunting is a choice to bully someone for whom you have contempt. It is about laughing *at* someone. Identifying taunting as bullying communicates the gravity and meanness of it to the bully and any not-so-innocent bystanders who might be inclined to join in the cruel game. Labeling it as bullying also lends credibility to the legitimate pain the bullied child is experiencing.

Teasing

- Allows the teaser and person teased to swap roles with ease.
- Isn't intended to hurt the other person.
- Maintains the basic dignity of everyone involved.
- Pokes fun in a lighthearted, clever, and benign way.
- Is meant to get both parties to laugh.
- Is only a small part of the activities shared by kids who have something in common.
- Is innocent in motive.
- Is discontinued when the person teased becomes upset or objects to the teasing.

When kids tease one another, there is a playfulness that is not present in taunting. Both kids tease one another equally—though one may be better at verbal teasing and the other at planting birthday candles that don't blow out. (Bullies get birthday candles that explode in the target's face, and take great pleasure in the target's pain and embarrassment.) If a child inadvertently says something that is hurtful to her friend, perhaps intending to wrap in humor something that is difficult to say outright, she picks up on her mistake by reading her friend's hurt and makes amends. The two are learning important lessons in relationship building and effective communication. They can practice with each other and safely learn the limits and boundaries of teasing, as well as the power of words. They share strong feelings of affection, compassion, and empathy. If they laugh at each other's foibles and mistakes, they are just as quick to be there to help the other clean up the mess. Good-natured ribbing reflects the closeness of two friends' relationship. Off-limits are attacks about race, ethnicity, religion, gender, sexuality, sexual orientation, sexual identity, physical attributes, or mental ability, weight, and allergies. Any attack is not teasing; it is taunting.

Taunting
- Is based on an imbalance of power and is one-sided: the bully taunts, the bullied kid is taunted.
- Is intended to harm.
- Involves humiliating, cruel, demeaning, or bigoted comments thinly disguised as jokes.
- Includes laughter directed *at* the target, not laughing *with* the target.
- Is meant to diminish the sense of self-worth of the target.
- Induces fear of further taunting or can be a prelude to physical bullying.
- Is sinister in motive.
- Continues especially when the targeted kid becomes distressed or objects to the taunt.

When a bully taunts her target, there is no playfulness in the attack, no matter how much the bully may protest, "I was just teasing." The bullied kid was probably targeted because the bully knew he or she would not strike back. There is no good-natured give-and-take. The taunt is intended to isolate the target. It is one-sided and intended to hurt and isolate the target. The words used are demeaning and cruel. The bully may laugh, and so might the bystanders. The target is embarrassed, humiliated, or shamed, living in fear of what will come next. There is no empathy, sympathy, or compassion; rather, there is glee, excitement, or amusement over the success of the attack. The motive of the bully is not to make a new friend, engage in friendly banter, or lighten a difficult situation; it is purely to belittle and demean another child and get pleasure from witnessing the pain.

We as adults are not always the greatest role models for our kids when it comes to discerning the difference between teasing and taunting. After unsuccessfully attempting to get a stray dog off a school bus in rural Kentucky, the driver asked the school administrator for help. The administrator rolled her eyes, laughed, and said, "You have *a lot* of dogs on that bus." Most of the students on the bus were children with special needs and poor. The bus driver was stunned, as he had come to know and care for the kids he transported to and from school each day. He was incredulous that any educator—even in apparent jest—would refer to them as dogs.

In Elmwood, Indiana, a noose was left next to a time clock at a company with only one black employee. No one admitted to leaving the noose, but some of the workers couldn't understand why the one employee it was intended for "couldn't take a joke."

During a stand-up routine in Nashville in 2011, comedian and *30 Rock* star Tracy Morgan flippantly commented that if his son were gay and talked in a high-pitched voice, Morgan "would pull out a knife and stab him." Some in the audience laughed with him, others were stunned into silence. He later made a statement: "I'm not a hateful person and don't condone any kind of violence against others. While I am an equal-opportunity jokester, and my friends know what is in my heart, even in a comedy club this clearly went too far and was not funny in any context."

The school administrator's comments, the workers' actions, and the comedian's poor attempt at "just joking" were not teasing. All three were mean and dehumanizing to the targeted groups.

One need only refer to the checklist to see that all of these cases had the characteristics of taunting, not teasing. The last two points in both lists will give parents, educators, and kids a good clue as to whether an activity is lighthearted bantering or a cruel attack. In teasing, the comment is innocent in motive and stops as soon as the person being teased objects or gets upset. The comment may have come at the wrong time, in the wrong place, or in the wrong circumstance. No harm was intended and, reading the other person's body language, the teaser stops. In taunting, the comment is sinister in motive and the bully continues, especially if the taunted person objects or gets upset. If everyone else is laughing and one child is scared or distressed, that is a good clue that what is happening is taunting.

A Little About Sex, a Lot About Contempt—Sexual Bullying

Sexist and sexual attitudes can collide with bullying. And all three means of bullying—physical, verbal, and relational—can be wrapped in sexual overtones. Because our sexuality is an integral part of who we are, sexual bullying cuts to the core of our being and can have devastating consequences. Peer-to-peer sexual bullying is one of the most widespread forms of violence in our schools today. But it is not only peer-to-peer. Students have targeted teachers and teachers have targeted students. The bullying ranges from sexual remarks, sexual gestures, inappropriate touching, and unwanted physical attention to sexual assault.

Verbal Sexual Bullying

Verbal bullying is the most common form of bullying, so it would make sense that the most common form of sexual bullying would be verbal. It can stand alone but is often the entrée to physical sexual bullying or relational sexual bullying and is too often the first step toward more vicious and degrading sexual violence. The nature of this type of bullying is different for boys and girls. The words used to bully boys tend to be derogatory terms defining them as "less than a boy"—that is, a girl (sissy, wuss, pussy, bitch, "you run like a girl")—or homophobic terms (gay, fag, queer, homo, "light in his loafers"). The words used to bully girls tend to objectify their bodies, demean their sexuality, or infantilize them (fat, dog, "eight," cunt, hole, pussy, lez, slut, whore, hooker, skank, babe, baby, chick, kitten).

Verbal bullying can also include threats to sexually violate the target, verbal assessments of the target's body, sexist or sexual jokes, or derogatory comments about sexual performance or lack of sexual activity.

Just as bullies who taunt their peers will argue that they intended no harm—were just teasing—so too do bullies who add sexist or sexual overtones to their bullying plead that they were only joking or flirting. If kids are taught the difference between teasing and taunting, they are more readily able to distinguish between flirting and sexual bullying.

Flirting
- Allows and invites both persons to swap roles with ease.
- Isn't intended to hurt the other person—is an expression of desire.
- Maintains the basic dignity of both persons.
- Is meant to be flattering and complimentary.
- Is an invitation to have fun together and enjoy each other's company.
- Invites sexual attention.
- Is intended to make the other person feel wanted, attractive, and in control.
- Is discontinued when the person who is being flirted with becomes upset, objects to the flirting, or is not interested.

Flirting has playfulness about it that sexual bullying does not. It is never intended to harm and is an invitation for two people to get to know each other better. As with any other invitation, it can be accepted or rejected—and the person who initiated the flirting honors either response.

Verbal Sexual Bullying
- Is based on an imbalance of power and is one-sided: the bully sexually taunts, the bullied kid is demeaned and degraded.
- Is intended to harm and exploit.
- Is invasive and intended to assert the status of the bully.
- Is intended to be degrading or demeaning.
- Is intended to express control and domination.
- Is intended to violate the boundaries of the target.
- Is intended to make the other person feel rejected, ugly, degraded, powerless, or uncomfortable.
- Continues especially when the targeted kid becomes distressed or objects to the sexual comment.

In sexual bullying there is no invitation—just an attack. The target is embarrassed, humiliated, and shamed and tends to feel powerless. It is not the intention of the bully to engage in healthy sexual flirtation with another person—the attack is meant to hurt. If the target protests, she is often labeled a "bitch" who is uptight and can't take a joke.

Physical Sexual Bullying

Physical sexual bullying can include, but is certainly not limited to, touching or grabbing in a sexual way, pinching, bra snapping, pulling down pants or pulling up skirts, brushing against a target in a sexual way, or sexual assault. It is important to note that criminal activity can have sexual bullying as one of its components. In October 2001, a sixth-grade girl in Denver, Colorado, was sexually bullied and assaulted in a middle school computer lab where twenty-four students were working in groups. A twelve-year-old boy held a knife to the girl's leg and offered three friends five dollars to be the first to fondle or grope their classmate. The three boys touched the girl all over her body, the girl's mother said in the complaint filed with the school district. According to the news report, "The teacher did not see what happened and thought the four boys and the girl were friends."

Several recent high-profile cases in which young girls were raped (criminal sexual bullying) by their peers and then targeted on- and offline after photos of the rapes were posted on the Internet, have brought to light the horrific consequences, beyond the rapes themselves, faced by these young girls and their families. Three of the girls committed suicide, talking before their deaths about being unable to bear the blaming, shaming, and stigmatization that they were forced to endure after the rapes. One young girl who was raped by a popular football player faced intense backlash from classmates and adults in the community. After the perpetrator was sentenced to two years probation and a four-month suspended jail term, and after enduring months of verbal attacks on- and offline, the young girl attempted suicide.

Sexual bullying doesn't stop at high school graduation. The 2007 "National Institute of Justice Campus Sexual Assault Study" found that 19 percent of undergraduate women and 6 percent of undergraduate men in the United States were sexually assaulted while in college. In 2014 the Pentagon released its latest "Report to the President of the United States on Sexual Assault Prevention and Response." This survey showed that of 5,061 reported cases of sexual assault and rape in the military in 2013, only 484 went to trial, with only 376 of those resulting in convictions. The 2012 version of the Pentagon report estimated that twenty-six thousand men and women were sexually assaulted, yet only 3,374 cases were actually reported. The statistic that is rarely reported, let alone given any press, is that one in one hundred men seen at the Veterans Health Administration hospitals have experienced "military sexual trauma." The statistic for women is higher: one in five, yet there are nearly six times as many men as women serving. The numbers are daunting.

At universities and in the military the issues around sexual bullying are the same as they are in high school. Rarely is the target believed, sometimes being blamed instead, and more often than not the bully gets away with the assault. Typically, it is the target who is vilified, gets called "fag" or "slut," and is forced to leave the school or the military, while the perpetrators remain.

Internationally, workplace bullying has become a recognized occupational health and safety issue. The Japanese courts have ruled that *ijime* (bullying) violates employers' obligation to provide a safe workplace and violates the rights of employees to be treated with respect in the workplace. All commuter rail and subway companies in Tokyo and Osaka have women-only cars because women were being groped and sexually harassed on their way to and from their "safe workplaces." Poster campaigns against *chikan* (groping) and tougher sentencing failed to slow the continual rise of reported groping on mixed-gender railway cars. It is interesting to note that male elementary school students and people with disabilities and their assistants can board women-only cars, because they, too, were being subjected to abuse on the mixed-gender cars.

In response to a marked rise in reports of sexual harassment and attacks on women commuting to and from work, railway companies in major cities in India and Indonesia have installed women-only railway cars. Creating a systematic and systemic change in the workplace can help to create a systemic change in societal attitudes toward bullying, but as we can see with the need for women-only railway cars, any true shift will require individual, societal, and organizational commitment to end the violence.

Relational Sexual Bullying

Add sexual overtones to all the ways kids use relational bullying to systematically diminish a bullied child's sense of self-worth—sexual rumors or sexual epithets on bathroom walls or lockers, shunning a target because of his or her sexual orientation or sexual identification, "scanning" a target's body, staring at breasts, leering, or making obscene gestures—and what you have is a hard-to-detect, easy-to-execute method of cutting to the core of the bullied kid. Add to all of these the displaying or circulating of sexually explicit material intended to shame or humiliate or degrade, the wearing of clothes or pins that have sexually offensive sayings or pictures, or the existence of sexually explicit graffiti, and you have the ingredients for creating what the Canadian Human Rights Commission (1991) and the United States Civil Rights Act of 1964 identified as a hostile environment that interferes with a student's ability to learn.

A Minnesota school principal ignored a girl's request to remove from a boys' bathroom stall sexually explicit and lewd graffiti about her. When the graffiti was not removed after two years of complaining, the girl filed a suit against the school district. The district reportedly settled the case for $15,000. Two years and $15,000 later appears to be a social commentary on a school climate that tolerates—if not invites—the dehumanization and degradation of a portion of its population who are required to be there every day.

In her 2001 book, *Schooling the Boys: Masculinities and Primary Education*, Christine Skelton suggests a whole-school approach to changing the sexist assumptions, gender stereotyping, gender myths, attitudes, and beliefs that underlie sexual bullying. She invites educators to ask the following questions:

1. What images of masculinity and femininity are pupils bringing with them into school and what types are they acting out in the classroom and the playground?
2. What are the dominant images of masculinity and femininity that the school itself reflects to the pupils?
3. What kind of role models does the school want and expect of its teachers?
4. What kinds of initiatives/strategies/projects should teachers be undertaking with children to question gender categories?

Perhaps we could all benefit from returning to the *Free to Be You and Me* book, children's song album, and musical special based on both that was broadcast on March 11, 1974. Actress and child-welfare activist Marlo Thomas set out to write something for her niece, Dionne, that would challenge the stereotypical gender roles and rigid racial stereotypes that were so ingrained in the children's literature Thomas read to Dionne. Thomas ended up creating something much bigger than one book for one niece. Forty years later, in the follow-up book, *When We Were Free to Be: Looking Back at a Children's Classic and the Difference It Made*, one of the original contributors to *Free to Be You and Me*, Letty Cottin Pogrebin, writes about the highly gender-differentiated world our young people are living in today and its consequences:

"Today too many girls hate their body images; some as young as eight already have eating disorders. Too many boys are becoming bullies or are being bullied. Very few gay teens feel free to be themselves. Too many kids are listening to rap songs, watching music videos, and playing computer games in which girls are demeaned, objectified, vilified, hyper-sexualized, beaten and raped. Too many children are victims of violence, incest, and sexual abuse. Too many adolescents are committing suicide. This isn't the world we envisioned forty years ago. It wasn't supposed to turn out this way. We've got to fix it. And some church leaders are also speaking out and saying, 'We've got to fix it.'"

Writing in the *Fort Worth Star-Telegram*, Reverend Fritz Ritsch called upon moderate Christian ministers to speak up about the intolerance, bigotry, and contempt around sexuality, sexual orientation, and sexual identification that is far too often cloaked in the garb of religion. Citing the recent "epidemic" of bullying-related suicides, he said, "[T]he bullying crisis has put a fine point on the need for moderates to challenge the theological bullies from our own bully pulpits. We cannot equivocate. Children are dying. We need to speak up. If not now, when?"

I was speaking with a group of grade twelve students in a human rights honors class and asked the girls why they called one another "slut." One girl responded that the other girl was her friend, and her friend knew the girl was just kidding because she wasn't a slut. I asked what a slut was to them. The same girl said, "A girl who sleeps around." I asked what they would call a boy who "slept around." While laughing, several of the boys responded at the same time, "A player." Yes, we've got a lot to fix; and yes, we've got to fix it if we are to ever eliminate sexual bullying. When told by a CBS reporter that some have accused her of being a radical feminist, the president of the Leadership Conference of Women Religious, Sister Florence Deacon, Order of St. Francis, responded, "I am, if you define feminism as the radical concept that women are human." To accept that boys and girls are equal and uniquely human is step one in stopping sexual violence.

A New York middle school teacher and author of *Sexual Respect Curriculum*, Peter Miner sums up the difference between healthy expressions of sexuality and sexual bullying: "Can you espouse the values of fairness and respect, and at the same time discriminate and injure? Sexist and sexually harassing behaviors are dissatisfying and therefore undesirable actions that hurt people and are unworthy of people of intelligence and integrity."

Racist Bullying: A Double Whammy

Just as sexist attitudes can collude with bullying, so, too, can racist attitudes.

In *The Anti-Bullying Handbook*, New Zealand professor Keith Sullivan, internationally recognized for his work in bullying prevention programs, describes what happens when this collusion takes place.

Rangi is working by himself in the classroom. The door opens. "What are you doing, Maori boy?" taunts David. "Did ya fall in the shit, black boy?" He struts closer. "Are you read-ing something? I didn't know you could read." "Hey, nigger," the other boys say as they start to filter in and see Rangi on his own. Instead of ignoring these taunts and provocations (as he has done four or five times over the last month), Rangi loses his temper. He turns on David. The two boys fight and Rangi is clearly the better fighter and is winning. David's friend Jim steps in, grabs Rangi around the neck, and pulls him away from David, throwing him on the ground. He helps David up. The duty [supervising] teacher arrives, and David and Rangi are taken to the deputy principal's office. David has been crying and says that he was just having fun and that Rangi went "psycho" and really hurt him. When questioned, Rangi is surly and insolent and is suspended from school for a week for fighting and being rude to the deputy principal. David's friends back him up and say that Rangi went "psycho" for no apparent reason. David is given a warning about fighting but is largely seen as the innocent party.

Rangi is identified by those in authority as the aggressor. He is not listened to. Instead, the boy with more credibility in the school is believed.

Dr. Sullivan went on to point out that although there is a strong element of racism in the bullying event, the school authorities had previously stated that racism did not exist at their school. They believe the bully and punish the bullied boy for fighting back. The boys will probably not bully Rangi again; rather, they will find someone they can bully more easily. Yet their racist attitudes have not been challenged. Rangi will probably nurse a grudge against the boys, rage against the injustice, and turn against the school because of its inability to address the problem justly.

The incident with David and Rangi demonstrates not only what often happens when a bullied child strikes back, but also what a bully tends to do when called to account:

1. Denies that he did anything wrong.
2. Trivializes the event: "I was just having some fun with him."
3. Counterattacks: "He just went 'psycho' on us."
4. Claims victim status by crying and accusing the other kid of starting the episode. This usually provokes the bullied child (who, in Rangi's case, had taken abuse for over a month before finally striking back. Rangi was surly and insolent when questioned).
5. Gets off the hook by casting the bullied kid as the bully. David is seen as the innocent party.
6. Counts on the support of the bystanders to deny, dismiss, or belittle anything the targeted kid says or does in defense of his actions. David's friends back him up, saying that Rangi went "psycho" for no apparent reason.
7. Intimidates others into going along with him.

The bully learned his lines well, mastered the ability to act the part of the wronged party, got others to collude with him, and played on both the emotions and biases of the adults. The cycle of violence continues.

Maori children are in the minority in this South Island school, as well as being oppressed First Nations people of New Zealand. Replace Maori with Dene, Inuit, Cherokee, Blackfoot, Navajo, Hopi, Lakota, Sioux, or any other racial or ethnic minority and you see a similar picture of what is happening in many schools across the United States and Canada.

In his 2002 book, *Racism: A Short History*, historian George Fredrickson summarizes the what, how, and why of racism: "Racism exists when one ethnic group or historical collectivity dominates, excludes, or seeks to eliminate another on the basis of differences that it believes are hereditary and unalterable." He goes on to explain that racism is a social behavior in which the dominant group, collectively, but not always singularly, oppresses the targeted group. The targeted group is seen as different from the dominant group, and different equals "less than." People in the dominant group can play any of the roles in the Bully Circle (page 146), with many playing the role of bully or the not-so-innocent bystander, and yet a few in the dominant group do challenge the racism, stand up for those who are oppressed, or resist the racism (the brave-hearted).

You've Got to Be Taught

Racist bullying doesn't just happen. Kids have to be taught to be racist before they can engage in racist bullying. Racist bullying takes place in a climate where children are taught to discriminate against a group of people, where differences are seen as bad, and where the common bonds of humanity are not celebrated.

Children systematically learn the language of racial slurs and the rules of bigoted behavior through thought (stereotype), feeling (prejudice), and action (discrimination). First, children are taught to *stereotype*—that is, to generalize about an entire group of people without regard to individual differences: [Insert a group] are hot-tempered, ugly, lazy, stupid, no good, crazy. . . .

Second, children are taught to *prejudge* a person based on this stereotype. Prejudice is a feeling: We don't like [_____].

Combine racist thought and feeling and you get children willing to *discriminate* against individuals in that group: "You can't play with us." "You can't come to our party." "We don't want you on our team." "Get out of here, you n——!" This is racist bullying and needs to be addressed as such.

It is only a short walk from racist discrimination to scape-goating a particular child—selecting someone to suffer in place of others or attaching blame or wrongdoing to a specific child when it is not clear who is at fault. Rangi was accused of starting the fight because "his kind" has hot tempers.

When it comes to racism, school policy, procedures, and pro-grams have to work hand in hand. Step one is to acknowledge that racism exists in our schools. Then we can be open to the possibil-ity that racist bullying is happening inside those walls as well. Two excellent resources are the Southern Poverty Law Center's website, www.SPLCenter.org, and the Facing History and Ourselves website, www.FacingHistory.org. Both provide educational material to deal with intolerance in general and racism in particular.

What Bullying Is Not

Although bullying is the focus of this book, it is helpful to know what bullying is not. The distinctions are not always that obvious at first glance. And even when we clearly identify what is not bully-ing, we run the risk of failing to designate certain acts of aggression as bullying, preferring to call them conflicts, or labeling them as "drama," and thus using language to reduce the gravity of the cruel acts. Bullying can hide behind myths and misperceptions. A pru-dent and judicious use of the term is critical. Failing to recognize an act as bullying, mislabeling it a conflict, overextending the term, or inappropriately labeling behaviors as bullying when they are igno-rant faux pas, impulsive acts of aggression, or conflicts can derail efforts to appropriately deal with real acts of bullying.

Ignorant Faux Pas

Using a racist, sexist, ageist, or physical-attribute or mental-ability stereotype is never a good thing to do, but it may not have the markers of bullying. Making statements such as the following often indicates an ignorance of the source or bias of the term, or apathy toward the group that is being marginalized, vilified, or discriminated against by the comment:

- I Jewed him down when I bought the car.
- I got gypped on that deal.
- How many (name a group) does it take to screw in a light-bulb?
- Don't be an Indian giver.
- She's got her dumb blonde act down.
- He runs like a girl.
- That's so gay.
- It's not over till the fat lady sings.
- He's as dumb as a doornail.
- They dagoed their car.
- That's so retarded.

What is needed is a brief tutorial on the stereotype or bias that the words convey, the possible effects they can have on others, and an admonishment to not use that phrase again—and to find a more creative, intelligent way to say what the young person really means. Often these phrases were learned at home, at school, or through the media, and the person spouting these words is oblivious to their origin or bias. These comments are crude and offensive and can set the stage for bullying, but they are not bullying.

Impulsive Aggression

Bullying does not include acts of impulsive aggression—in other words, aggression that is a spontaneous, indiscriminate striking out, with no intended target. Such aggression is usually reactionary and emotionally charged. It can be related to a physical or mental disability, and must not be dismissed or excused, but it is not bullying. Spontaneous, deliberate, indiscriminate striking out also may be a response by a bullied kid to an attack by a bully, but it is not bullying (more on this in the next chapter).

Conflict

Conflict—even handled poorly—is not bullying. Normal childhood behaviors such as sibling rivalry or one-on-one fighting with siblings or peers with competing claims is not bullying. Conflict is a normal, natural, and necessary part of our lives. It involves either a disagreement or clash between people, their ideas, goals, or principles. Conflict is inevitable in our homes, schools, workplaces, and communities, and so is the pain and discomfort that goes along with it. But conflict can be resolved and made less painful if it is dealt with directly, creatively, responsibly, and non-violently—not passively or aggressively. People who avoid conflict or always give in end up either passive, likely to take all kinds of abuse lying down, or seething with suppressed anger and rage. The former are likely to be vulnerable targets for bullies; the latter direct their hostilities outward in acts of violence against others or inward against themselves. When conflict is viewed as a contest—something that one person has to win and the other will inevitably lose—emotional or physical aggression often becomes a tool of choice. The other option is flight—avoiding conflict at all cost, playing the peacemaker. Neither is productive. It is our job to figure out how to reach fair, equitable, and just solutions and resolutions to our own conflicts and to help our kids do the same. No easy task, to be sure.

Sometimes it takes a mediator who is neutral and impartial to help the two parties arrive at a solution they both see as fair, equitable, and just. Adults can teach young people through example, guidance, and instruction that violence is an immature, irresponsible, and unproductive technique to resolve conflict, and that using non-violent tools to resolve conflict is a mature and courageous act. When conflict is viewed not as a contest but as a crisis, i.e., a sudden change or turning point in a situation, young people can learn not to attack aggressively or flee from the conflict. They can instead embrace it, seeing it as a challenge and opportunity to grow and change. Conflict then becomes a cooperative challenge, a process, and a movement back and forth between two or more people.

Unresolved conflict can escalate to armed confrontation. Criminal activities that may have begun as a conflict and escalated to a serious physical assault, a serious threat of physical assault, or an assault with a weapon require legal intervention as well as disciplinary procedures and therapeutic intervention, but they are not bullying.

Ignorant faux pas, spontaneous aggression, and conflict do not bear the markers of bullying. They are issues that parents and educators must recognize and deal with effectively in order to create a more deeply caring community for our kids. Each one of these issues can contribute to the breakdown of healthy human relationships if they are dismissed, ignored, or left to fester.

Hate Crimes—Criminal Bullying

It is important to note that some violent activities *do* bear the markers of bullying as well as of criminality. These are commonly called hate crimes: criminal acts against a person, group of people, or property in which the bully chooses the target because of the target's real or perceived race, religion, sexual orientation, national origin, disability, gender, or ethnicity. Not only do these require legal intervention, they require disciplinary procedures and therapeutic intervention that address the elements of contempt and arrogance that are packaged with the violence. They are not faux pas, nor are they spontaneous acts of aggression, and they certainly do not require conflict resolution techniques.

In November of 2013, three students from San Jose State University in California were suspended from school and charged with the racial bullying of their roommate, seventeen-year-old Donald Williams Jr., after they continually and systematically tormented him from September through October. They clamped a U-shaped bicycle lock around his neck and claimed they had lost the key, called him "three-fifths" and "fraction," hung a Confederate flag in their suite, wrote a racial slur on their white board, and barricaded Williams in his room on several occasions. The other four suite-mates saw and heard what was going on but failed to stand up for their bullied roommate, or to speak out against the attacks, or to report the bullying to school personnel. As of May 2014, four of William's suite-mates have been formally charged with misdemeanor hate crime and battery.

The terms "three-fifths" and "fraction," used by Williams's suite-mates, refer to the way the U.S. government once counted African Americans—as a fraction (three-fifths) of a person. These comments did not indicate an ignorance of the source or the bias of the word or phrase. These young men knew what these words meant and chose them specifically to demean, denigrate, and dehumanize Williams.

One of the problems that allowed the racist bullying to continue and reach the level of a hate crime was the university's failure to see the bullying for what it was. According to the claim filed, when Williams complained to the resident advisor, the advisor met with Williams and his suite-mates—not to stop the bullying but rather to "smooth out relations between the group." Viewing it as a conflict to be resolved, the advisor had all of the young men sign a "Roommate Living Agreement." It was Williams who insisted that "No bike lock of shame" be added to the agreement. This should have been a clue to the resident advisor that the problem was not a conflict to be resolved. Going along with the conflict charade, Williams's roommates signed the agreement and at the same time ramped up their plans for his continued harassment. The bullies were not held accountable until one month later and, according to the claim, the target of their cruelty was subjected to "further racial indignities."

Mislabeling

It is in the interest of bullies to create a context ("We were just joking." "It was only a prank.") that diverts attention from the true nature of their goals and behaviors. The rhetoric of conflict lends itself to this effort (for example, the creation of a Roommate Living Agreement). This is not an isolated incident of confusing bullying with conflict.

While researching bullying prevention programs for the first edition of this book, I was concerned that many of the programs developed for schools had as their foundation conflict resolution solutions. People who complete such well-intentioned bullying prevention programs become skilled at handling different kinds of conflict and learn effective anger management skills, but they still have no clue how to identify and effectively confront bullying. It is disturbing how often school districts' procedural handbooks mention the use of a mediator "to resolve" a bullying issue, as if it is a conflict. In doing this we are asking targeted students to be willing to reach some sort of "agreement" with the perpetrators. In conflict, both parties must be willing to compromise or give something up in order to come to a resolution. The bullies are already in a position of power and have robbed the targets of their sense of well-being, dignity, and worth. How much are we asking the targets to give up?

With slumped shoulders and an air of frustration and hurt, twelve-year-old Celeste complained to her teacher that one of her classmates had tripped her, called her gross names, locked her out of a chat room, and smashed her art project. The teacher put the two girls together to "resolve" this conflict. The bully made lots of excuses: "I didn't mean to hurt her feeling. . . . I'm sorry if you were offended. . . . She just fell over my feet. . . . We didn't know we had locked her out of the chat room. I fixed it this morning. . . . I didn't have anything to do with smashing her art project. It fell on the floor." Meanwhile Celeste sat there with her arms crossed, looking like a member of the Dixie Chicks: "I'm not ready to make nice." Frustrated by the failure of the conflict resolution tools, the teacher told Celeste that she needed to get along with the classmate who had supposedly apologized and wanted to "make nice." But Celeste knew that the bully hadn't meant what she said, and that the teacher had not really believed what Celeste had told her about being targeted. Celeste knew that as soon as the teacher was out of sight, the bullying would continue and probably get worse—and it did. The next time the bully attacked, she did it with an even bigger smirk on her face, knowing she had gotten away with it before. Celeste would never again tell the teacher about the bullying that continued. She drew further into herself and her grades began to slip.

Gorillas in Our Midst

Just like Donald Williams Jr.'s resident advisor and Celeste's teacher, we as observers can have a disinclination to see and acknowledge bullying for what it is, i.e., contemptuous and cruel behavior; or to accept that young people—especially "nice kids"—are capable of this kind of cruelty. Our unwillingness to see this is abetted by a common phenomenon of observation.

In a 1999 research project conducted by Daniel Simons and Christopher Chabris, subjects were asked to view a seventy-five-second video titled *Gorillas in Our Midst: Sustained Inattentional Blindness for Dynamic Events*. On the video, two teams—one dressed in white, one dressed in black—passed two basketballs around. The subjects were to count the number of passes between players wearing the same color. About forty-five seconds into the video, a woman wearing a gorilla suit walks through the group of players, stops briefly to pound her chest, and then walks out of the video frame—spending a total of nine seconds on the screen. Subjects who were counting the passes were then asked if they had seen the gorilla. Only 36 percent reported that they had. The other 64 percent experienced what is known as "inattentional blindness," the inability to detect unexpected objects to which we aren't paying attention.

If we aren't tuned in to the possibility that the gorilla is in our midst—that bullying is happening in front of us, or behind our backs—expecting to see only conflict or drama, and armed with the policies and procedures to deal with just those, we will end up retargeting the target and emboldening the bully. Once bullying is framed as a conflict, the range of responses is restricted to consent-based alternatives for resolving that supposed conflict. And "nice" kids are fully capable of being mean. Even after six teens from South Hadley, Massachusetts, were charged with complicity in the death of their classmate, Phoebe Prince, one of the school administrators in the district was quoted in *Newsweek* magazine as saying that "these were nice kids, from nice homes." Nice maybe, but definitely cruel to their classmate. If, in our minds, "nice" is equated with "incapable of being mean," the gorilla will not just be pounding its chest, it will be leaving in its wake a trail of bullied kids—some bullied to death.

It does not matter if it is mild, moderate, or severe: Bullying is not normal, natural, or necessary. It is antisocial and needs to be addressed as such. This is why current zero-tolerance policies (those that attempt to respond to a one-on-one fight, bullying, and assault with one solution—expulsion) are really zero-thinking policies. Such policies are about efficiency and finding fault, not about effective solutions for breaking the cycle of violence. What needs to be found is a social solution to this antisocial activity. Bullying is not a party to any form of conflict resolution, be it negotiation, truce, or reason. Both bullying's inception and its solution lie elsewhere.

Understanding the ways and means of bullying, and understanding what is and is not bullying are step one and step two in breaking the cycle of violence. Step three is to understand the makeup of the three characters in this tragedy: the bully, the bullied, and the not-so-innocent bystander. The scene is set. The actors enter.

> *How fragile are the bonds of civility and decency that keep*
> *any kind of human community from utter collapse.*

—**Rabbi Richard L. Rubenstein**

chapter four

The Bully

Can we not teach children, even as we protect them from victimization, that for them to become victimizers constitutes the greatest peril of all, specifically the sacrifice—physical and psychological—of the well-being of other people? And that destroying the life or safety of other people, through teasing, bullying, hitting, or otherwise "putting them down," is as destructive to themselves as to their victims.

—**Lewis P. Lipsitt,**
Children and Adolescent Behavior Letter,
Brown University (May 1995)

Bullies come in all different sizes and shapes: Some are big; some are small; some bright and some not so bright; some attractive and some not so attractive; some popular and some absolutely disliked by almost everybody. You can't always identify bullies by what they *look* like, but you can pick them out by what they *act* like. They have their lines and actions down; their roles are often rehearsed at home. Sometimes they take their cue from the movies they see, the games they play, the kids they hang with, the school they attend, and the culture that surrounds them. To the untrained eye, it may look as if they are only teasing, just pretending, having a good old-fashioned fistfight, or just siblings doing the usual rivalry stuff. They are not. They are involved in serious acting with serious consequences for themselves, the kids they bully, and the community as a whole.

The Makeup of a Bully

There are lots of reasons some kids use their abilities and talents to bully other people. No one factor tells the whole story. Bullies don't come out of the womb as bullies. Inborn temperament is a factor, but so, too, are what social scientist Urie Bronfenbrenner called "environmental influences": children's home life, school life, and the community and culture (including the media) that permit or encourage such behavior.

Four things we know for sure about bullies:

1. They are taught to bully.
2. They bully because they can.
3. They choose to bully.
4. They chose whom to bully.

They make a choice to use their leadership skills to manipulate, control, dominate, and humiliate those whom they see as a threat to their status, or those they see as being less than themselves.

Just as bullies come in all sizes and shapes, there are different *kinds* of bullies. If your child is doing the bullying, he might recognize himself in one or more of these categories. For the target of a bully, it is helpful to know the tools of the trade that a certain kind of bully uses. As a potential witness, resister, and defender, it will be easier for your child to stand up for a peer and against an injustice if she knows how that injustice is being perpetrated.

There are seven kinds of bullying roles kids can choose to play:

1. **The confident bully**

   The *confident bully* doesn't walk onto the scene; he swaggers onto it, throwing his weight around figuratively and literally. He has a big ego (as opposed to a strong one), an inflated sense of self, a sense of entitlement, a penchant for aggressive behavior, and no compassion for his targets. He feels good only to the degree that he feels a sense of superiority over others. Peers and teachers often admire him because he has a powerful personality and strong leadership skills. This does not mean that he has a lot of friends. Friendships are based on trust, loyalty, and mutual respect, not typically characteristics of any bully. Such a savvy bully knows how to play the game so he is not caught.

2. **The social bully**

   The *social bully* uses rumor, gossip, verbal taunts, and shunning to systematically isolate her selected targets and effectively exclude them from social activities. She is jealous of others' positive qualities and has a poor sense of self, but she hides her feelings and insecurities in a cloak of exaggerated confidence and charm. Devious and manipulative, she can act as if she is a caring and compassionate person, but it is only a guise to cover for her lack of true concern for anyone she targets and a tool to get what she wants. She may be popular, but she is not someone other kids would want to confide in, lest they, too, become a target for her bullying. She uses her full charm to gain favor with those she feels can help her.

Both the confident bully and the social bully are also known as "high-status social bullies" who use their leadership skills to manipulate their peers and charm the adults around them. Seeing these two characters as strong leaders who are "nice kids," adults often dismiss the complaints of those they target, because "these are nice kids, they come from nice homes and would not intentionally hurt anyone." The targeted kid is not believed and the high-status bullies become even more emboldened.

3. **The fully armored bully**

    The *fully armored bully* is cool and detached. He shows little emotion and has strong determination to carry out his bullying. He looks for an opportunity to bully when no one will see him or stop him. He is vicious and vindictive toward his target but charming and deceptive in front of others, especially adults. He appears to have what is known as a flat affect—that is, a cold and unfeeling demeanor; in reality he has buried his feelings so deep in a place of darkness and growing angst that even he has trouble finding and identifying them.

4. **The hyperactive bully**

    The *hyperactive bully* struggles with academics and has poorly developed social skills. He usually has some kind of learning disability, doesn't process social cues accurately, often reads hostile intent into other kids' innocent actions, reacts aggressively to even slight provocation, and justifies his aggressive response by placing blame outside of himself: "He hit me back first." The hyperactive bully has trouble making friends.

5. **The bullied bully**

    The *bullied bully* is both a target and a bully. Bullied and abused by adults or older kids, she bullies others to get some relief from her own feelings of powerlessness and self-loathing. Least popular of all the bullies, she strikes out viciously at those who hurt her and at weaker or smaller targets. The bullied bully is often the one most seriously impacted by bullying. She is at high risk for depression, gripping social anxiety, and drug usage, carrying both the damaging effects of being bullied and of being a bully.

6. **The bunch of bullies**

The *bunch of bullies* is a group of friends who collectively do something they would never do individually to someone they want to exclude or scapegoat. Bullying, done by a group of "nice" kids who know that what they did was wrong and that it hurts their target, is still bullying.

7. **The gang of bullies**

The *gang of bullies* is a scary lot drawn together not as a group of friends, but as a strategic alliance in pursuit of power, control, domination, subjugation, and turf. Initially joining to feel a part of a family of sorts, to be respected and to be protected, in their zeal they become so devoted to their group that they disregard their own lives, the carnage they inflict on their victims, and the overall consequences of their actions. Added to this zeal is a lack of empathy and remorse.

Although their ways and means of bullying may be different, bullies have these traits in common. They all

1. Like to dominate other people.
2. Like to use other people to get what they want.
3. Find it hard to see a situation from the other person's vantage point.
4. Are concerned only with their own wants and pleasures and not the needs, rights, and feelings of others.
5. Tend to hurt other kids when parents or other adults are not around.

6. View weaker siblings or peers as prey (bullying is also known as "predatory aggression"—a scary term, to be sure, but not as scary as the actual behavior it defines).
7. Use blame, criticism, and false allegations to project their own inadequacies onto their target.
8. Refuse to accept responsibility for their actions.
9. Lack foresight—that is, the ability to consider the short-term, long-term, and possible unintended consequences of their current behavior.
10. Crave attention.
11. Get pleasure from inflicting pain on their targets.

In order to practice being bullies, kids need to find other kids to bully. Whom they find may surprise you. The next chapter looks at "the bullied"—who they are, how they respond, and the potential impact of bullying on their lives.

> *Hatred deforms the hater more than the hated. As if any enemy could be more hurtful than the hatred with which he has incensed against him; or could wound more deeply him whom he persecutes, than he wounds his own soul by his enmity.*

—Saint Augustine (fifth-century bishop)

chapter five

The Bullied

Don't laugh at me, don't call me names,
Don't take your pleasure from my pain.
I'm a little boy with glasses
The one they call a geek,
A little girl who never smiles
'Cause I have braces on my teeth
And I know how it feels to cry myself to sleep
I'm that kid on every playground
Who's always chosen last
A single teenage mother
Tryin' to overcome my past
You don't have to be my friend
But is it too much to ask: Don't laugh at me
Don't call me names
Don't get your pleasure from my pain . . .
Don't laugh at me, I'm fat, I'm thin, I'm short, I'm tall
I'm deaf, I'm blind, hey aren't we all.

—Steve Seskin and Allen Shamblin,
"Don't Laugh at Me"

Just like bullies, kids who are bullied come in all sizes and shapes. Some are big, some are small; some bright and some not so bright; some attractive and some not so attractive; some popular and some disliked by almost everybody. The one thing that all kids who are bullied have in common is that they were targeted by a bully (or by a bunch of bullies). Each one was singled out to be the object of scorn and thus the recipient of verbal, physical, or relational bullying, merely because he or she was different in some way. Bullies need targets on whom they can heap their aggression, and the differences identified as the justifications for the attacks are spurious at best, contemptuous excuses at worst.

Targets can be just about anybody:

1. The kid who is new on the block.
2. The kid who is the youngest in the school—and thus usually smaller, sometimes scared, maybe insecure. Bullying escalates when a new class enters middle school or high school.
3. The kid who has been traumatized—who is already hurt by a prior trauma, is extremely sensitive, avoids peers to avoid further pain, and finds it hard to ask for help.
4. The kid who is submissive—who is anxious, lacking in self-confidence, and easily led and who does things to please or placate others.
5. The kid who has behaviors others find annoying.
6. The kid who is unwilling to fight—who prefers to resolve conflicts without aggression.
7. The kid who is shy, reserved, quiet or unassuming, timid, sensitive.
8. The kid who is poor or rich.
9. The kid whose race or ethnicity is viewed by the bully as inferior, deserving of contempt.
10. The kid whose gender, sexual orientation, or sexual identification is viewed by the bully as inferior, deserving of contempt.
11. The kid whose religion is viewed by the bully as inferior, deserving of contempt.

12. The kid who is bright, talented, or gifted—targeted because she "stands out"—in other words, is different.

13. The kid who is independent and unconcerned about social status, doesn't conform to the norm.

14. The kid who expresses emotions readily.

15. The kid who is fat or thin, short or tall.

16. The kid who wears braces or glasses.

17. The kid who has acne or any other skin condition.

18. The kid who has superficial physical attributes that are different from those of the majority.

19. The kid with physical and/or mental disabilities—such children are two to three times more likely to be bullied than other kids because they have an obvious disability and thus a ready excuse for the bully; often they are not as well integrated into classes and thus have fewer friends to come to their aid; and they lack verbal and/or physical skills to adequately defend themselves against the aggression. A child with attention deficit hyperactivity disorder may act before he thinks, not reflecting on the possible consequences of his behavior and, purposely or inadvertently, annoy a bully.

20. The kid who has a serious food allergy.

21. The kid who is in the wrong place at the wrong time—attacked because the bully wanted to pick on someone right there, right now.

The myths that abound in our society about targets—that they are weak and pathetic, frail, insecure, loners, in a "dance" with a bully, asking to be bullied, had it coming, deserving of what they got, "losers deserve to lose"—all feed into the rationalizations kids (and many adults) make for not putting the onus for the bullying on the bully, or for joining in, for turning away from the targets, or worse, for blaming the targets for what happened to them. Many kids who are targeted are deeply caring, respectful people who have a strong sense of fair play and a low propensity to violence. According to Tim Fields, author and cocreator of BullyOnLine, (www.BullyOnline.org), the bullies "see these qualities as vulnerabilities to be exploited." He goes on to say, "No one *deserves* to be bullied."

Kids who have behaviors that annoy or amuse their peers still have a right to be treated with dignity and respect, just like anyone else. Granted, they may need to change their behaviors, or, as in the case with children who have Asperger's syndrome (mild autism), may need to memorize the clues that other kids read instinctively so as to not so readily be made the fool by peers who think it's okay to play tricks on them. We need to ask why kids would feel they have a right to disregard, scorn, or hate another kid simply because that child was different in some way from themselves. Why would kids take their pleasure from another kid's pain?

In *Protecting the Gift* by Gavin de Becker, Dr. Mary Arneson details her experiences as a child with mild autism:

It is a world of people who act friendly and then turn out to be enemies. School is a place where people do mean things all the time, for no reason. The things that matter most, or are the source of most comfort, are objects of ridicule. For example, the autistic child dresses to please herself. In my case, the problem was that girls simply did not wear roomy shoes, and I simply did not wear shoes that hurt . . . so I chose boys' tennis shoes. . . . Other kids could have ignored this, but they didn't. What I remember, instead, is a girl phoning me and saying that she really admired my shoes I wore and asking where she could get some. Unsuspecting, I told her; not realizing that my believing anyone could admire those shoes was the funniest thing she and the other girls listening on the line could imagine.

Kids with autism often walk with an unusual gait, have narrow, focused interests, and don't read social cues well. They are easy targets for kids to mimic their gait, mock their interests, and persuade them to act in ways that get them in trouble—entertainment for the bullies.

A recent development in bullying is the number of children with food allergies who have been targeted by their peers—at times with life-threatening consequences. An October 2010 study published in the *Annals of Allergy, Asthma and Immunology* found that one in three children with food allergies had been targeted by their peers, with half of the bullying being physical. Dr. Scott Sicherer of the Jaffe Food Allergy Institute at the Mount Sinai School of Medicine in New York City found that children with food allergies in grades six through ten were twice as likely as their non-allergic peers to be bullied.

Kids have reported having allergens stuffed into their mouth or peanut butter smeared in their hair. Seven-year-old Owen was threatened by a classmate who said he was going to force Owen to eat a peanut; sixteen-year-old Chelsea had a panic attack at school when a classmate shoved a peanut butter sandwich in her face; twelve-year-old Erika Dacunha fled her classroom when she saw that her peers had put pistachios in her desk and around the classroom just to see what would happen to her.

In her story, "A Teen's Story of Allergy Bullying—and Bravery," (full text available online at http://allergicliving.com/2013/07/16/a-teens-story-of-allergy-bullying-and-bravery/) Erika recounts that, when caught, her peers claimed that she "was an inconvenience. They wanted to be able to bring nuts to school—so they were trying to use 'population control'!" Her peers weren't the only source of her fear and pain. "When I was in grade three, the parents of my school community held a meeting. The topic? Whether I should be removed from the school. The parents said my needs, which included avoiding bringing my allergens into the classroom, would inconvenience their children and dip into the school's funds. Some argued that if I was 'that sick' I should be home-schooled."

It can be argued that the bullies did not have a full understanding of the consequences of their taunting; what can't be argued is the delight they got out of seeing their classmates traumatized and fearful.

Alexandra Shea tells of the power bullies can have over kids who are different from the "norm." Describing herself as an "admittedly shy, reclusive, and somewhat peculiar only child," she wrote of her fears about going to summer camp. Number four on her list:

Them—the junior capos who run the social underground in these rustic gulags. *They* are the bully-princesses who have always abounded in Grade 6 female society. Their hair is perfect, their clothes ditto, and *They* decide who is in and who is condemned to the outer darkness, the subject of ridicule, whispers, and ostracism. I knew instinctively on which side of the great divide I would fall. . . . I had a gut instinct that books were not highly regarded as a suitable pastime and that bookish kids came just after rabies-riddled raccoons in the pecking order. Oh yes . . . I was an odd child indeed.

—Alexandra Shea,
"What I Didn't Do at Summer Camp,"
the *Globe and Mail*, May 28, 2001

Almost all of us have been on the receiving end of some sort of bullying, even if we ourselves were bullies—in fact, especially if we were bullies. When a bully wants to put someone down in order to feel superior herself (or to confirm and keep her already superior status), it doesn't take much to find an excuse to target someone. As you will see in chapter 8, bullies learn to be bullies in large part by the way they were treated by bigger or more powerful people in their lives. In her book *For Your Own Good*, internationally renowned psychiatrist Dr. Alice Miller writes that "it should be very obvious that someone who is allowed to feel free and strong from childhood does not have the need to humiliate another person."

To feel free and strong is a necessary ingredient for anyone to thrive. As shown in "Scenes from a Tragedy" on page 16, kids who bully, who are targets, and who are not-so-innocent bystanders are all bound up in the cycle of violence and weakened in some way by the experience. The myths about who is the target of bullying often are based on what a bullied kid looks and acts like *after* having been bullied repeatedly.

Once the bully has targeted her, how she responds will influence whether or not she moves from target to victim (succumbing to the bullying). Alexandra Shea was definitely affected by the "bully-princesses"; they were one of the four reasons she wanted to stay away from camp. Yet she did not succumb to their ridicule, whispers, and ostracism. She writes in her article, "With time and tender mercy, I got better on my own. I now live a life replete with friends and abounding with joys. I am no longer shy." She also suggests that the bully-princesses don't always change when they grow up: "They are still with us, under a veneer of social civility, a thin one."

If a kid succumbs to the attack—gives the bully what is demanded by showing distress, fear, or apathy; or fails to respond assertively (or aggressively)—he changes emotionally, mentally, and physically. He becomes someone he was not before the attack; and all future attacks will be against this ever-weakening target. The guilt, shame, and sense of failure felt by a target unable to cope with the brutalization contribute to the destruction of his sense of well-being. As he becomes more isolated from his peers, has trouble concentrating on schoolwork, and develops survival strategies instead of social skills, his life changes radically. How bystanders respond to both the bully and the target have a tremendous influence on how emboldened the bully becomes and/or how weak the target gets.

Evan Ramsey, a target who became a victim, will be spending the rest of his life in prison. Trapped in the rigid brick-wall social system of Bethal Regional High School in a remote town in Alaska, shy, small-framed Evan Ramsey was the target of abuse for years. Speaking in 2001 to writer Ron Arias for a *People* magazine article, "Disarming the Rage," he described the bullying: "Everybody had given me a nickname: Screech, the nerdy character on *Saved by the Bell*. . . . I got stuff thrown at me, I got spit on, I got beat up. Sometimes I fought back, but I wasn't that good at fighting." At first he reported the incidents to his teachers. "After a while [the principal] told me to just start ignoring everybody. But then you can't take it anymore."

On February 19, 1997, Evan walked into the high school with a twelve-gauge shotgun and killed schoolmate Josh Palacios and the principal, Ron Edwards. Evan was tried as an adult and sentenced to 210 years in prison. From his cell in the correctional center in Seward, Alaska, he admits, "I felt a sense of power with a gun. It was the only way to get rid of the anger." Eligible for parole when he is eighty-six years old, Evan spoke a truth kids who have been bullied relentlessly know in their hearts and try to get adults to understand: "I would have had a different life if I hadn't been treated like that."

Another teenager was sentenced to eight and a half years for smuggling a duffel bag full of guns and bombs into Southside High School in Elmira, New York, on February 14, 2001. After years of being a target for bullies, Jeremy intended to go on a killing spree but realized he couldn't kill innocent people and surrendered peacefully to the police. He said he knew what he did was wrong and that he deserved to be punished. "I truly believed everyone hated me, I felt confused, alone, and desperate. . . . I know in my heart I am not a killer."

In an interview for ABC News, Rachel, a teenager from Littleton, Colorado, said she could relate to the loneliness, abuse, and resentment felt by kids who plotted killings at their schools in retaliation for the cruel form of entertainment bullies enjoyed at their expense. Classmates tormented Rachel for five and a half years. "They actually had a contest. They'd high-five each other if they came up with the best name to describe how ugly I was. They'd kick me in the back of my knees and give me small bruises or they tripped me." A quiet girl, she became more withdrawn after each episode, locking herself in her room after school and crying. It was only after she transferred to another school that she could escape her tormentors. "I finally felt human again."

Rachel was able to move to a new school. Elizabeth wasn't as fortunate. She spent a few years as a ward of the court and received her schooling in a psychiatric facility. On March 7, 2001, Elizabeth brought her father's gun to school and shot another girl, wounding her in the shoulder. The shooting victim was Elizabeth's former friend, who had joined with the other girls who had taunted her repeatedly. Making a daily practice of shunning and excluding her from their social circles, the bunch of bullies felt no remorse for what they had done. In fact, some failed to see how "just teasing her" could get her that upset. They didn't get it. Elizabeth, on the other hand, has expressed remorse and has taken full responsibility for her actions.

Shame, Secrets, and Sorrow

How could these situations reach such a point without any intervention, without an adult noticing? Why didn't these kids just tell somebody? In each of these stories, adults did know; kids did ask for help. Few got any relief. Parents are often the last to know. At the arraignment for Elizabeth, her father told reporters, "We had no way of knowing how much she was taunted."

If your child is a target of a bully, don't count on him telling you about it outright: "Hey, guess what happened to me today!" It's not going to happen. Kids have many reasons for not telling adults about a bullying situation:

1. **They are ashamed of being bullied.**
   The bully intends to make the target feel unworthy of respect, unpopular, isolated, and shamed. The bullying is often directly related to the target's race, ethnicity, age, physical or mental ability, or sexuality (including sexual orientation and sexual identification)—things that are intimately connected to the core of a target's being, or are things they can't change, such as a food allergy or their family's economic status. Most targets are caring, sensitive people who would not bully someone else, and who can't figure out why someone would be so cruel to them for no good reason.

   Boys are less likely than girls to tell an adult. Boys are culturally inculcated with the idea that they are supposed to "take it," "be strong," and "go it alone," in concert with "Don't cry" and "Don't go running to Mama," two of society's traditional admonitions. Girls and boys are both unlikely to report sexual bullying and instead "put up with it," seeing it as an ugly part of the social and school culture that isn't going to change any time soon. Younger children are more likely to tell than older kids. Younger kids still think they can ask an adult to help and expect that adults will help. Older kids know that's not necessarily true and often have experience that would validate their thinking.

2. **They are afraid of retaliation if they tell an adult.**

Bullies fuel this fear with threats. The fear and the implied or actual threats of retaliation combine to foster the "code of silence" that enables bullies to get away with their brutalizing activities. In his memoir, U.S. Senator Scott Brown wrote about being repeatedly sexually assaulted as a teen by a camp counselor. His mom and his wife were stunned by the revelation and asked why he had never told anyone. He wrote, "He said that he would kill me, and make sure nobody would believe me."

3. **They don't think anyone *can* help them.**

Feeling more and more isolated by the bullying, they believe that they are in this alone. Bullies are too powerful, too sneaky, and too smart to be stopped. If a school's policy is that in order for something to be dealt with, it must have been seen, children may write off any school personnel effectively dealing with the bullying. Most bullying is done under the radar of adults and won't be seen by them.

4. **They don't think anyone *will* help them.**

They are told to try to get along with the bullies, to just stay out of their way, to "ignore" them, to fight back, and not to be a "wimp." The problem with trying to get along with bullies is that they aren't interested in getting along with the target. The problem with staying out of the bullies' way is that they will hunt down the target, and once again the target will have failed to stop the bullying. The problem with "ignoring" is that it is almost impossible to do. The taunts, the exclusion, the rumors, the punches all eat at the target's sense of well-being. Fighting back often makes the situation worse. Bullies are cowards; they are not ignorant. They picked on the target because they knew they could beat him or her, and the target's ineffectual attempts to fight back will only reinforce the "wimp" label.

5. **They have bought into the lie that bullying is a necessary part of growing up.**
   It might hurt like hell, but the hell is part of the landscape of childhood.

6. **They may believe that adults are part of the lie, since it is not only kids who are bullying them.**
   Some of the adults in their life may bully them, too. These adult bullies might have even given other kids "permission" to torment them, or at least sanctioned such behavior.

7. **They have learned that "ratting" on a peer is bad, not cool, "juvenile"—even if that peer is bullying them.**
   "Sucking it up" and just letting it go is supposed to be a more "mature" response to getting verbally abused, physically abused, or shunned.

8. **They fear that parents and educators will take the bully's word over theirs.**
   This is not a misperception on the part of the target. Often bullies can spin tales of deception and lies about the target being weak, pathetic, or the villain—and certainly not the one being abused.

The bottom line is that often targets are fearful and mistrusting of those they could tell.

Kids might not tell an adult outright that they are being bullied for any or all of the reasons listed above, but they usually give us clues. We just need to be tuned in to them. If your gut says it's happening, it probably is.

Warning Signs

1. **Shows an abrupt lack of interest in school or a refusal to go to school.**

   According to a National Association of School Psychologists report, 160,000 children in the United States miss school every day for fear of being bullied. Why voluntarily get in the path of the school bullies?

2. **Takes an unusual route to school.**

   Going north and three blocks east to get to a school that is south of your home makes a lot of sense if going directly south will put you in the path of a bunch of bullies who have promised to beat you up, take your jacket, or relieve you of your lunch money.

3. **Suffers a drop in grades.**

   It's hard to concentrate on schoolwork when you are trying to figure out how to avoid the bullies, shaking in fear of what will happen next, and still recovering from the last attack. Later in the bullying cycle, your time and energy is used up plotting schemes to get revenge instead of doing a math assignment.

4. **Withdraws from family and school activities, wanting to be left alone.**

   When you feel isolated, shamed, scared, and humiliated, you just want to curl up in a ball and not talk to anyone—or lock yourself in your room and cry.

5. **Is hungry after school, saying he lost his lunch money or wasn't hungry at school.**

   The bully takes great pleasure in extorting lunch money. The lunchroom ranks third behind the playground and hallways in the order of places where bullies attack their targets, so it's a good place to avoid, even if you do have your lunch money.

6. **Is taking parents' money and making lame excuses for where it went.**

   Once again the bully separates you from your money. The threats of retaliation can convince you that stealing from your mom's purse or your dad's wallet poses a lesser risk to body and mind than not showing up with the money for the bully.

7. **Makes a beeline to the bathroom when she gets home.**

   Since bathrooms are number four on the list of places bullies like to attack, you figure it's best to "hold it," even at risk of a bladder infection. A bladder infection can't possibly hurt as much as having your head dunked in a swirling toilet or seeing your reputation attacked via insulting graffiti on the mirrors over the sinks.

8. **Is sad, sullen, angry, or scared after receiving a phone call or an e-mail.**

   You don't know how to tell your mom or dad that the girls on the other end of the phone line called you ugly names and then all laughed before hanging up. You are ashamed to talk about the obscene lies the boy in your English class wrote about you and sent to everyone on his e-mail list. You are paralyzed with fear after opening your e-mail. The bully assures you there is no escaping his taunts. What could your parents possibly do that would help and not make it worse?

9. **Does something out of character.**

   You would rather get caught skipping school than caught in the schoolyard by the bunch of bullies who circle around you every day and "pretend" to be playing. You would be willing to pull your pants down at recess if those girls promise to quit taunting you and will let you into their social circle.

10. **Uses derogatory or demeaning language when talking about peers.**

    If you're being called ugly names, poked, shoved, shunned, and laughed at, you won't have any terms of endearment for the kids who started the bullying or for those who joined in or looked the other way. Who's left to talk about?

11. **Stops talking about peers and everyday activities.**

    If you're being bullied, you have no everyday activities that are not tainted with pain, frustration, fear, and terror. What's left to talk about?

12. **Has dishevelled, torn, or missing clothing.**

    You don't like to resolve conflict by duking it out, and it wasn't a one-on-one fight between equals with competing claims. But saying you got in a fight sounds better than saying you got beaten up, called ugly names, and threatened with further beatings if you told. Besides, the last time you told your dad about the bullying, he told you to fight back. Or you surrendered your favorite jacket rather than risk an attack, but saying that you "accidentally" left it in the locker room will go over better at home than admitting how you really lost it.

13. **Has physical injuries not consistent with explanation.**

    Saying that you walked into a locker sure sounds better than admitting you were shoved into one. Saying you sprained your ankle running to class beats revealing that those girls tripped you in the bus aisle, and then laughed as you limped back to your seat. "I don't know how I got that black eye; I must have fallen out of bed," rings less painfully than recalling how you were held down and kicked in the face on the way to school.

14. **Has stomachaches, headaches, and panic attacks, is unable to sleep, sleeps too much, and is exhausted.**
    Bullies can be real pains in the brain and in the body. The body responds to the stress of being targeted by turning on its chemical defense system so you can fight or flee. But with daily attacks, this system can never shut down. Adrenaline keeps getting released. The body stays on hyper alert, churning up the stomach, twitching the limbs, and numbing the brain. Constantly resisting and fearing the bully taxes the mental and physical defenses. Eventually the system breaks down and the mind and body collapse into a state of exhaustion.

15. **Creates art that depicts severe emotional distress, inner turmoil, or outright violence.**
    This is no Picasso's Blue Period. In fact, it's all black and blood red, and not because there were no other colors available. A sudden, unexplainable shift in your child's artwork to content that depicts violence directed at specific people or depicts a specific plan for violence should not be dismissed as a period piece or a phase. Coupling this art with destructive, violent, and cruel music, games, or movies will not soothe the pain or ease the distress, and can quickly ramp up the inner turmoil to an unbearable level that will likely be expressed in more than a piece of art.

Kids speak in five ways: with body, face, eyes, tone of voice, and words. Sometimes their words are an excuse or cover for what they are really trying to say. Don't dismiss changes in your child's behavior as merely a phase, something that will pass. Be alert to the frequency, duration, and intensity of any changes. Bullying can have long-term emotional, mental and physical consequences. When you see warning signs, listen beyond the words and look beyond the actions to see what is really going on "under the mask of normal."

Bullycide and Mayhem

Many kids, humiliated, embarrassed, battered, and shamed, wear that mask of normal every day, but underneath the fake smiles and nervous laughter is crushing hurt. If the pain is not relieved, the child may go into a tailspin, and the signs you will begin to see are far more alarming than those listed above. Tremendous shame brought on by rejection and humiliation can drive kids to implode or explode. James Garbarino, professor of human development at Cornell University and author of *Lost Boys: Why Our Sons Turn Violent and How We Can Save Them*, writes of the devastating effects of attacks on the core of a person's existence: "Shame imposes this fear that one will cease to exist, the prospect of psychic annihilation. Nothing seems to threaten the human spirit more than rejection, brutalization, and lack of love. Nothing . . . can equal insults to the soul." He goes on to explain that kids who are shamed are vulnerable to committing violence and aggression, because such acts are a way of saying that they are not a cipher; that they do exist. In a tormented child's mind, the threat of psychic annihilation combined with a need to somehow respond to the injustice perpetrated by the actions of the bully and the inactions of peer and adult bystanders leaves him one choice—to strike out.

Violence doesn't just happen. It is not unpredictable, nor does it come out of nowhere. It is the tragic ending of what is often a long, dramatic story, with small hints, red flags, and cries for help along the way.

In *Bullycide, Death at Playtime: An Exposé of Child Suicide Caused by Bullying*, Neil Marr and Tim Field coin the term *bullycide* to more accurately describe when bullied children choose to kill themselves rather than face one more day of being bullied. At least sixteen children every year in the United Kingdom choose death over being battered by their peers. According to a 2014 paper from the U.S. Centers for Disease Control and Prevention, 8 percent of youths in American high schools reported making a suicide attempt in the previous twelve months. Of youths between the ages of ten and twenty-four, 4,600 succeeded in 2013. There are no statistics about how many of those 4,600 deaths were actually bullycides.

Suicide is complicated. After Phoebe Prince's death, newspaper articles suggested that her death was not the result of the merciless bullying she had experienced at the hands of her peers. In an attempt to absolve those charged, it was argued that Phoebe had serious emotional issues, that she was depressed.

> My response to the press and school district personnel was: I don't know if Phoebe would or would not have killed herself without the relentless bullying that she experienced. I do know that had those who targeted her not bullied her; if school personnel had responded to the first reports of Phoebe being targeted by her peers and held those peers accountable; if their parents would have intervened; if Phoebe hadn't been weakened by other issues in her life, thus making her more vulnerable to succumbing to the bullying, she may or may not have killed herself that January. But I do know that the last five months of her life would not have been so miserable. The kids who were charged with complicity in her death were not found guilty of causing her death, but they must live with and be accountable for what misery, pain, and humiliation they did cause her. And those who turned a blind eye must live with what they could have done.

With the approval of Phoebe's parents, E. J. Fleming wrote *Tread Softly: Bullying and the Death of Phoebe Prince. Tread Softly* takes the reader on a powerful journey through the backstory of the bullycide of Phoebe Prince, a bubbly, bright, talented young girl who emigrated from Ireland to the small community of South Hadley, Massachusetts. Cutting through the news reports, rumors, and innuendos, E. J. Fleming writes a compelling story of the roots, ways and means, and aftermath of bullying that went unabated even after Phoebe's death.

There is no question that the death of Brian, a fifteen-year-old who loved to write poetry, was a bullycide. On March 28, 1994, Brian walked into his economics class, placed a gun to his head, announced to his classmates, "I can't take this anymore," and pulled the trigger. His mother said he had been taunted and tormented by his peers for years. "A lot of times the more popular or athletic kids would make him a target. They would slap Brian in the back of the head or push him into a locker. It just broke him." The poem Brian wrote before his death, found by his parents after his funeral, attests to the violence done to him. He writes of being seen by his peers "as an insignificant 'thing,' something to be traded, mangled, and mocked." He would choose to retreat into the darkness of death because "[i]n the shadows, their evil eyes cannot stare my soul into oblivion. . . . I am free to move without their judgmental eyes on me. . . . I can sleep without dreams of despair and deception. In the shadows I am home."

Brian was a quiet, caring, and talented boy. The relentless attacks by his peers steadily broke his spirit and helped destroy his sense of self. One can only wonder how many other children choose the darkness of death over the brutality of their peers.

Speaking about the possible connection between bullying and suicide in young people, Young-Shin Kim, MD, the lead author of the

Yale School of Medicine 2008 research paper "Bullying and Suicide: A Review," noted: "While there is no definitive evidence that bullying makes kids more likely to kill themselves, now that we see there's a likely association, we can act on it to try to prevent it." Analyzing thirty-seven studies on the topic from thirteen countries, including Canada, the United States, the United Kingdom, Germany, South Korea, Japan, and South Africa, she and her fellow researchers found that "almost all studies identified a connection between being bullied and suicidal thoughts, with victims between two and nine times more likely to report experiencing this state of mind."

We do know that some kids stuff down their pain for a long time and then strike back. As many as twenty teens in an American high school of eight hundred students might be considered "high risk" for shooting others at school, according to a Harris poll underwritten by New York's Alfred University. Two thousand and seventeen students in grades seven through twelve were asked about school violence, including whether they had ever thought about shooting someone at school. Eight percent of the teens said they had thought about it, and another 10 percent said they had thought about carrying out a shooting at school. Alfred University researchers then asked about access to guns. Twenty students in every eight hundred had considered a school shooting *and* had access to a gun. Those students are most likely to be boys, in grades eleven and twelve, *who don't feel valued at home or at school* and who have *a perceived low quality of life*, based on their responses to the questions asked by the surveyors. Because of stricter gun controls, the gun issue is not as great in Canada, but with many ways to wreak havoc besides using guns, communities in both countries have reason to be concerned.

A March 2001 ABC News/*Good Morning America* poll of five hundred high school students across the nation found that when students identify a potentially violent classmate, it is generally a boy and one *who has been bullied*, rather than a bully. Seven in ten say the potential attacker they can think of is a boy; 29 percent think of both girls and boys. Just 2 percent have only a girl in mind. Three-quarters say it is more likely to be a person who is picked on than one who picks on others. Research confirms what these teenagers are saying. In a 2002 study done by the U.S. Secret Service, in over two-thirds of the thirty-seven school shootings since 1974, the children who did the shooting all had been "persecuted, bullied, threatened, or injured."

Warning Signs for Predicting Violent Juvenile Behavior

The following are two assessment tools listing warning signs of possible violent juvenile behavior. These tools are intended to be used to determine if there may be a problem in the making, a tragedy brewing. They are not intended as checklists to be used for accusing a child or targeting a child for exclusion. These indicators are warning signs—red flags. It is important to be alert to both the *accumulation* and *combinations* of indicators. Some of these signs are part of the profile of "the bully," some are more descriptive of "the bullied," and some can be found in both. In my own work with young boys and girls who were troubled and/or violent, I found that they all had stories of hurt, abuse, neglect, or outright rejection. They expressed a feeling of hopelessness that was often masked by anger. They spoke of horrific injustices and violations. They came to the program in which I was involved after they had harmed themselves or harmed others—too late for warning signs to be noticed. In retrospect, the signs were all there for anyone willing to look and listen.

The kids whose tragedies are listed in the introduction of this book all had stories containing small hints, red flags, and cries for help. But for many of them, the two lists below serve only as psychological autopsies after their deaths. Far better to use these indicators to assess the need for support and intervention before the havoc is wrought.

In his book *Protecting the Gift: Keeping Children and Teenagers Safe (And Parents Sane)*, Gavin de Becker, a leading expert on predicting violent behavior, shares a list of preincidence indicators (PINS) that might precede teen violence:

1. Alcohol and drug abuse
2. Addiction to media products
3. Aimlessness (constantly changing goals and ambitions, unrealistic expectations, and lack of perseverance and self-discipline to reach the goals)
4. Fascination with weapons
5. Experience with guns
6. Access to guns
7. Sullen, angry, depressed (SAD)
8. Seeking status and worth through violence
9. Threats (of violence or suicide)
10. Chronic anger
11. Rejection/humiliation
12. Media provocation (widely publicized major acts of violence can stimulate people who identify with the perpetrators and the attention they receive)

He adds that many of those who commit extreme acts of violence have not learned the seven key abilities people need to effectively manage life, described by Daniel Goleman in his book, *Emotional Intelligence*:

1. To motivate ourselves
2. To persist against frustration
3. To delay gratification
4. To regulate moods
5. To hope
6. To empathize
7. To control impulses

The lack of any of these seven could be a pre-incident indicator as well. It is important to note that four of these key abilities are difficult to develop if you are the target of bullying. It's difficult to motivate yourself even to get out of bed in the morning if all you have to look forward to is a day of being bullied. It is hard to persist against frustration day in and day out when your emotional, mental, and physical well-being are under threat of attack from the moment you leave for school until you get home again; when it matters not what precautions you take or concessions you make to avoid a confrontation. It's hard to regulate moods when you are ignored, shunned, sneered at, kicked, and the subject of malicious rumors. You're on a roller coaster of fear, despair, anger, frustration, and sadness. It's easier to regulate moods if you feel some sense of control over your life, when you have options available to you, and when joy, laughter, and a sense of belonging counterbalance other feelings. It's difficult to be hopeful when every day is filled with hurt and pain, rejection, and attacks. The most you can hope for is that somehow the bullying will end. If you've been bullied for a long time, you've given up any hope of anyone helping you, and you've certainly given up any hope of being able to make the bullying stop on your own.

Professor de Becker also notes that kids "at risk of committing terrible violence don't necessarily have a history of getting into trouble. . . . This means that if several pre-incidence indicators are present in a given boy, one's concern should not be turned into denial just because someone says, 'Oh, he's never been in trouble.'" This is especially true for kids *who are the target of a bully*. When life seems intolerable, as it often does to kids who have been bullied relentlessly, only one or two indicators may signal serious trouble. Add SAD to media provocation, mix with a life that seems intolerable—thanks in large part to rejection and humiliation—and you can have a bright kid—called "a loner" by his peers and someone who "seemed like he didn't even exist"—who commits suicide by flying a plane into a building.

The assessment tool for predicting violent juvenile behavior developed by the National School Safety Center at Pepperdine University has many of the same indicators as Gavin de Becker's PINS, worded differently. Both lists include indicators omitted by the other. As parents and educators, we need all the help we can get to be aware of possible danger signs. When there is concern about the potential for violence, using indicators from both lists will not magnify the risk or blow it out of proportion. Rather, the two together can make for a clearer picture of the danger.

In the National School Safety Center's assessment tool below, a "yes" answer for each statement is assigned 5 points. The total score determines a child's predilection for violent behavior.

Profile

_____ Has a history of tantrums and uncontrolled outbursts.

_____ Characteristically resorts to name-calling, cursing, or abusive language.

_____ Habitually makes violent threats when angry.

_____ Has brought a weapon to school.

_____ Has a background of serious disciplinary problems at school and in the community.

_____ Has a background of drug, alcohol, or other substance abuse or dependency.

_____ Is on the fringe of his peer group with few or no close friends.

_____ Is preoccupied with weapons, explosives, or other incendiary devices.

_____ Has previously been truant, suspended, or expelled from school.

_____ Displays cruelty to animals.

_____ Has little or no supervision and support from parents or a caring adult.

_____ Has witnessed or suffered abuse or neglect in the home.

_____ Bullies or intimidates peers or younger children.*

_____ Tends to blame others for diffculties and problems he causes himself.

_____ Consistently prefers TV shows, movies, or music expressing violent themes and acts.

_____ Prefers reading materials dealing with violent themes, rituals, and abuse.

_____ Reflects anger, frustration, and the dark side of life in school essays or writing projects.

_____ Is involved with a gang or an antisocial group on the fringe of peer acceptance.

_____ Is often depressed and/or has significant mood swings.

_____ Has threatened or attempted suicide.

* I would add to this list:

_____ Has been bullied by peers or by older children.

Code

5–20 points: Youngster is potentially at risk for juvenile misbehavior.

25–50 points: Youngster is at risk and needs significant amount of positive support, mentoring, role modeling, and skill building. **55 points and above:** Youngster is a "ticking time bomb." The child and immediate family are at risk. Seek help from social and health services, other youth service professionals, and law enforcement.

We need to go beyond these indicators and look behind the scenes at the lives of kids who turned violent to learn how their individual makeup, their life experiences, and their environment influenced their violence. The reasons for acts of violence are as complex as the children who carry them out. Parental support, home life, peer groups, bullying, media violence, and accessibility to guns all play some sort of role. If the assumption made by teenagers is that potential attackers in their schools are kids who were picked on—and the statistics seem to bear this out—then keeping children from becoming targets of bullying would substantially reduce the risk of future acts of violence and would certainly reduce the number of kids who, like Brian, chose death over facing the brutality of their peers.

Commenting in *O Magazine* on the case of Elizabeth, the young girl who shot her classmate, Phillip C. McGraw, PhD, advised:

As parents, we must take the blinders off, think the unthinkable, and see what is happening in the painful downside of a generation that's losing its way. Acts of violence are never justifiable; but no matter how flat you make the pancake, it has two sides. The factors that led to this tragedy include acts of both commission and omission. When students reject, isolate, and psychologically torture their classmates, these children, like wounded animals, will strike back: an act of commission. They have accountability, as do those who stand idly by and allow this infliction of pain: an act of omission.

Those who join in the bullying, cheer the bully on, stand idly by, or are afraid to step in are all part of the problem. In the next chapter we look at the not-so-innocent bystanders: who they are and how what they do (or don't do) can influence both kids who bully and kids who are bullied.

Let us not look back in anger or forward in fear, but around in awareness.

—James Thurber

chapter six

The Not-So-Innocent Bystander

Twelve to one:
What chance had Angus? They surrounded him,
Pulled off his coat and trousers, socks and shoes,
And, wretched in his shirt, they hoisted him
Into the huge wastepaper basket; then
Poured ink and treacle on his head. With ropes
They strung the basket up among the beams
And as he soared I only saw his eyes
Look through the slats at us who watched below.

—Sir John Betjeman,
Summoned by Bells, 1960

The not-so-innocent bystanders are the third group of players in the tragedy. They are the supporting cast who aid and abet the bully through acts of omission and commission. They can stand idly by or look away, or they can actively encourage the bully or join in and become one of a bunch of bullies. Whatever the choice, there is a price to pay. Actively engaging with the bully or cheering him on causes even more distress to the child who is bullied, encourages the antisocial behavior of the bully, and puts the bystanders at risk of becoming desensitized to the cruelty or becoming full-fledged bullies themselves. When kids observe the aggressive antisocial activities of a bully, they are more likely to imitate those activities if they see the bully as a popular, strong, and daring role model. It is not uncommon for preteen and teen boys and girls to use verbal, physical, and relational denigration of a targeted child to elevate their own status in their peer group. The apparent lack of negative consequences coupled with a bounty of prizes such as elevated status among peers, applause, laughter, and approval (or in some cases monetary rewards) for the bullying contribute to the breakdown of the bystanders' inner controls against such antisocial activities. Add to these conditions a group of peers who are caught up in this drama and you have a third ingredient: a decreased sense of individual responsibility. The bully is no longer acting alone; the bystanders have become a bunch of bullies who together denigrate the target further. This spiralling down equally reduces the guilt felt by the individual kids and magnifies the negative attributes hung on the target. "But Mom, he is such a cry baby. He whines when we just look at him." "She's such a dork; she wears such stupid clothes and walks around with her head hung down. She won't even smile." (Rarely do people make the connection that the target's performance and/or attitude is what it is in part because he or she is being bullied.)

The lack of sanctions for bullying, the breakdown of inner controls, the reduction of feelings of guilt, and the magnification of a target's negative attributes all contribute to the cultivation of a worldview that reinforces stereotypes, prejudices, and discrimination. That, in turn, corrupts the bystanders' empathy, sympathy, compassion, and perspective taking (walking in another's shoes)—four essentials for successful peer relationships.

Standing idly by or turning away have their own costs. Injustice overlooked or ignored becomes a contagion that infects even those who thought they could turn away. The self-confidence and self-respect of the bystanders are eroded as they wrestle with their fears about getting involved and with the knowledge that to do nothing is to abdicate their moral responsibility to their peer who is the target.

In Sir John Betjeman's poem, Angus peered through the slats of the basket at those who watched from below. One can imagine the hopelessness and desperation in his eyes, compounded by the knowledge that those who observed his humiliation and spoke not a word of protest or raised a hand to stop it abandoned him. The cruelty was riveting to watch but distressing to contemplate. Yet contemplate it Betjeman did, over the years, before he put into words his own unease, his burden of guilt, and Angus's pain. No one is left untouched by a bullying episode.

The Bullying Circle—The Trap of Comradeship

> *There must have been a moment at the beginning, where we all could have said no. But somehow we missed it.*
>
> **—Tom Stoppard,**
> *Rosencrantz and Guildenstern Are Dead*

Author William S. Burroughs makes the provocative statement "There are no innocent bystanders" and then asks the equally provocative question, "What are they doing there in the first place?" The Bullying Circle (see illustration on page 146) was illustrated by my son, Joseph, and is adapted from the Bully Circle, with permission from creator Dan Olweus, PhD, of the University of Bergen, Norway, one of the world's leading researchers on bullying and peer harassment. The Bullying Circle indicates who these not-so-innocent bystanders are and what they are doing or not doing in a bullying scenario. Starting with the bully/bullies on the left side of the circle and moving counterclockwise in order of complicity are the various characters surrounding the target.

A. **Bully/Bullies**—Plan, instigate, and/or start the bullying and take an active part.

B. **Henchmen**—Do the bully's bidding by taking an active part but do not actually plan or instigate the bullying.

C. **Active Supporters**—Cheer the bully on and seek to reap the social and/or material gains that result from the bullying.

D. **Passive Supporters**—Enjoy the bullying but do not show open support. Get pleasure from the pain inflicted on the target.

E. **Disengaged Onlookers**—Merely observers who say "It's none of my business," turn a blind eye, and pretend they don't see what's happening.

F. **Potential Defenders**—Oppose the actions of the bullies and know that they should help the target but don't, for a variety of reasons and excuses.

This vicious social arrangement makes the bullying possible by inviting the merger of role and person that, in turn, creates the capacity for internalizing the cruelty and shaping later cruel behaviors. In other words, each person in the scenario becomes a character actor—someone who specializes in playing the role of an unusual or distinctive character. Slipping into the role offered in the Bullying Circle, it is easy for bystanders to become invested in the logic and cruel practices of the bully and become not just complicit but "owned by it." In this tight-knit circle, characters find that the more cruel acts they perform or condone, the more their reputation is enhanced among their participating peers and with the bully.

For young people, it is these insidious day-to-day changes in attitudes, beliefs, and prejudices that begin the slow descent into what Sebastian Haffner, in his book, *Defying Hitler*, labels a "trap of comradeship." This is the trap in which a culture of cruelty flourishes when these not-so-innocent bystanders discard their garb of personal responsibility as they further dehumanize the targeted peer. One of the most disturbing aspects of this comradeship is how a group of kids begins to behave as a collective entity, ignoring or belittling anything that could disturb their collective self-satisfaction. This collectivity is the "and" in Arthur Eddington's mathematical formula: "We used to think that if we knew one, we knew two, because one and one are two. We are finding that we must learn a great deal more about 'and.'" The bullies and the bystanders become a cruel combination that is more than the sum of its parts. All of the incidences of hazing on pages 52–53 demonstrate how a group of young people can get caught in the trap of comradeship; dehumanize their targets; laugh at their pain; and ostracize, belittle, or humiliate anyone who registers a complaint.

However, there is also an "or" which has the potential to radically change the formula—and thus the outcome. The fourth character, directly across from the bully, the antithesis of the bully, gives us hope that kids can break out of this trap.

G.   **The Brave-Hearted**—Dislike the bullying and help or try to help the target. This character wears three different and vital garbs—those of resister, defender, and witness. This character is the one who actively resists the tactics of the bully, stands up to the bully, speaks out against the cruelty, and/or protects, defends, and speaks for those who are targeted. The cycle of violence can be interrupted when even one person has the moral strength and courage to resist the bully, defend those who have been targeted, or give witness to the cruelty (document it and/or report it) in order to get it stopped. This character is an awkward and embarrassing reminder that such choices are possible. This is the young girl who sits with the new girl when the high-status social bully in grade eight says to all the other girls, "I don't like the new girl. You want to be in my group, don't eat lunch with her." This is the young boy who steps in to protect the smaller boy when the bully says to all the other boys in the locker room, "Look at that weird kid. Let's throw him in the shower with his clothes on." These are the two boys who buy fifty pink shirts and invite their schoolmates to wear pink in support of a younger boy who was taunted by a group of bullies simply because he wore a pink shirt on the first day of school. All of these brave-hearted kids do what they do at the risk of being taunted themselves by the bullies and their henchmen: "Miss Goody Two-shoes, you're next!" Or, "What! Are you just like him?" Yet they do it, not only knowing that it is the right thing to do, but caring enough about the targeted kid to do something to make the bullying stop.

In *Olweus' Core Program Against Bullying and Antisocial Behavior: A Teacher Handbook*, the author explains the usefulness of this bullying circle as a tool for teachers, parents, and students in discussing ways to counteract and prevent bullying and the importance of kids being able and willing to move to the right side.

A 1995 Toronto, Ontario, study supported Dr. Olweus's observation that the majority of peers do not come to the aid of a targeted classmate. D. J. Pepler and W. M. Craig examined the roles of peers in bullying episodes observed in urban school playgrounds. Their study revealed the following:

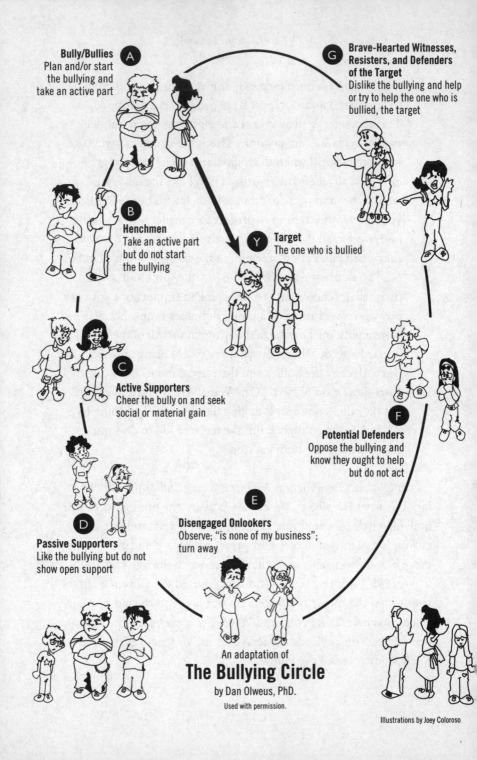

Bully/Bullies
Plan and/or start the bullying and take an active part — A

Henchmen
Take an active part but do not start the bullying — B

Active Supporters
Cheer the bully on and seek social or material gain — C

Passive Supporters
Like the bullying but do not show open support — D

Disengaged Onlookers
Observe; "is none of my business"; turn away — E

Potential Defenders
Oppose the bullying and know they ought to help but do not act — F

Brave-Hearted Witnesses, Resisters, and Defenders of the Target
Dislike the bullying and help or try to help the one who is bullied, the target — G

Target
The one who is bullied — Y

An adaptation of
The Bullying Circle
by Dan Olweus, PhD.
Used with permission.

Illustrations by Joey Coloroso

1. Peers were involved in some capacity in 85 percent of the bullying episodes.
2. Peers reinforced the bullying in 81 percent of the episodes.
3. Peers were more respectful and friendly toward the bullies than the targets.
4. Peers were active participants in 48 percent of the episodes.
5. Peers intervened in only 13 percent of the episodes at which they were present.

The question that begs to be asked: "Why would 81 percent of the kids who would not instigate bullying be so willing to become a part of the attack or turn a blind eye to the plight of the targeted child?" There are a few valid reasons and lots of excuses.

The four reasons most often given for not intervening:

1. *The bystander is afraid of getting hurt.* The bully is bigger and stronger and has a reputation that justifies the fear; so jumping into the melee doesn't appear to be a smart thing to do.
2. *The bystander is afraid of becoming a new target of the bully.* Even if the bystander is able to intervene successfully, there is a chance she will be singled out later for retribution. Bullies are quick to disparage and malign anyone who tries to intervene.
3. *The bystander is afraid of doing something that will only make the situation worse.* In Santee, California, Andy's friends were afraid that if they told administrators about Andy's threats to harm the kids who bullied him, he would be expelled from school. In hindsight, expulsion would have been much better than a life sentence for murder.
4. *The bystander does not know what to do.* He hasn't been taught ways to intervene, to report the bullying, or to help the target. Just as bullying is a learned behavior, so must children be taught ways to stop it, and care enough to want to stop it.

As legitimate as they are, these reasons do not shore up the self-confidence or self-respect that is eroded when a child witnesses a bullying incident and is unable or unwilling to respond effectively to stop the cruelty. All too often these fears and lack of skill can turn into apathy—a potent friend of contempt. Contempt grows best in a climate of indifference. And contempt, as we saw in chapter 4, is what bullying is about.

Bystanders have more excuses than valid reasons for not intervening. These excuses help poison the social environment, increasing the likelihood that bystanders will side with the bully and eventually assume the role of bullies themselves. They include but are certainly not limited to these nine:

1. *The bully is my friend.* Kids are less willing to intervene when the bully is seen as a friend, even if this friend is being unfair, disrespectful, or mean.

2. *It's not my problem! This is not my fight!* Socialized not to interfere in other people's affairs, to do their own work, and to look out for number one, bystanders can excuse themselves by claiming to be minding their own business. This is also known as indifference. In her prologue to *Rescuers: Portraits of Moral Courage in the Holocaust*, Cynthia Ozick writes of the inherent danger of such an excuse: "Indifference finally grows lethal . . . the act of turning away, however empty-handed and harmlessly, remains nevertheless an act."

3. *She is not my friend.* Kids are more willing to intervene when the targeted kid is a friend. Bullies often select kids who have few friends.

4. *He's a loser.* In a highly competitive culture it is easy to write off targets as losers. Bystanders fear they might lose their own status in their group if they are even seen with the targeted child, let alone seen defending her.

5. *He deserved to be bullied, asked for it, had it coming.* Why stop something that is warranted? He didn't even stand up for himself, so why should anyone else stand up for him? This excuse appears to get the bystander off the hook, but it fails to take into account the basic principle that bullying is about contempt. No one deserves to be stripped of his dignity and self-worth. Targeted kids cannot always act alone to successfully fend off a bully or bunch of bullies.

6. *Bullying will toughen him up.* Bullying does not toughen up a target; it humiliates and often enrages him. (See chapter 1, "Three Characters and a Tragedy.")

7. *Kids have a deeply embedded code of silence.* Who wants to be called a snitch or a rat, blamed for getting someone else in trouble? What isn't considered in this excuse is the immorality of silence in the face of malice.

8. *It's better to be in the in-group than to defend the outcasts.* In a clique, once the leader of the pack identifies a kid as a target, the rest of the group tends to fall mindlessly in line, doing the bully's bidding without much consideration for the rights and feelings of the outcast. The in-group becomes so tightly connected and single-minded that there is no room for protest, dissent, or differences. The need for approval and acceptance within such a clique is so strong that even if the bystander felt the momentary urge to protest the harm being done to a targeted kid, that urge would be quickly squelched. When cliques are the norm, there is a clear demarcation of "us," "them," and "kids below us and them," those deserving of contempt and certainly not worthy of concern: "Columbine is a good, clean place except for those rejects. Most kids don't want them here."

9. *It's too big a pain in the brain.* A bystander must weigh the pros and cons of remaining faithful to the group versus siding with

the targeted kid. This mental calculation can create tremendous intellectual and emotional tension. The fastest way to reduce the tension is to magnify the pros of marching lockstep with the group and magnify the cons of helping out the bullied kid. Add the four legitimate reasons above to excuses number one through eight and the answer seems simple—don't get involved. Added bonus—the headache is gone. To a kid—and to many adults—standing up and speaking out can be complicated, risky, difficult, and painful.

Taken together, these reasons and excuses contribute to the erosion of civility in peer group interactions. When civility is diminished, it is replaced by a false sense of entitlement, an intolerance toward differences, and a liberty to exclude that allow kids to harm another human being without feeling empathy, sympathy, compassion, or shame. This erosion of civility also erodes kids' ability to communicate, negotiate, and compromise—three vital skills necessary for solving problems, resolving conflicts, and reconciling differences peaceably.

As mentioned, on November 10, 2000, fourteen-year-old Dawn-Marie hanged herself with her dog's leash in her bedroom. She left a note naming three girls she said were "killing her," because of bullying. In a landmark case that charted new legal territory for holding bullies to account, on Tuesday, March 26, 2002, in Abbotsford, British Columbia, one of those girls was found guilty of uttering threats and of criminal harassment. Another girl was found not guilty of uttering threats; the third girl chose to enter into an aboriginal restorative justice program that was suggested to the judge by Dawn-Marie's mother as a constructive alternative to serving time.

In an article in the *Globe and Mail*, Rod Mickleburgh wrote about testimony given during the trial of the first girl: "They accosted the 14-year-old, threatening to beat her up—once in a very public location before other students. Dawn-Marie was frightened and often in tears over the threats. She tried not to walk home alone. She visited the school counselor." The provincial court judge, Jill Rounthwaite, took aim at the bystanders—those who supported Dawn-Marie's tormentors, gathering around them "without recognizing that by doing so, they added to their power and intimidation. . . . I was particularly dismayed that none of the bystanders had the moral strength or the courage to stand in front of Dawn-Marie and tell them to stop, go away; leave her alone."

The Good Bird's Club

I have the joy and honor of serving as an advisor on resilience and bullying for *Sesame Street*. Developing the concept of the Bullying Circle for preschoolers, the *Sesame Street* writers created a powerful episode called "The Good Bird's Club." Big Bird is elated when he receives an invitation to join the club. But the leader of the club, Pigeon, taunts him about his looks, and Pigeon's henchmen, Blue Jay and Robin, support the taunts with their laughter. Big Bird finds out that in order to be included he must change his bright yellow feathers and his feet, eyes, and beak. Wanting desperately to be included, he begs Abby, *Sesame Street's* fairy-in-training, to cast a spell and change him. She tells him she likes him just the way he is, but Big Bird persists. Reluctantly, Abby helps Big Bird make the changes, but soon realizes that Pigeon is bullying Big Bird and is never going to let him join, no matter how much he changes. Both Abby and Elmo go to an adult, Chris, who convinces Big Bird that he shouldn't have to change who he is to join a club. Chris's message to Big Bird is that "you are special and wonderful the way you are."

Young children watch as Big Bird goes from a happy bird to

a dejected one as he becomes a shell of his former self, trying to please Pigeon. Just as young people would be, Abby and Elmo are conflicted about what to do, and soon realize that one way they can stand up for Big Bird is to tell a trusted adult who can support Big Bird and help all of them create The Happy to Be Me Club, which everyone can join. The website www.SesameStreet.org/parents/top-icsandactivities/topics/bullying has activities parents and educators can do with young children to help them understand the dynamics of bullying and what roles they can play to stop it.

Bullying creates a climate of fear that makes kids feel unsafe. It is important that kids of all ages recognize that they are responsible for helping to create a safe, caring, respectful, and bully-free environment.

> *In one way or another, as a supporter, as a perpetrator, as a victim, or one who opposed the ghastly system, something happened to our humanity. All of us South Africans were less whole. . . . Those who were privileged lost out as they became more uncaring, less compassionate, less humane, and therefore less human. . . . Our humanity is caught up in that of all others. We are human because we belong. We are made for community, for togetherness, for family, to exist in a delicate network of interdependence. . . . We are sisters and brothers of one another whether we like it or not, and each one of us is a precious individual.*

> **—Archbishop Desmond Tutu,**
> *No Future Without Forgiveness*

chapter seven

The Brave-Hearted—The Witness, Resister, and Defender

You can't let people in need down. You can't turn your back to people who need your help. There must be some sort of decency in a man's life and that wouldn't have been decent to turn my back. So there's no question of why or why not. You just did. That's the way you were brought up. That's the way of tradition in my country. You help, of course . . . could you have retained your self-respect if you knew that these people would suffer and you had said, "No, not at my table?" No. No way. So that's not a problem—you just have to do it. And nothing else.

—Preben Munch-Nielsen,
A Dane who, as a seventeen-year-old, rescued Jews during World War II; quote posted at the United States Holocaust Memorial Museum in Washington, D.C.

Bystanders are rarely acknowledged for their not-so-innocent involvement in bullying, nor are they recognized as the potent forces they can become to stop bullying. Stifling a bully requires a simple ethical principle: do the right thing on behalf of the targeted individual, regardless of the actions of the bully or other bystanders. Witnesses, resisters, and defenders confound and disturb those who are unquestionably obedient to the bully and cruel to their targeted peer. Rescuers like Preben Munch-Nielsen were confounded and disturbed as well, but for a different reason. In telling his story as a rescuer he mused, "That your fellow citizens should be doomed because their human value was considered nothing because of their race is an impossible thought." To him, the Jews he rescued were Danes just like him, (I and Thou and We) not the "vermin and bacteria eating at the fabric of our society," that the Nazis made them out to be.

Just as courageous was a young German naval attaché, Georg Duckwitz, who leaked in advance to the Danes the Germans' plan for the deportation of Jews. Georg Duckwitz committed this act of conscious disobedience to save lives, willing to accept whatever penalty might be imposed as a consequence.

What is the makeup of these people who are willing to speak out against injustice and stand up for others who are targeted? Why are they willing to heed the call when the rest of their peers turn a blind eye? How do they summon the courage to take a risk, to take a stand? Do these initial acts of courage change the person doing the act? Most important, what can we learn from them?

Providing proof of the existence and power of good, and the possibility of defying the perceived inevitability of a given harm, people young and old have refused to violate their own ethics and have done the right thing simply because it was the right thing to do—often at great cost to themselves.

"I'd Do It Again"

I met seventeen-year-old Brittne Friar from Brady, Texas, when we appeared on a talk show to discuss bullying and its impact on both the people who were bullied and those who tried to intervene. Brittne was the senior class president, cheer captain, and homecoming queen. When she saw a new student, fifteen-year-old Patricia, being targeted by their peers supposedly for dating a senior, Brittne stepped in to stop the cruelty. The schoolmates turned on Brittne, verbally and physically attacking her and, on one occasion, trying to run her off the road on her way to school. They tormented her online and taunted her in the hallways. Reporting the incidents to school officials did little to stop the bullies and their henchmen. It reached the point where Brittne no longer felt safe at school and didn't want to go. Three months before her graduation, Brittne moved to a high school in another district, forfeiting her role as valedictorian and losing her eligibility for some scholarships. When asked by the host if she regretted stepping up to help her peer, Brittne replied emphatically, "I'd do it again!"

At times, witnesses, resisters, and defenders do the right thing at great cost to themselves and to their families; yet they know in their minds and hearts that doing the right thing is really the *only* thing they can do.

Describing American soldier Joseph Darby's decision to hand over to superiors damning pictures of prisoner abuse by fellow soldiers at Abu Ghraib prison in Iraq, Darby's sister-in-law Maxine Carroll said Joseph "didn't realize that he had done anything that was super special. The way he looks at it, he was just doing his job." A neighbor, Gilbert Reffner, said, "He was brought up to know right from wrong." In an interview on BBC Radio 4's *The Choice*, Darby talked about how handing over the photographs had changed his life forever. Although promised anonymity, his identity was revealed "by accident" by then Secretary of Defense Donald Rumsfeld. Darby was afraid of retribution not only from the soldiers in the photos but also from other soldiers. Most of the soldiers in his unit were supportive of his actions but others called him a traitor for "putting American soldiers in prison over Iraqis." He was quickly removed from Iraq and lived under police protection for six months. The animosity in his hometown was so great that he and his wife had to relocate to a new town. In the BBC interview he commented, "I've never regretted for one second what I did when I was in Iraq, to turn those pictures in."

Pink Shirts

Just as repeated acts of cruelty strengthen and help perpetuate acts of cruelty in the name of comradeship, so, too, do repeated acts of courage strengthen and perpetuate acts of kindness. Those who resist, defend, and give witness to the suffering of others often say that they were changed by their own actions and that, in some cases, their actions encouraged others to become witnesses, resisters, and defenders, too.

In September 2007 at Central Kings Rural High School in Cambridge, Nova Scotia, a grade nine student, Charles, was taunted with sexual slurs and threatened with a beating by some of his schoolmates for wearing a pink shirt on his first day of secondary school. Hearing about the bullying, two grade twelve students, David Shepherd and Travis Price, bought fifty pink shirts and got online to urge their schoolmates to join them in their "sea of pink." The next day, hundreds of students showed up in pink to show solidarity with Charles. According to a CBC News report, Charles walked into the school and was overwhelmed by the support. David Shepherd said, "Definitely it looked like there was a big weight lifted off his shoulders. He went from looking right depressed to being as happy as can be." Talking about those who targeted Charles, David, who himself had been targeted in grade school, said, "If you can get more people against them . . . to show that we are not going to put up with it and support each other, then they are not as big a group as they think they are." This simple act of kindness and support has morphed into a Pink Shirt Day movement throughout North America.

From Target to Witness

Some of those who were initially targeted and decided to stand up for themselves became role models for others who were being bullied, empowering them to stand up for themselves and for others who were being bullied, and to speak out to stop the injustice.

A powerful novel in verse, *Stickboy* is a haunting, furious, deeply moving yet humorous journey told in the first person by Canadian poet and writer Shane Koyczan, who, after being tormented for years by his classmates, grabbed his grandfather's gun to get revenge on those who had bullied him. His grandmother intercepted him as he was leaving the house. Both this novel and his anti-bullying poem that became a TED lecture, "To This Day: For the Bullied and the Beautiful," give testament to the profound and lasting effects of relentless bullying on a human being, and to the resilience to move beyond the hurt and the pain, yet be forever changed by it. Shane Koyczan is an advocate and role model for others who have endured the pain, humiliation, anger, and depression of being bullied. He is also a thorn in the side of those who think that bullying is harmless kids' stuff.

So, too, is Benjamin Tarasewicz. As a kid with autism, Benjamin was regularly tormented by some of his peers who zeroed in on the "quirks" of his disability. In his autism blog, Benjamin writes:

> I know what bullying feels like. When I was in middle school, I actually gave my very first autism "presentation and talk-back" to kids in health class because I hoped that explaining about autism would help them be more kind. I wanted kids to appreciate me and my talents instead of taunting me about my differences.

I never dreamed that I would go on to speak with hundreds of kids my age, helping them to understand that "being different" doesn't mean that someone is less of a person. Actually, being different can give you insights and thoughts that others wouldn't come up with—sometimes such ideas can change the world! Think of people like Albert Einstein and Temple Grandin. . . . I'm doing what I can to teach about kindness and compassion, and one of my big dreams is to give my autism presentation in an events center filled to the top with people—I want to make an impact like a meteor!

A gifted performer, he gives presentations on living with autism, moving listeners to both laughter and tears with his personal story. His message inspires introspection, understanding, and compassion, but at the same time can make you angry that anyone would feel like it is okay to treat a kid with autism as less of a person.

In recognition of his advocacy work, Benjamin has received numerous awards and has been featured in the news and on TV. He blogs about his own journey at benjaminbreakingbarriers.wordpress.com.

Wanting to replace unfamiliarity with understanding and promote a positive perspective about Asperger's, Dr. Frank Gaskill of Southeast Psych in North Carolina and Ryan Kelly cowrote a graphic novel about a boy with Asperger's, *Max Gamer* (www.MaxGamerOnline.com). Max uses his special abilities to become a superhero. Gaskill explains that "Max has special abilities, but rather than having them become burdens, they become ways to help himself and other people around him. He's awesome, just like most Aspies I know are awesome. Max is an awkward and bright Aspie who helps others. His big sister, Sara, loves and hates him all at the same time, while keeping an eye on her Facebook 'friends' count. Grandpa Miles connects with Max on their shared love of history—he specializes in WW2 while Max knows details about every U.S. president." In her endorsement of the book, renowned doctor of animal science and author of *Different . . . Not Less,* Temple Grandin said, "This comic would have helped me when I was a teenager who was being teased." And it can help kids with Asperger's and their siblings and peers begin a dialogue about Asperger's and what it means to accept and celebrate differences.

Standing Up

The cycle of violence can be interrupted when even one person has the moral strength and courage to stand up—or stay seated as Rosa Parks did. When a whole group of people is willing to say no to the tyranny of bullies, the cycle of violence can be broken.

Rosa Parks refused to get up from her seat on the bus—no small act of resistance in light of the consequences (arrest and a fine)—and set in motion a massive boycott of the Montgomery, Alabama, city-owned bus company. Led by Martin Luther King Jr., the boycott lasted 382 days and helped bring about the Supreme Court decision that outlawed racial segregation on public transportation in the United States. When she appealed her conviction, Rosa Parks commented in an interview, "I didn't have any special fear. It was more of a relief to know that I wasn't alone."

The four thousand–member strong Coalition of Immokalee Workers (CIW) was formed in 1993 by a few field hands who began meeting in a church hall in Immokalee, Florida—the tomato capital of the United States. One of the main spokespeople for the group is Lucas Benitez. In his article "Politics of the Plate: The Price of Tomatoes," Barry Estabrook writes about the symbolism for Benitez of a crumpled shirt covered in dried blood:

> One day in 1996, a 16-year-old Guatemalan boy named Edgar briefly stopped working in the field for a drink of water. His crew boss bludgeoned him. Edgar fled and arrived at the coalition's door, bleeding. In response to the CIW's call for action, over 500 workers assembled and marched to the boss's house. The next morning, no one would get on his bus. "That was the last report of a worker being beaten by his boss in the field," said Benitez. The shirt is kept as a reminder that banding together, progress is possible.

Just as there is an ordinariness to those who commit cruel acts, there is an ordinariness to those who become witnesses, resisters, and defenders. By studying the words and actions of people who not only did not succumb to the intoxicating madness around them but instead railed against it, we can begin to see a way out of the morass of contempt, find a way to rewrite the script, create new roles, and write ourselves a different ending. These people acted in spite of the culture of fear, greed, and/or contempt that they were up against. Since our story about who we are in today's social and cultural climate is part and parcel of our human nature *and* our social and cultural climate, breaking the cycle of violence involves looking for ways of being in our homes, schools, and communities that will reduce the harm we do to one another. For bullying to stop and for trust to be established (or reestablished), a cultural change within society is often as necessary as reflecting on and possibly changing our own behavior.

In the next chapter, we'll explore how families can help raise decent, caring, responsible, resilient kids who can act in their own best interest, stand up for themselves, exercise their own rights while respecting the rights and legitimate needs of others, act with integrity, and have the moral strength and courage to stand up to and speak out against injustices—to be that fourth character, the brave-hearted.

> *Unless someone like you cares a whole awful lot, nothing is going to get better. It's not.*

—**Dr. Seuss,**
The Lorax

part two

Breaking the Cycle of Violence and Creating More Deeply Caring Communities

Healthy families and communities give individuals the experience of a life that extends beyond selfish interests. They are the arenas in which we learn responsibility to and for others. They provide individuals with a web of trust and social support that is desperately needed in this transient, swiftly changing society. They combat personal insecurity with a simple, ancient message: "You are not alone." When people are part of an effectively functioning community, they feel responsible in a way that isolated individuals never can.

—John W. Gardner,
"National Renewal," a speech given for
the National Civic League

chapter eight

It Runs in the Family

Our most important task as parents is raising children who will be decent, responsible, and caring people devoted to making this world a more just and compassionate place. We can fashion for ourselves and our children a warmer, kinder world that will dispel the darkness and isolation.

—**Neil Kurshan,**
Raising Your Child to Be a Mensch

The bully, the bullied, and the not-so-innocent bystanders—chances are your child is involved one way or another in this daily drama. Breaking the cycle of violence that this antisocial activity creates involves recasting the roles of each of these characters, rewriting their scripts, and changing the theme of their play. Stopgap methods such as grounding, removing privileges, and spankings to punish the bully and rushing in to rescue the bullied kid provide only temporary solutions and often make matters worse. The bystanders are rarely acknowledged for their involvement or recognized as the potent force they can be to stop the bullying. The Danish activist Preben Munch-Nielsen's words sum up what I think is step one in breaking the cycle of violence and creating more deeply caring communities: "That's the way you are brought up. That's the way of tradition in my country." In *The Altruistic Personality*, Samuel and Pearl Oliner wrote that the majority of rescuers of Jews during World War II also referred to the way they were brought up and to the example of parents in explaining their actions. These heroic people were not "moral heroes, arriving at their own conclusions about right and wrong after internal struggle, guided primarily by intellect and rationality." On the contrary, "what most distinguished them were their connections with others in relationships of commitment and care." These were people who had internalized community and family norms—who talked the talk and walked the walk. When asked how long it took for them to make their decision to help, more than 70 percent said, "Minutes." Helping others was not a decision they made just in those minutes; it appeared to be a habitual response to everyday events in their ordinary lives.

How can we make acting courageously and treating others kindly, fairly, and justly habitual responses to everyday events? It is one thing to *know* what to do; it is another to actually *do* it. Moral education involves not only learning a virtue, but also knowing what constitutes virtuous behavior and having the strength to act accordingly. A kid must *want* to be the kind of person who acts courageously—or kindly, or fairly, or justly—must know *how* to do it, and must be *willing* to do it. We can teach kids the how, but unless they believe that they are decent, caring, and responsible human beings, the *want* and the *will* won't be there.

The strength of our children's "connections with others in relationships of commitment and care" is determined in part by the kind of family they grow up in. The school and community also play an important role, but home is where kids get the first lessons of their moral education.

Three Kinds of Families

In my book *kids are worth it!: Raising Resilient, Responsible, Compassionate Kids*, I identify three basic kinds of families: brick-wall, jellyfish, and backbone. What distinguishes them is the kind of structure that holds them together. This structure affects all the relationships of the family: child to parent, parent to child, parent to parent, child to child, and the way the family as a whole relates to the outside world. Your examination of the three types of families will help you identify things that are happening in your home that are helping your children become decent, caring, and responsible persons; and things that are getting in the way. The keys are becoming conscious of the messages you are giving your children, directly or indirectly, and becoming aware of the emotional and physical environment you are creating for yourself and your children.

Both the brick-wall family and the jellyfish family help create bullies, bullied kids who when attacked have few inner resources to fend off the bully, and bystanders who aid and abet the bully or stand on the sidelines, powerless to act. In contrast, backbone families provide the support and structure necessary for children to develop and nurture their innate ability to care and their desire and will to do good—all of which are suppressed in brick-wall families and ignored in jellyfish families. Backbone families help children develop self-discipline, and even in the face of adversity and peer pressure, they retain faith in themselves and in their ability to make a difference.

The Brick-Wall Family

In the brick-wall family, the building blocks—the bricks—that are cemented together to make the family are a concern with order, control, obedience, adherence to rules, and a strict hierarchy of power. Kids are controlled, manipulated, and made to mind. Their feelings are often ignored, ridiculed, or negated. Parents direct, supervise, mini-lecture, order, threaten, remind, and worry over the kids. The brick-wall family is in essence a dictatorship, perhaps a benevolent one, but a dictatorship nevertheless. Power in a brick-wall family equals control, and all of it comes from the top. It can be a great training ground for the child who would become a bully or the proving ground for the bullied child to affirm her own lack of worth, lack of ability, and lack of personal resources to fend off the bully.

The following is a short list of characteristics of a brick-wall family relevant to the cycle of violence (for a complete list, see *kids are worth it!*):

1. *Absolute parental authority, enforcement of order, and a need to win.* Sometimes the techniques are obvious, blunt control tools. ("You will obey me or else." "You do what I tell you to do.") Often the techniques are subtle, though no less damaging. ("Move over, let me show you the right way to do it." "Can't you do anything right?") Children learn to do what they are told to do without questioning the person making the request or demand, or questioning the purpose or consequences of the deed. Bullies learn to "boss" others around, vulnerable kids learn to "take it," and bystanders learn to "follow the leader" and assume they are powerless to change the status quo.

2. *Rigid enforcement of rules by means of actual, threatened, or imagined violence.* Brute force is often used, and failure to meet expected standards is "corrected" with some form of physical punishment. ("I don't care if you are twelve, you're

not too big to paddle." "Open your mouth—I told you if you said that word again, I would wash your mouth out with soap.") Physical punishment is easy and swift and may stop the misbehavior immediately. But if our goal is to develop inner discipline—that is, discipline motivated by inner rather than outer controls—it fails miserably. Not doing something because you might get hit is not the same as not doing something because it is wrong to do. Research has shown that the majority of bullies and kids who readily succumb to the bullying come from homes where harsh physical punishment is used consistently (or used randomly and arbitrarily, as found in a jellyfish family). Punishment increases anger and aggression and greatly inhibits the development of empathy. Hitting children demonstrates to them that it's all right for people to hit people—especially for bigger people to hit smaller people or stronger people to hit weaker people. The bully is likely to take this technique to school and victimize smaller or weaker peers. Targeted kids who succumb to the bullying often lack inner resources to fend off the bully— having had these resources (a strong sense of self and an ability to respond assertively) quite literally beaten out of them.

3. *Attempt to break the child's will and spirit with fear and punishment.* ("Don't give me any excuses. Just get out there and play hockey." "Stop crying, or I'll give you something to cry about.") A strong will and spirit can buffer a targeted child from taunts. They also help kids come to the aid of another, in spite of what others in the group may do. A broken will and spirit leaves both the targeted child and the not-so-innocent bystander feeling helpless and hopeless. It is that same broken will and spirit that can prompt a bully to put someone down so she can feel "up."

4. *Use of humiliation.* Parents employ sarcasm, ridicule, and embarrassment to manipulate and control behavior. ("How could you be so stupid?" "You're such a cry baby. No wonder no one will play with you." "If you are going to act like a girl, you are going to dress like one.") Bullies learn to use these tongue-lashing and name-calling tools to manipulate and control the behavior of both the bullied child and the bystanders. When feelings, thoughts, and preferences are ignored, ridiculed, or punished, kids can come to believe that there is something profoundly wrong with them, and they begin to act as if that is true, which can make them a vulnerable target for a bully. ("He's such a wimp." Could it be that he has learned to be passive to avoid his parents' wrath? "Why does she just stand there and take it?" Could it be that she has heard these same comments directed at her at home? For a vulnerable target, the negative messages the bully dishes out are reruns of what she has heard at home.)

5. *Extensive use of threats and bribes.* Parents alternate between the carrot and the stick. Kids never know which to expect. It is counterproductive to promote any virtue—such as tolerance, honesty, trustworthiness, compassion, or kindness—in the absence of choice. Bribes and rewards and their flip side, threats and punishment, stunt the child's ability to make a choice. "If you share your toys with your brother, you can pick a treat at the grocery store" (bribe). "You will share your toys with your brother or you will spend the rest of the afternoon in your room" (threat). "You can pick out a toy in the store since you shared a toy with your brother" (reward). "I'm locking up all of your toys since you obviously can't share with your brother" (punishment). None of these provides an opportunity for a child to willingly

choose to share. All seem to demonstrate that we are operating from an attitude of fear rather than faith. If we don't
give our child a reward for sharing, we worry, "Will she ever
learn to share? Will she continue to share if we don't reward
her each time she shares? Will we create a selfish brat if we
don't try to entice her to share or punish her for refusing to
share?" External motivation merely manipulates a child into
performing a specific task. It does not inspire anyone to be
tolerant, compassionate, honest, trustworthy, or fair. Even
when bribes and threats appear to work, children who "do
to please" have no deep understanding of the deeds they
have done, they often have little or no commitment to what
they are doing, and most important, they fail to gain genuine
concern for their siblings or peers. Deeds are done merely or
mostly for the payoff. Children who "do to please" can easily
become overly dependent on others for approval and recognition, lacking self-confidence and a sense of responsibility—
ideal traits for a bystander who willingly joins with the bully
or stands on the sidelines.

6. *Heavy reliance on competition.* Parents encourage or force
children to compete in order to get them to perform or
excel. ("Let's see who can run the fastest to the car." "Why
can't you be like your brother?" "If you try harder, you can
beat her.") Bullying is about contempt—a powerful feeling of dislike toward someone considered to be worthless,
inferior, or undeserving of respect. Brick-wall parents want
their kids to feel good about their individual successes at the
expense of honoring the normal empathic feelings that they
experience for their siblings and peers who lose. Empathy is
an innate ability all children have, but it must be nourished.
The dark side of competition is that it can negatively affect

kids' feelings toward their siblings and peers, stifling the development of this empathy. Rather than celebrate diversity and honor differences, heavy reliance on competition trains kids to see others as obstacles to their own success or as adversaries. It also separates kids into winners and losers. If the bully is seen as a winner (who won at the expense of the dignity and self-worth of the targeted child), bystanders are more likely to side with the winner and not want to be seen with the loser, let alone come to his aid.

7. *Learning takes place in an atmosphere of fear.* Mistakes are considered bad, and there is no margin for error. Perfection is the goal. ("If you wet your pants, you will go back to wearing diapers, just like a baby." "There is no excuse for this B on your report card.") Fear of making a mistake can lead to the false bravado of the bully ("I can do that; I just don't want to."), the feeling of unworthiness of the targeted child who didn't stand up for himself the first time he was bullied ("I must have done something wrong to bring this on."), and the inaction of the bystander who is afraid to take a risk and worries about not doing the right thing ("What if I do something that makes matters worse?").

When parents demand obedience and rule by fear, kids are taught at a very young age not to express their true feelings. Spontaneous expressions of joy, concern, and happiness are stifled, because *the parents stifle all feelings.* Eventually the child becomes so wary of her parents that *no* feelings are expressed spontaneously; she must first "check in" with her parents to see if the feeling is okay. Feelings of anger, fear, sadness, or hurt are not just stifled, they are directly punished or denied. Forbidden to express these emotions themselves, kids get stuck in them. Sometimes they even refuse to acknowledge that they are angry or hurt and have no way of getting rid of the energy produced by those feelings. The energy builds up inside, like steam pressure in a boiler. Eventually one of three things results:

- **Passive-destructive acts against the self.** These acts signal a poor sense of self or even self-hatred. A passive-destructive person often avoids dealing openly with feelings or blames others for "causing" them. "I'm not sad." "It didn't hurt." "It's his fault." Instead of solving the problem, these acts negatively impact the person who has the problem.
- **Aggressive acts against others.** An aggressive person tries to control others with verbal, physical, or relational bullying. These acts don't solve the original problems. Instead they create new ones.
- **Passive-aggressive acts (a combination of the other two).** These acts combine the first two in a creative way that signals that the person is responsible neither for himself nor to others. She doesn't deal with people or issues directly, but uses devious ways to hurt them, making sarcastic remarks or put-downs and declaring she was just kidding, spreading rumors, or pretending to care while in reality intending to harm. She harbors her anger and uses the negative energy to attack targets who may be more popular, pretty, smarter, or kinder.

8. *"Love" is highly conditional.* In order to get affection and approval, children are expected to do as they are told and are shunned when they are disobedient. ("Go away. I don't like little girls who hurt their brother." "I expect you to play

hockey. Three generations have done it, and I'm not letting you cop out just because you don't like getting hit. No kid of mine is a quitter.") When love is conditional, it is not really love at all. Kids who must constantly earn their parents' approval are so busy "doing to please" that they don't have the time or energy to figure out who they are and what unique gifts they bring to life. They depend on others to affirm their worthiness or unworthiness. They are willing to do whatever is asked of them by a dominant peer to get his or her affection and approval.

9. *Teach what to think, not how to think.* If children are taught what to think, they are more easily manipulated and more likely to do something to please someone else rather than do what may be good for them or for someone in need. ("Why don't you wear the red dress? You look better in it than that blue one." "Don't you think you should wear a coat?" "Don't play with him. He's not our kind.") If children are told what to think and not taught how to reason through a problem nor allowed to make their own choices and decisions within reasonable limits and with adult guidance, they will be unable to "think outside the box" to come up with viable alternatives to bullying someone else to get their own needs met or to succumbing to a bully, or to summon the inner resources required to intervene effectively on behalf of a bullied peer.

From the outside, a brick-wall family often seems to be a close-knit unit. But this is only a facade. Underneath the surface is a volatile mixture of anger, rage, degradation, and frustration, held in place by brute force, coercion, or intimidation and waiting to explode—ideal conditions for creating bullies, vulnerable targets, and reluctant bystanders. Brick-wall families give kids little opportunity to find out who they are, what they can do, and who they can become. Children both witness and experience firsthand aggressive, antisocial behaviors exhibited by their parents. It is no wonder that they use these same skills in an attempt to get their own interpersonal needs met. Their prosocial behaviors are often ignored or viewed as a means to some selfish end. Children are not allowed to express their opinions and feelings. Intimidated, coerced, threatened with physical violence, or actually abused, some children seek out others to control as they were controlled; others store up their rage and resentment and let it all loose in acts of violence against themselves or their peers; some become compliant and apathetic, easily led, manipulated, or dominated by any authority figure—including the town bully; and still others become so weakened that they have no inner resources to defend themselves against a bully or to seek help.

The Jellyfish Family

The opposite of the brick-wall family is the jellyfish family, one that lacks a firm structure yet, like the brick-wall family, stifles the healthy display of feelings and emotions, albeit in different ways. In the jellyfish family, a permissive, laissez-faire atmosphere prevails. Children are smothered or abandoned, humiliated, embarrassed, and manipulated with bribes, threats, rewards, and punishments. They become obnoxious and spoiled and/or scared and vindictive. They don't receive the many affirming life messages that enable kids raised in a backbone family to view themselves and the world around them with optimism. (Kids who are optimistic view setbacks, mistakes, and negative social interactions as things they can control or at least do something about, rather than be immobilized and victimized by them. They are more apt to look for ways to solve problems than to place blame or give up.)

Jellyfish families can be divided into two types, jellyfish A and jellyfish B. In jellyfish A, because of her own upbringing, a parent doesn't know how to create a healthy structure, consistency, and safe boundaries for her children. She was likely brought up in either a brick-wall family or a family combining brick-wall and jellyfish parenting styles. She is frightened of repeating the abuse she knew but doesn't know what to put in its place. She becomes extremely lax in discipline, sets few or no limits, and tends to smother her children. Since her own needs were never honored, she has trouble recognizing them in herself and thus confuses her children's needs with her own unfulfilled needs. She has difficulty distinguishing between what her children really *need* and what they might *want*— sometimes substituting lavish gifts for spending meaningful and necessary time with her kids.

A jellyfish A parent tends to become enmeshed in her children's lives, always there to smooth out problems and rescue them from any adversity. Research has shown that kids who are dependent on their parents to get them out of any and every situation, or who are regularly rescued by them, are more vulnerable to the antics of a bully and more willing to give in to his demands. When a parent rushes in to take care of a bullying situation for her child, she not only bolsters the bully, but also sends a clear message to her child that she believes he does not have the ability to assert himself. (By no means am I implying here that an adult should never intervene. In fact, if adults see or hear of a bullying problem, they must intervene. It is the *way* a jellyfish parent intervenes that is the problem.)

In a jellyfish family, there is no structure at the critical points of a family's day-to-day life—mealtime, bedtime, chores, and recreation. When the lack of structure results in absolute chaos, major problems develop. In frustration or panic, the jellyfish A parent tends to revert to the only parenting techniques she knows— threats, bribes, and punishments: "I'm throwing that ball in the trash if you can't share it." "I'll take you to get a treat if you get in the car right now." "That's it. I've had it. All of you to your rooms. If you are going to fight at the table, you don't need dinner." In calmer moments, there are lots of apologies and attempts to assuage the guilt the parent feels for acting just like her own parents: "I shouldn't have lost my temper yesterday. I bought you a better ball than the one I threw away." "I'm sorry I didn't let you eat last night. I'll take you to any restaurant you want." When the parent vacillates between brick-wall and jellyfish, the children are left so disoriented and confused that they easily lose any sense of who they are and what they are capable of doing. They often seek comfort, support, and recognition from anyone—including cults and gangs of bullies—willing to give them a sense of belonging and some kind of security and consistency.

In jellyfish B, the parent physically or psychologically abandons his children, forcing them to fend for themselves. The parent has personal problems that keep him centered almost totally on himself. He may be incapable of caring for his children because of his own lack of a strong sense of self or because of drug, alcohol, sexual addiction, or a mental disorder. Or he may simply be too involved in getting his own life together to be concerned about the welfare of his children. They may have all the material possessions they could want but receive no nurturing, cuddling, or warm words of encouragement—only coldness. This deep sense of loss and grief shows itself not in bruises or broken bones, but in a broken heart—a hopelessness and despair. Children begin to believe that if anything is to get done, they must do it themselves; they can count on no one. They feel unloved and abandoned and begin to mistrust others.

Since their needs have been ignored or discounted, they learn to lie and to manipulate people to get their basic needs met.

Five major characteristics of the jellyfish family contribute to the cycle of violence:

1. *Punishments and rewards are arbitrary and inconsistent.* One day a child is punished for hurting his sister; the next day the same behavior is ignored; the following day he is rewarded for not hitting his sister all afternoon. The child who was hit begins to believe that she can count on no one in the family to protect her. Home is not a safe place, so why should she expect the playground to be any safer? What good does it do to tell adults about the problem? Her sibling doesn't develop inner controls for his feelings and impulses. He learns there aren't always negative consequences for his behavior, so he is willing to take his chances on not getting caught.

2. *Second chances are arbitrarily given.* When a child makes a mistake, is mischievous, or creates mayhem, she is sometimes held accountable and sometimes not. ("I know I told you if you dented the car, you'd have to pay for it. I'll pay this time, but next time you will have to pay for it yourself, trust me." "I'm going to pretend I didn't see you hit him. I told you that you would have to go to time-out if you hit him; next time you will." "That was an ugly thing to do to your sister; I don't want to see that again.") This inconsistency interferes with the child's developing a strong sense of responsibility for his own actions.

3. *Threats and bribes are commonplace.* When threats and bribes are used in an attempt to control behavior, children learn ways to avoid getting caught doing something wrong and ways to get caught doing something good. It's all about get-

ting caught—learning to work the system for the payoff—not about making and keeping friends, owning up to and fixing mistakes, or being kind and helpful because it is the right thing to do. Children don't learn how to get their own needs met without manipulating others. If everything is a deal, they won't develop the necessary skills to be a friend. Being able to get your own needs met in a healthy way and developing strong friendships are two major antidotes to bullying.

4. *Emotions rule the behavior of parents and children.* When emotions rule, it is difficult for children to develop their own inner voice (personal moral code) that speaks to them before they act—a critical element of self-control over selfish and aggressive impulses. They act without thinking about possible consequences and alternative responses. If anger is the most common emotion felt, children will begin to see hostile intent even in the benign mistakes of others. This can prove to be a problem for both the bully and the bullied child. The bully will look for an excuse to hurt someone; the bullied child who has impulse control problems will provide that excuse by purposely or inadvertently annoying the bully. Bystanders governed by emotion are easily caught up in the frenzy of the crowd and go along for the ride or are paralyzed by fear. Either way, they are of no help to the bullied child.

Kids are not taught how to identify or responsibly express their feelings. Often the adults both express their own feelings and respond to their child's feelings in extreme ways. The parents will either smother the child or try to own the feelings for her, not encouraging her to work through her own feelings, thereby protecting her from the consequences of the expressions of her feelings. "She didn't mean to hurt him." "Your child probably provoked him. It is not my child's fault." Smothered kids are unable to develop the strong social skills necessary to thwart a bully's attack. Smothered kids fail to develop the social skills so honored by their peers: a sense of adventure and exploration, physical play, and healthy risk taking. They don't get the opportunities to practice constructive conflict resolution skills. They don't develop the confidence or self-awareness needed to recognize or fend off the inappropriate advances of a bully. If the jellyfish parent rescues the child from difficult emotions and situations, the child learns to be dependent on others to define her own feelings. She also becomes helpless at solving her own problems and is quick to lay blame on others. "He made me mad." "She looked at me funny." "It's not my fault."

If the parent abandons or neglects the child, totally disregarding his feelings, the child learns to put aside or bury feelings of fear, hurt, sorrow, and anger. He learns not to trust others and to manipulate them to get what he needs. One abandoned or neglected child puts himself up by putting others down; he feels good by making others feel bad. He coolly and swiftly disposes of anyone who gets in the way of his getting what he wants. Another who is abandoned or neglected becomes absolutely self-sufficient, allowing no one to get close to her. Still another becomes so needy, constantly seeking others to make him feel safe, loved, and secure, that he becomes a prime candidate for the role of henchman for a bully.

5. *"Love" is highly conditional.* In order to get affection or approval, children must please their parents; they feel an obligation to make their parents feel good. Recognition and affection must be earned. Just like children from brick-wall families, they depend on others to affirm their worthiness or

unworthiness. Since they feel unworthy, they may see others as just as unworthy and may feel no qualms about hurting others, reasoning, "If I have no worth, neither do they." Or, having no way to deflect an attack, they may be so vulnerable that a bully's verbal abuse cuts to the core of their being. They are willing to do whatever is asked of them by a dominant peer to get his or her affection and approval or to make the bullying stop.

Both jellyfish A and jellyfish B families can help create a bully, a vulnerable target, and a bystander. With no restraints on their aggressive behavior, some children will take over the family, terrorizing siblings and parents alike. Others, overwhelmed by a deep sense of loss, have no resources to fend off a bully. Some will readily join with the bully just to join with somebody. Others will stand back, too helpless to intervene, too hopeless to think it would matter if they did.

Kids may survive, but they cannot thrive in a brick-wall or a jellyfish environment. They need the boundaries and guidelines of a flexible, open, and adaptable backbone structure—not the harsh, rigid, unyielding structure of a brick-wall family. And kids need the stable environment created by a backbone family, one that is conducive to creative, constructive, responsible, and compassionate activity, not found in the chaotic and unstable jellyfish family.

The Backbone Family

Backbone families come in many shapes, sizes, and colors. They don't come from any particular background or social strata. They don't live in special neighborhoods. They aren't necessarily headed by older parents or by younger parents. They are not necessarily religious or nonreligious, nor are they of any specific race or ethnic origin. They are characterized not so much by what they do or don't do as by how they balance the sense of self and the sense of community in all that they do. Interdependence is celebrated. There is no cycle of violence here, only an ever-growing circle of caring.

Backbone families can also be described by what they are not: They are not hierarchical, bureaucratic, or violent. Backbone parents don't demand respect—they demonstrate and teach it. Children learn to question and challenge authority that is not life-giving. They learn that they can say no, that they can listen and be listened to, that they can be respectful and be respected themselves. Children of backbone families learn to love themselves and have empathy for others. By being treated with compassion, they learn to be compassionate toward others, to recognize others' suffering, and to be willing to help relieve it. The backbone family provides the consistency, firmness, and fairness as well as the calm and peaceful structure needed for children to flesh out their own moral code. Rather than being subjected to power expressed as control, and in return attempting to control others or giving up and allowing others to control them, children feel empowered. With the freedom to be themselves, they have no need to control or manipulate others, hold anyone in contempt, or subjugate themselves to a bully.

The following are fifteen characteristics of a backbone family:

1. *Parents develop a network of support for their children through six critical life messages given every day:*

- I believe in you.
- I trust you.
- I know you can handle life situations.
- You are listened to.
- You are cared for.
- You are very important to me.

Through love, acceptance, and encouragement, children in backbone families are recognized, valued, and esteemed. They are able to fend off the verbal attacks of a bully, believe they are capable of responding assertively in a variety of confrontations, and are willing to ask for help when they don't know what to do. They know they will be listened to when they need to be heard. Nothing they say or do will be taken lightly, dismissed, or shamed.

Kids who receive these six critical life messages daily are able to develop a healthy, secure attachment with a parent. This attachment allows children to further develop their own innate abilities to be optimistic, to persevere, and to be generous. Optimism—the attitude of someone who feels positive and confident—is critical to dealing effectively with setbacks, mistakes, and negative social interactions. Optimistic kids view setbacks, mistakes, and negative social interactions as situations they can manage or do something about, rather than be immobilized and victimized by them. They are more apt to look for ways to solve problems than to place blame or give up. Perseverance—steady and continued action or belief over long periods despite difficulties or setbacks—increases kids' confidence and gives them the strength to take risks to help others. Generosity—willingness to give help or time freely—enables kids to go beyond themselves and lose preoccupation with their own needs and wants. The development of these three innate abilities helps kids mitigate and modulate innate aggressive tendencies and helps nurture kids' empathy, sympathy, and compassion for their peers.

2. *Democracy is learned through experience.* At family meetings, either formal or informal, all family members are aware of events, schedules, and problems and are invited to participate as fully as possible in planning activities, fixing schedule

problems, and resolving conflicts. Children see that their feelings and ideas are respected and accepted and that it is not always easy to juggle the needs and wants of all members of the family. As the children grow in responsibility and decision-making abilities, their opportunities for both are increased. Family meetings help children see their own needs and wants in relationship to others'. They become aware of what it takes to work together as a group, honor differences, and resolve conflicts peacefully.

3. *An environment is created that is conducive to creative, constructive, and responsible activity.* The physical, emotional, and moral environment in a backbone family is not rigid or unbending, nor is it cluttered with mixed messages or poor role models. Prosocial behaviors are modeled and taught. Children are encouraged to explore, play, take healthy risks, and resolve conflicts assertively and peacefully. Mistakes are viewed as opportunities to learn and grow, not as reasons for rebuke.

4. *Discipline is handled with authority that gives life to children's learning.* When kids create mischief or act irresponsibly, they are shown what they have done wrong, are given ownership of the problem, and are offered ways to solve the problem. Their dignity is left intact. The goal of the parent is to help children develop their own self-discipline that enables them to be decent, responsible, caring people.

5. *Rules are simply and clearly stated.* In establishing the rules, parents draw on their own wisdom, sense of responsibility, and perception of their children's needs, constantly increasing opportunities for their children to make their own age-appropriate decisions, assume age-appropriate responsibilities, and learn to set their own emotional, physical,

moral, and ethical boundaries. ("You can decide which bike helmet you would like to buy. If you want to ride your bike, you must wear a helmet." "It's your job to walk the dog this week." "You can dislike what that boy does; it does not give you the right to call him ugly and hurtful names." See consequences below.)

6. *Consequences for irresponsible behavior are either natural or reasonable.* They are also simple, valuable, and purposeful. There is no need for threats, bribes, or punishment. ("You will need to replace your friend's jacket that you borrowed and lost" [reasonable, simple, valuable, and purposeful]. "You hurt that boy in your class. You need to fix what you did, figure out how you are going to keep it from happening again, and find a way to heal with him. And let's look at a decent and respectful way you can tell him what he is doing that is annoying you" [reasonable, simple, valuable, and purposeful].)

7. *Children get second opportunities.* This is not the same as the arbitrary second chance without responsibility used in the jellyfish family. Kids are clearly given responsibility and a reasonable consequence for not following through. When they blow it—and kids will—they are given a second opportunity to try again, *after* they have experienced the consequences for blowing it the first time. ("You can drive the car again after you contact the insurance company and make plans for repairing the damage done to the back fender. Until then you will need to walk, ride your bike, or take the bus.") By being held accountable for what they do and being able to fix the problems they create, they are less likely to place blame for their behavior beyond themselves and onto their peers.

8. *Children are motivated to be all they can be.* They are accepted
    as they are and invited and encouraged to be more than they
    thought they could be. Learning takes place in an atmosphere
    of acceptance and high expectation. ("I know Jill's behavior
    bothers some of your friends. But it is not right to invite
    everyone else in the group to your sleepover and exclude
    her. I know you can figure out how to make your slumber
    party work. I'm here to help if you need it.") They are held
    to high standards of conduct not to please their parents,
    but because their parents believe they are capable of being
    decent, responsible, caring people. They are taught to act
    with civility—that is, to treat someone with the same dignity
    and respect they would want for themselves, even if they
    don't actually like that person—to be willing when necessary
    to set aside their own wants and concerns for the larger good,
    to criticize, to hold accountable (but always with regard for
    the humanity of the other person), and to resolve differences
    respectfully.

9. *Children receive lots of smiles, hugs, and humor.* All three are
    given freely and without conditions attached. Children learn
    that touch is critical to human bonding by watching par-
    ents give affection to each other and by receiving loving and
    caring touches themselves. They see their parents enjoying
    life and sharing laughter *with* them, not laughing *at* them.
    They are less likely to laugh at their peers if they themselves
    are not the butt of someone's joke at home.

10. *Children learn to accept their own feelings and to act respon-
    sibly on those feelings through a strong sense of self-awareness.*
    Parents are empathic and emotionally available to them,
    modeling appropriate ways to express the full range of emo-
    tions. ("I am sad that he is moving to a new town. I will miss

him." "It's okay to cry, son. I am sad, too, that their family won't be our neighbors anymore. You and Sam had many wonderful times together. Let's think of something to do that will make the move a little easier for him." "I am so angry at Sara. She told everyone I was a slut." "Susan, it's okay to be angry with Sara; what she did was cruel. Let's look at what you can do with your anger that would be constructive, and think of what steps you can take to confront her.") Kids learn to acknowledge and honor their own feelings. They also learn that they don't need to act on every emotion they have. Their own empathy is nourished, perspective taking is developed, and acts of compassion are encouraged. When their feelings are recognized and validated by their parents, children are less likely to become enmeshed in the feelings of their peers. Critical to responding to peers empathetically is the ability of children to see their own feelings as separate from those of their peers and to respond to the sadness, fear, or hurt without becoming so sad, fearful, or hurt that they themselves are overcome or immobilized. They are able to see the pain, know what that feeling is like, and respond in a way that will relieve that pain.

11. *Competency and cooperation are modeled and encouraged.*
Parents demonstrate the ability to do a variety of tasks, and they help their children learn new skills. They show their children how to work and play with others. They show them how to become competent, cooperative, and decisive. ("Let's figure out a bike trip for this weekend. I'll check the bikes this time. Who wants to fill the water bottles, make the snacks, or map out the bike path route? Let's think of someone we can include to ride our extra bike." "We're inviting the new neighbors over for dinner, because that's what you do when

new people move in." "When a new kid comes to class, what can you do to help him feel included?" "What can you do if your friends don't want him to eat at your lunch table?") Competition is recognized as a reality in their lives, but kids are taught to celebrate their own success *and* to acknowledge the empathy they feel for those who lose.

12. *Love is unconditional.* Because they are children and, for no other reason, they have dignity and worth—simply because they are. ("I love you." "You are fun to be with." "I'm here if you need me.") Kids who feel loved, wanted, and respected are more willing to celebrate differences and welcome others into their circle of caring.

13. *Children are taught how to think.* They are encouraged to listen to their own intuition, to be spontaneous, to be creative in thoughts and actions, and to reason through problems. They are spoken with, not to; listened to, not ignored. They are encouraged to challenge authority that is not life-giving, as well as to respect the true wisdom of their elders. They are given a thirst for knowledge of the old and a spirit of curiosity to discover the new. ("When you have a gut feeling about something, trust your own intuition." "You'll figure out a way to solve that problem; I know you can do it." "Can you tell me how you feel about it and what you think we can do to fix it?" "I hear what you are saying. I hadn't thought of it that way." "If someone in a position of authority asks you to do something that is unkind, unjust, unfair, hurtful, or dishonest, you need to listen to your own conscience." "You can stand up and speak out when you see an injustice being committed. If one of your classmates is bullying another child, there are several ways you can be helpful in stopping the bullying. Let me show you some of them.")

Children are taught to figure out a good course of action when facing a moral dilemma. They are able to bring together objective "rightness" (what to think) and subjective "discernment" (how to think) to figure out what could be a good course of action to end a bullying situation. Then the "what to think" and "how to think" are used to connect actions (What can I do?), intentions (Why am I doing it?), and the circumstances of a situation (to whom, when, where, how, potential intended and unintended consequences, and possible alternatives). This course of action becomes a way of life for them.

14. *Children are buffered from the possible impact of a bully, or from the need to become a bully, by the daily reinforcement of the messages that foster a strong sense of self:*

- **I like myself.** Kids know they are loved unconditionally, and are capable of taking full responsibility for their own thoughts and actions. When a bully taunts them, they can do positive self-talk: "I am a good and capable and compassionate human being. That kid who is calling me names is mistaken, having a bad day, and/or trying to get her own needs met in a mean way."
- **I can think for myself.** Kids who can think for themselves are less likely to be manipulated by a peer or go along with the crowd. Given lots of opportunities to make choices and decisions with adult guidance, not adult directives, they are able to step in when everyone else is stepping away, to speak up when everyone else falls silent, and to withstand criticism for their actions.
- **There is no problem so great it can't be solved.** Kids who are encouraged to solve problems tend to be competent and resilient in the face of adversity. Realities are

accepted. Problems are solved. "You have a classmate who is bullying others" (reality). "Let's look at some ways you can help the child who is being bullied" (problem to solve). "You said the bully seemed to be all alone. Maybe not too many people have been nice to him. Do you think you could invite him to join the rest of you at the lunch table?" (problem to solve). "That was a hurtful thing to say to her" (reality). "We need to talk about what would make you want to put someone else down so cruelly" (problem). "What do you think you can do to make proper amends?" (problem to solve). "I will follow up with you to talk about how it turned out."

15. *The family is willing to seek help.* Problems are not denied or hidden. Parents recognize when they need to seek advice from elders or trained professionals and receive the advice with an open mind and heart. ("Our son is bullying other children. What can we do to help him change his behavior and his heart?" "My daughter is having trouble standing up to her classmate who likes to hurt younger kids on the playground." "My son is a target of the town bully. What can we do to help him and to stop the violence?")

Being a backbone parent isn't easy. There are no quick fixes, no sure answers, just lots of opportunities to grow. If you aren't already one, *becoming* a backbone parent takes time and effort but is well worth both. If you identified yourself in the brick-wall or jellyfish family system or a patchwork of all three, remember that you cannot change everything overnight. You might need help and support to make the changes that will be necessary. You might be able to find that help in a supportive neighbor, friend, or mentor. Sometimes a family therapist or counselor can help you make sense of where you have been, where you are going, and what you can do to get there. If you are currently punishing or rescuing your children, you can change your attitudes, behaviors, and habits. In turn, you will change your relationship with your children, which will in turn affect the way they relate to their siblings and peers.

If we want to influence and empower our children to break the cycle of violence, our daily behavior needs to flow from that belief. If we make disparaging comments about people in our community, we are teaching our children intolerance, bigotry, and hatred. If in our words and actions we demonstrate acceptance, kindness, and compassion, our children will tend to do the same. If our children witness us standing up for values we believe in and speaking out against injustices, they are more likely to transfer those lessons to their own everyday experiences than if we tell them they must never bully or make them "share" with their sister "or else."

Growing up in a hostile, cold, and punitive household will not eliminate the possibility of a child becoming a decent, caring, responsible person; however, such an environment will significantly reduce the chances of it happening. In creating a warm, caring, nurturing environment for our children, we get no guarantee that they will become decent, caring responsible people, but in such an environment the possibility becomes much more likely.

> *When a family is free of abuse and oppression, it can be
> the place where we share our deepest secrets and stand
> the most exposed, a place where we learn to feel distinct
> without being "better" and sacrifice for others without
> losing ourselves.*

> **—Letty Cottin Pogrebin,**
> *Family Politics*

chapter nine

Is There a Bully in the House?

> *When people have learned to desanctify each other, to*
> *treat each other as means to our own ends, to not feel*
> *the pain of those who are suffering, we end up creating*
> *a world in which these terrible acts of violence become*
> *more common. . . . I categorically reject any notion that*
> *violence is ever justified. It is always an act of desanctifi-*
> *cation, not being able to see the divine in the other.*
>
> **—Rabbi Michael Lerner,**
> "Our Estrangement from God,"
> *From the Ashes*

None of us wants to think that our child is bullying other kids. But if you are worried that your child might be a bully, you can stop worrying and look carefully at the clues that give you cause to be concerned. It is important to remember that bullying is not about anger or conflict; it's about contempt—a powerful feeling of dislike toward somebody who is considered worthless, inferior, and undeserving of respect. Rabbi Lerner calls it "desanctification, not being able to see the divine in the other." Pierre Teilhard de Chardin called it "dehumanization," not being able to see the humanity in the other person. No matter what it's called, it is easy for you to check to see whether the behavior that is causing you concern has the four markers of bullying: imbalance of power, intent to harm, threat of further aggression, and terror. Along with those four markers, you may sense in your child an attitude of entitlement to control, dominate, subjugate, or otherwise abuse another person; an intolerance toward differences; and a mistaken assumption that he or she has the liberty to exclude someone not deemed worthy of respect or care. The punch your son gave his playmate was not born of anger or frustration; it came from calculated aggression. He seemed to have no empathy, sympathy, compassion, or shame. In fact, he displayed an air of indifference as he calmly explained to you that his playmate was a big crybaby. Your daughter held her younger brother's arm behind his back and twisted it until he screamed in pain. The look on her face seemed to be one of pleasure—the smile was really a smirk. Seeing you come into the room, she quickly grabbed her brother and tried to soothe his pain. But you saw that smirk before your daughter saw you. The teacher called to say your son and a group of his friends circled a young boy in the school cafeteria, squirting him with ketchup and calling him "fag." No, it was not playful teasing, and yes, it was your son who seemed to be leading the pack. While driving carpool, you overheard your daughter and friends laughing about the ugly prank they pulled on the new kid. Your son referred to the new girl in school as if she were a prime cut of meat. You are stunned. He says that's the way all the kids talk; where have you been?

Terrorizing, intimidating, shunning, tormenting, and ridiculing are not sibling rivalry or peer conflicts. They are acts of bullying. It is important that you not make light of what happened and write it off as "usual stuff" between siblings or playmates. It is just as important that you not try to justify, rationalize, or minimize. "The other boy was aggravating my son." "The girls were just playing around. They didn't mean to hurt the new kid." "Everyone gets teased." Letting your child get away with such behavior does not serve her well. You are subtly saying that you don't expect much more from her, thus giving her a ready-made excuse for being cruel or violent.

It is also important that you not punish your child. Punishing your child will only teach him to be more aggressive and hurtful. He will undoubtedly master the art of doing his bullying in ways that are sneaky or "under the radar" of even the most observant and aware adults. More important, punishment degrades, humiliates, and dehumanizes the children who are its objects. (Sounds like bullying to me.) Punishment is preoccupied with blame and pain. It does not consider reasons or look for solutions. It preempts more constructive ways of relating to a child. It drives people further apart, and it enables the parent and child to avoid dealing with the underlying causes of the bullying. The overriding concerns of punishment are: What rule was broken? Who did it? and What kind of punishment does the child deserve? Punishment deprives the child of the opportunity to understand the consequences of her actions, to fix what she has done, or to empathize with the child she has harmed.

Studies of the background of bullies and their most vulnerable targets conclude that physical punishment (and/or neglect) played a big role in the lives of both. What has not been researched is the part more subtle forms of punishment play. I suspect that these have a negative impact as well. Following are the most common:

- Isolation ("If you twist his arm again, you will stay in your room for the rest of the day.")
- Embarrassment and humiliation ("If you are going to act like a one-year-old, you will have to dress like one as well. Go get me a diaper.")
- Shaming ("Shame on you for hurting him.")

- Emotional isolation ("Don't come to me for a hug—you were a bad girl to hurt your brother.")
- Grounding ("You can't go over to your friend's house, watch TV, or use the phone until you learn to treat your brother better.")

Note how these subtle forms of punishment resemble relational and verbal bullying. Embarrassment, humiliation, and shaming might make a parent feel good about doing something besides physically punishing, but they are unlikely to change the behavior of the bully. He will probably avoid taking responsibility for the wrongdoing, concentrating more on how badly he is being treated than on what he did that initiated the punishment. With both these and physical punishment, children are robbed of the opportunity to develop their own self-discipline—the ability to act with integrity, wisdom, compassion, and mercy when there is no external accountability for what they do.

Can a child feel ashamed of what he has done? Yes, but he can't be shamed into feeling ashamed or guilty or remorseful. Those feelings must come from the inside, not from the outside. It is okay—in fact, it is important—to feel guilty about something done intentionally to harm someone else. That's what having a conscience is all about. But the feeling of guilt won't be there unless the feeling of empathy has been cultivated. Empathy and guilt go hand in hand. Your son must care about others' feelings and be able to "walk in their shoes" before he can feel guilty about hurting them or treating them unfairly. Your role is not to shame him, it is to let him know that what he did was wrong and that you care enough about him to help him make it right. When you care this much about your son, he will be more ready to transfer this caring to others. Activist and author Carl Upchurch explained how important this caring is to empathic connection: "I think that they matter because you think that I matter."

If you know your child is bullying his siblings or peers, you will need to act immediately and decisively. Consider your own behavior. Is there anything you are doing to encourage or support the bullying? If the answer is yes, as discussed in the last chapter, you can change your attitudes, behaviors, and habits. In turn, you will change your relationship with your child, which in turn will affect the way he relates to his peers and siblings.

If the answer is no, there could be other socializing influences that are giving rise to your child's bullying—peer relationships or social and educational environments such as day care and school. Since bullying is about contempt, excuses such as emotional, physical, or mental handicaps are just that—excuses. Bullying is a purposeful, thought-out activity intended to harm someone who is seen as inferior or unworthy of respect and concern. Being hyperactive, having an attention deficit, or showing signs of neurological damage may contribute to a child's aggressive behavior, but they do not "cause" a child to have disregard, loathing, or hate for someone else. Those states of mind and heart have to be learned.

Whether the answer is yes or no, know that you can do something to stop the bullying. In his book, *Parents Under Siege*, Professor James Garbarino reminds us that as parents "we are *responsible* for our children's actions; we are not necessarily to *blame* for them." It is good if you can stop the bullying in the early stages before the lines of the role are mastered and your child is typecast as the bully. But it is never too late to change the dynamics. Just as your child was capable of being disrespectful and malicious and callous, so is he capable of being respectful, kind, and compassionate. He learned to bully; he can learn more prosocial ways to act with his peers. The list of traits bullies have in common on page 111 can be summed up in what bullies are not good at: caring about others, being kind to siblings or peers, sharing, getting along, and making friends. Helping your child develop these skills will go a long way toward helping your child take on a new, more constructive role. There needs to be a change in both your child's thinking and behavior.

There are things you can do:

1. Intervene immediately with discipline. (The three Rs: restitution, resolution, and reconciliation)
2. Create opportunities to "do good."
3. Nurture empathy.
4. Teach friendship skills—assertive, respectful, and peaceful ways to relate to others.
5. Closely monitor your child's TV viewing, video game playing, computer activities, and music.
6. Engage in more constructive, entertaining, and energizing activities.
7. Teach your child to "will good."

1. Intervene immediately with discipline.

Discipline is not judgmental, arbitrary, confusing, or coercive. It is not something we *do to* children. It is a process that gives life to learning; it is restorative and invites reconciliation. Its goal is to teach, guide, and help children develop self-discipline—an ordering of the self from the inside, not imposition from the outside. In disciplining a child who has bullied someone, we are concerned not with mere compliance ("Don't bully. Say you're sorry and then just leave him alone"), but with inviting him to delve deeply into himself and reach beyond what is required or expected. When a child has developed his own moral code, committed himself to acting kindly and justly, believes he has both the ability to control his behavior and a choice in how he behaves, and takes responsibility for his own actions, he will be able to get his own needs met while treating others with the same dignity and regard with which he would like to be treated.

Discipline provides the tools necessary to begin the healing process when serious material or personal harm has occurred. It deals with the reality of the situation, not the power and control of the adult. It helps change attitudes and habits that led to the bullying and promotes genuine peace in the home.

The process of discipline has four steps that the act of punishment does not have:

1. It shows the bully what he has done wrong—no mincing words, soft-pedaling it as a conflict, or minimizing the activity. ("Gee, everybody calls people names in the lunchroom.")
2. It gives him ownership of the problem—no excuses ("We didn't mean to hurt him; we were only teasing"), no blame shifting ("James started it; I didn't"), no buts ("But he is such a loser"), no "if only" ("If only he wouldn't act like that, then we wouldn't bother him").
3. It gives him a process for solving the problem he created—restitution, resolution, and reconciliation; in other words, he must fix what he did, figure out how to keep it from happening again, and heal with the person he has harmed.
4. It leaves his dignity intact—he is not a bad person; what he did was despicable; nonetheless, we believe he is capable of being a decent, caring, responsible kid.

Discipline is a constructive and compassionate response to bullying that takes into consideration the intent, the severity of the deed, and the restorative steps needed to help the bully take on a new, more prosocial role. It will involve your time as well as your child's time. However, the time you take is well worth it as your child begins to realize that all of his actions have intended and unintended consequences. He will learn that he is quite capable of taking responsibility and ownership for what he did and just as capable of taking full responsibility for the harm he caused, not because he fears reprisal, but because it is the right thing to do.

Arm-Twisting and Discipline

When you walked in on your daughter twisting her brother's arm, twisting her arm in turn to teach her a lesson, isolating her, embarrassing her, shaming her, telling her you don't love little girls who are mean to their brother, or grounding her won't teach her to not harm her brother; rather, it will teach her to do it in a way that she won't get caught next time. Punishment will likely enable her to see herself as a victim of your punishment rather than as the agent of her brother's pain. Dismissing it or hoping it was a passing aberration will invite your daughter to bully even more. The constructive alternative is the four steps of discipline, with the three Rs—restitution, resolution, and reconciliation—being an integral part of the third step.

You can clearly state what she did and affirm your belief that she is capable of fixing the mess she made. "You twisted your brother's arm. You hurt him and you need to make amends for this hurt. I'll walk through the three Rs with you. I know you can handle this."

The first R, restitution, means fixing what she did. Had she broken her brother's favorite toy, she would have needed to fix or replace that toy. Material damage is usually easier to repair than personal damage. The pain felt by her brother, the fear he may have of his sister hurting him again, and his lack of trust that she will treat him kindly are harder to fix than putting together the pieces of a broken toy.

An apology is in order, but it is requested, not demanded. If you demand an apology, you will get either an insincere "I'm sorry" or repeated insincere apologies after repeated arm-twistings. Such obligatory repentance doesn't heal any rift. A sincere apology is more likely to be forthcoming if the child has seen it modeled or has been the recipient herself of a sincere "I'm sorry."

No matter how heartfelt, just speaking the words *I'm sorry* is not enough. An elementary school teacher explained it to her students with a vivid example. She hammered a nail into a block of soft wood. As she hit the nail repeatedly, she asked her students to think of times when they physically hurt someone, verbally taunted them, or shunned them. With the claw of the hammer, she pulled the nail out of the wood. Holding up the nail, she said, "This is the 'I'm sorry,' but it's not enough." Holding up the block of wood, she asked the students, "What are we going to do about the hole the nail left in the wood?" To repent honestly and unconditionally means to assume responsibility for the deed, admit the wrongness of what has been done, express a strong desire not to do it again, assume responsibility for the damage, and begin to mend the torn relationship.

Repentance cannot be forced upon your daughter, but you can help her arrive at repentance by helping her work her own way through the three Rs. Repentance is not a goal in itself. Rather, it is a by-product that comes about only as she works through the whole process of reconciliation.

The second R, resolution, means figuring out a way to keep the incident from happening again. In other words, how can your daughter create herself anew—not apart from what she has done, or in spite of what she has done, or because of what she has done? Creating anew involves integrating the destructive act (twisting her brother's arm) and all its results and implications into a new beginning. It happened. She can't go back and undo the deed. Wishing it hadn't happened isn't productive, either. She needs to be able to figure out what she actually did (no, it wasn't an accident; she intended harm), what she did to bring it about (yes, she was jealous, and yes, she was angry—not at her brother, but at the fact that he never seemed to get in trouble and she seemed to always get into trouble), and what she can learn from it (I am capable of hurting someone when I feel jealous or angry, when I disregard his feelings, and when I don't try to see the situation from his point of view. I can get my own needs met in a way that doesn't hurt my brother; it's all right to be upset or angry, it is never all right to twist his arm to hurt him). It is at this point that you can talk with your daughter about being aware of the consequences of her actions—the impact her actions have on her brother (it hurts to have your arm twisted), the impact they have on her relationship with her brother (no one likes to be around people who hurt them), and the impact they have on her (twisting arms is a lousy way to play with other people; soon I will have no one who will want to play with me. I want to and can be a decent, caring, responsible kid who is fun to have as a sister). You can help your daughter work through her feelings and help her practice more prosocial behaviors (see number two on page 204). If her actions were motivated by jealousy—disregard or contempt for a sibling is often rooted in jealousy—it is important that you examine the way you treat both kids. It is easy to cast siblings into fixed roles of the "bully" and the "bullied," with each being perceived by you and each other in those roles and acting accordingly.

The third R, reconciliation, is a process of healing with the person you have harmed. It involves a commitment by the offender to honor her plan to make restitution and live up to her resolutions. It also involves willingness on the part of her brother to trust, risk, and rebuild a relationship with her. After making restitution and coming up with practical resolutions, it is helpful if your daughter offers her time and talent to her brother. ("Your brother didn't get off to such a great start today getting his arm twisted. What can you do to help him have a better day?" "He likes to be pulled in the wagon.") Your daughter pulls your son in the wagon. This serves two purposes: one, the bullied brother can experience the goodness of his sister; and two, the bullying sister can experience her own ability to be good and do good. ("I messed up. I am a decent, caring, responsible person who can fix what I did wrong, figure out how to keep it from happening again, and heal with the brother I have harmed".)

Kids would most likely be inclined to stop at step two and be done with the whole ordeal. It is important that this third step take place. It is up to the adult to orchestrate it. With your daughter who has not yet become typecast in the role of bully—she's just practiced it a few times—this step can happen fairly quickly and help her readily assume a more prosocial role. Her brother, who has not been the target of relentless bullying by his sister, will probably be willing to hop in the wagon and go for a ride. The cycle of violence has been halted, and a strong circle of caring is being created.

This is not the case when you are faced with a situation where the teacher calls to tell you your son has been tormenting another child relentlessly and the other child has no desire ever to be in contact with your son, let alone take part in a reconciliation, no matter how much your son expresses true remorse, tries to make restitution, and comes up with great resolutions. Too often, kids who have bullied and the kids they have bullied are forced into conflict resolution workshops—but remember, bullying is not about conflict; it is about contempt. There is no conflict to be resolved. The bully merely puts on his charm for the adults and shows the obligatory remorse—this is just another act with new lines. The bullied child gets no relief, no support, and the bully learns no genuine empathic or prosocial behaviors. There is a chance the bully will seek revenge or the target will recant his story out of fear of that revenge. The bullying will likely continue.

Your son can work on all of the above up to the point of reconciliation and then must be willing to be patient in waiting for the bullied child to be open to true reconciliation with him. Time, in and of itself, does not heal relationships, but it does take time to heal. Even if your son went to the other boy with a heartfelt apology and offer of restitution, the bullied boy might need more time to become stronger himself before he can reconcile. The *intention* behind asking for time is not to hurt your son, make him feel the same pain he inflicted, or make him suffer as much as he made the other boy suffer. The time may be needed for the target of your son's bullying to face the hurt, vent his emotions, and begin to release any grudges and destructive feelings, so that he not only reclaims his own peace of mind, sense of security and safety, and sense of well-being, but also can begin to open his heart and his hands to reconciliation with your son.

Your son can show respect by honoring the distance that may need to be kept during this waiting period. If anyone is to be inconvenienced at this point, it is to be your son. He may have to steer clear of any situation that would put the two of them together, whether it is in the hallway, in the science class, or at the soccer game. He may have to do home study if the child he bullied is too fearful to be in the same school as your son. He may have to be more closely supervised and restricted to certain areas of the playground. His actions will probably be closely monitored. Your son may balk at these conditions. You can gently remind him that it was he who did the bullying.

When the other child is ready, he and your son can come together to look for creative solutions to solving the problems that they face in order to be reconciled. This is not the same as seeing the bullying itself as a conflict. The problems that need to be solved relate to how the two can live together in the school community *after* the bullying has stopped and *after* the bully has worked through the steps of discipline.

2. Create opportunities to "do good."

It's not enough to tell your son what he cannot do; he needs to figure out what he can do. With your guidance and supervision, he can find opportunities to behave toward others in caring and helpful ways. In the process of reconciliation, he will be doing something good for someone he has harmed. What your child can do now is to practice "doing good" *before* he even thinks of harming someone else, not just after the fact. The more times he behaves toward others in caring and helpful ways, the less likely he will be to want to treat them (or anyone else) with disregard. You can brainstorm with your child ways to be helpful at home, in the neighborhood, and at school. "Your brother is having trouble with his multiplication tables. You've got them down pat. Do you think you could help your brother learn them?" "Mrs. Smith has been ill and her garden is overgrown with weeds. Do you think you could clean it up for her?" "The school is looking for crossing guards. You are a quick thinker and very observant. Do you think you could do that job?" You can also invite your child to join you in doing something helpful in your community. "Habitat for Humanity is having a house raising this weekend. They need all the help they can get. The organizers said they needed people who could lift two-by-fours. You're strong, I know they would appreciate your help, and I would enjoy working side by side with you."

Giving your son chores to do, such as dumping the trash, and important responsibilities to assume, such as feeding the dog, may not sound like ways to help your child learn to "do good." Not only do these ordinary activities help children develop the ability to organize their own resources, experience closure on a task, organize their time, set goals, and build skills necessary for working through more complex tasks, they send a special message to kids: "You are an important member of our family; we need you, and we are counting on you to help out." Kids need to believe that they can make a contribution, can make a difference in their families, neighborhood, and school. "Doing good" is a step beyond helping your child get his own needs met. It also helps your child learn to notice and care about the rights and needs of others, which in turn helps him to nurture his ability to empathize with others.

3. Nurture empathy.

Empathy is the core virtue around which all other virtues are built. From empathy can flow sympathy, which in turn can blossom into compassion for another human being who is suffering. (See "Empathy, Sympathy, and Compassion," page 40.) In her book, *Building Moral Intelligence*, Michele Borba describes empathy as "the ability to identify with and feel another person's concerns. . . . Empathy is what enhances humanness, civility, and morality. Empathy is the emotion that alerts a child to another person's plight and stirs his conscience. It is what moves children to be tolerant and compassionate, to understand other people's needs, to care enough to help those who are hurt and troubled."

Empathy is an inborn quality in human beings. Our emotional states are influenced by the emotional states of those around us. Even newborns respond to the distress cries of other infants. By the time they are one year old, children can be observed trying to comfort someone who is sad or hurt. Still not fully able to understand the other child's feelings as being separate from their own feelings, one-year-olds try to comfort the other child by doing what would comfort themselves. They go and get their own mom, even if the other child's mother is present, or give their own favorite toy to the child in distress. By two years of age, they are capable of understanding that feelings have causes and that as toddlers they are capable of doing things to help someone feel happy or sad. By four years of age, most children can take another person's perspective—a critical milestone in being able to reflect on the impact of their own behavior on other people and to come to the aid of someone in distress. By the time they are six or seven, children are more emotionally capable of responding effectively and more intellectually capable of responding constructively. They are able to more accurately identify what the other person is feeling, able to see what the other person needs to relieve his stress, and capable of doing what is needed to relieve the others person's suffering.

In his book, *Empathy and Moral Development: Implications for Caring and Justice*, Professor Martin L. Hoffman explains that at the most advanced stage of empathy, a person is able to process nonverbal and verbal messages, situational cues, and the knowledge of the other person's life condition. A person can then imagine the emotions and experiences suggested by that information and reflect on all of it. "In this way they gain understanding and respond affectively to the circumstances, feelings, and wishes of the other, while maintaining the sense that this person is separate from themselves." Such a level of empathy would prevent your son from coldly and callously harming his classmate or prevent your daughter from maliciously twisting her brother's arm. They would both be able to see other children as worthy of the same regard as they, and be able to look ahead to see what pain their actions would cause for the other children. They would also be more willing to stand up and speak out when anyone else was treating another child unfairly or unjustly.

Bullies tend to have poor perspective-taking skills, seeing incidents only from their own point of view and being concerned only about their own feelings. The language of a bully is, "You will give me what I want. I don't care how you feel," or "I do care how you feel: the worse, the better." If your child is bullying others, he does not lack empathy. It is still there, perhaps buried inside him or corrupted. It is going to take time and effort to uncover it or restore it to its healthier form.

Your child can learn to recognize his siblings' or peers' sadness, hurt, or dejection and identify with their distress. He can also learn to imagine how it would feel if he were in their shoes and know how to extend kindness and help. You can begin to help him by sharing your own feelings, explaining why you feel the way you do, responding empathetically to him, helping him become aware of how his hurtful behavior affects others, teaching him principled moral prohibitions against hurting others, and helping him develop his perspective-taking abilities.

Feelings and thoughts lead to action. By using everyday situations, you can teach your child to first recognize and label his feelings and identify his thoughts: "How did you feel when you failed your exam?" "How did you feel when you helped your teammate score that goal?" "How did you feel when you shoved that boy into the locker?" "How did you feel when you helped your sister?" "How did you feel when you twisted your brother's arm?" "What were your thoughts about your teammate scoring that goal?" "What thoughts did you have about the boy you shoved into the locker?" "What did you think about your ability to help your sister?"

The next step is to help him take on another person's perspective. One way to do that is to have your child walk in another's shoes, to feel what the other person felt, and to think about what the other person thought: "How do you think your teammate felt when you helped him?" "How do you think your sister felt when you helped her with her homework?" "How do you think the boy felt when you shoved him into the locker?" "Why do you think the other boy didn't tell anyone you pushed him against the locker?" "What do you think he would tell you if he could?" "Why do you think your brother didn't want to share his toy with you?" "Why do you think I am upset by that phone call from the school?"

The next step is to help him recognize his own feelings and thoughts and take on the other person's perspective *before* he acts. "What did you feel before you shoved him into his locker?" "The next time you have those feelings, what can you do with them that will eliminate the possibility of your classmate being hurt by your actions? What can you do with those feelings that is more constructive?" "What did you feel before you twisted your brother's arm?" "What can you do the next time you feel that way?" "What was it that you felt you needed?" "How can you get what you need without hurting someone else?" "Can you imagine what the other child would think and feel if you called him such ugly names?" "Is there another way you could tell him what is bothering you?" "Would you want that said to you if you were in his shoes?" "What else could you do with your thoughts and feelings that would acknowledge your own wishes and still respect the dignity and worth of the other child?"

4. Teach friendship skills—assertive, respectful, and peaceful ways to relate to others.

There may be many reasons your son bullied his peer. It's okay to look for *explanations* as long as they are not seen as *excuses*. He may not have known how to be assertive or respectful, aggressively throwing his weight around and grabbing whatever it was that he wanted. He may not have known how to peacefully resolve inevitable peer conflicts. As he reacted aggressively to his peers, they began to see him as someone to fear and to stay away from or to "hang" with so as to avoid becoming one of his targets. Getting into the habit of acting tough and mean, he found himself with an inflated ego, not a strong sense of self; with acquaintances, not friends. Your child may have resorted to bullying because he couldn't figure out another way to make friends in a new situation. Anything he tried made matters worse, not better. He might have figured, "If I can't be the best, I'll be the worst."

To have friends, he needs to be a friend. In fact, one of the strongest buffers a child can have against being a bully is being a good friend. It is impossible to be a good friend and a bully at the same time. Being a friend is about caring and sharing. To learn how to be a good friend, your child first needs to understand three basic principles of any healthy relationship:

1. You control only 50 percent of the relationship with your classmate; he controls the other 50 percent. You can't *make* him play with you; you can only *invite* him to play. The choice to play with you or not is his to make. He doesn't have to accept your invitation to play.

2. You can *influence* 100 percent of the relationship. *How* you ask him to play can make a big difference in how your classmate responds. Yelling, berating, pushing, or hitting him will greatly reduce the chances of his ever wanting to play with you. Asking, sharing, complimenting, and encouraging him will greatly increase the likelihood that he will want to join in your activity.

3. "No" is a complete sentence. If your classmate doesn't want to play, no matter how respectfully you asked, no matter how much you want him to play, you must honor his "No" and go find someone else to play with you.

Knowing that you control 50 percent of a relationship and the other person controls the other 50 percent, that your words and actions influence the whole relationship, that you both can choose to accept or reject each other's invitations, and that "No" is a complete sentence can serve all three characters—the bullied, the bully, and the not-so-innocent bystander—who are trying to change roles and break the cycle of violence. A child who is annoying you is only *inviting* you to pounce back; you don't *have* to accept the invitation. His annoying you never justifies bullying him. A bully's taunting is only an invitation to feel bad or to react aggressively or passively; you can turn it down. The bunch of bullies can invite you to join in the bullying of another child; you can say no and can invite the targeted child to join you in a more productive and creative endeavor. You could even invite the bully to join you (more on that later).

One of the hardest things for young people to grasp is the complexity of their social scene. In the insightful and humorous book *Cliques, Phonies, & Other Baloney*, Trevor Romain reminds kids that they always have a choice about their friendships. All kids want to feel they belong. But they don't need to be in a clique and, in fact, may not want to be in a clique. They can decide that being popular with their friends is the only popularity that really matters. "It's up to you. If you have one or two good friends, that's great. But you don't have to stop there. Use your people skills to make a few more friends. After all, you can never have too many people who care about you and like you for who you are." He goes on to give kids ways to be a good friend and thus keep friends:

The Top Ten Ways to Keep Your Friends
1. Show them kindness and respect.
2. Stick up for them.
3. Be supportive when your friends need help or advice.

4. Tell the truth (but be kind about it).
5. If you hurt a friend, say you're sorry.
6. If a friend hurts you and apologizes, accept the apology.
7. If you make a promise, keep it.
8. Put some effort into your friendships; otherwise your friends might feel neglected.
9. Don't try to change your friends—accept them the way they are.
10. Treat your friends the way you want them to treat you.

And one more thing: always be thankful for your friends.

A bully tries to boss or scare kids into doing what he wants them to do. ("If you want to play with me, you can't play with her.") A kid who wants to be a friend invites others to share in a relationship and then honors their acceptance or rejection of the invitation. Once someone accepts the invitation, a friend is careful to be assertive, respectful, and peaceful in his behavior in order to keep her as a friend.

5. Closely monitor your child's TV viewing, video game playing, computer activities, and music.

In 374 B.C., Plato wrote of his concern about negative influences on children's socialization: "And shall we just carelessly allow children to hear . . . tales which may be devised by casual persons, and to receive into their minds ideas for the most part the very opposite of those which we should wish them to have when they are grown up?" All forms of media have a profound effect on the way our children perceive the world in which they live. Media technology has become so powerful that we cannot afford to be laissez-faire about its consequences on our kids. Too much media involvement and too little "real life" social interaction and engagement stifle the development of social skills necessary to relate in a decent, caring, and responsible way. Much of what is called entertainment certainly doesn't teach the basics of civility. Cruel, raunchy, crude, violent images and lyrics prevent the nurturing of empathy and respect, two critical elements of that civility. Teachers have reported an increase in "mob mentality" among kids who routinely watch "trash TV." Hoping to provoke a peer to lash out, students gang up and taunt her unmercifully with vile comments about her looks, behavior, sexuality, or intellectual ability. So much for a thirty-minute character education lesson on the virtues of compassion, empathy, or respectful language. The television is a far more persuasive instructor than any class lecture on the importance of such virtues.

Research has shown that children who are regularly exposed to media violence are apt to become *desensitized* to real-life violence. As a consequence, they are less likely to be sensitive to the pain and suffering of others and thus less likely to respond to someone in need or to help out in a crisis. They are more likely to be *numb, apathetic,* and *callous* when they become aware of or see a peer being harmed. They are more willing to tolerate ever-increasing levels of violence in their everyday world. They become habituated to a violent, crude, and rude society, taking it for granted and unable to visualize a life that is different.

The video culture of violent fantasy seduces many emotionally vulnerable kids. When they are saturated with vivid media images glorifying violence as the legitimate solution to problems, they fail to learn peaceful conflict resolution skills. When they repeatedly play point-and-shoot video games that portray other people as adversaries, as prey, or as targets, they become desensitized to the act of shooting human beings, and the natural inhibition to killing people is broken down.

In the media, perpetrators of violence are almost always men.

Young boys are being reinforced to commit acts of rape, murder, and sadism. Rapist and sadistic "entertainment" encourages denigration and subjugation of girls and women—talk about teaching contempt! Violence combined with sex is seen as fun, as sport. Add to the violence racist stereotyping, extreme competitiveness, greed, selfishness, and callousness and you have an instruction manual for bullying. In media, people are often divided into "bad" people and "good" people—them and us. It is almost impossible to develop the ability to walk in another's shoes, respond compassionately, or see someone as an equal when they are "not one of us." (In his provocative TED lecture, "The Demise of Guys: Why Boys Are Struggling and What We Can Do About It," and in his book of the same title, psychologist, Dr. Phil Zimbardo looks at how online porn and video addiction is robbing our young boys of the ability or willingness to "navigate real-life relationships, school, and employment" and more importantly, ways parents and educators can help to get "them back on track.")

Kids *imitate* the violence they see and hear. There is a clear correlation between exposure to violence and the development and display of aggressive values and behavior. Kids who habitually watch media violence tend to behave more aggressively and use aggression to try to solve problems. There is no correlation between what happens in real-life violence and the unreal media violence. In the media there are often no negative consequences for the perpetrators. If the perpetrator is viewed as a "good guy," violence is actually cheered and rewarded. Rarely is remorse shown, and even more rarely does a violent program send any kind of anti-violence message.

Just as there are good movies and television shows, there are some fun games and fantasy games like *Myst*, one of the highest-selling games in the industry, which invite kids into a world that requires them to solve a mystery or accomplish a goal. There are many others that require little more than quick, aggressive, violent responses to a perceived threat. These games reward kids for their speed in reacting and for their quick reflexes. The reactive portions of their brains are strengthened. The abilities to reflect and respond are not reinforced; in fact, they are stifled. What are often reinforced are stereotypes, which in turn invite discrimination that can result in real-life discrimination. In the 1999 article "Culture Quake" published in *Mother Jones* magazine, Paul Keegan describes the game *Quake III*: "[It] gives you only a few seconds to enjoy the medium before you get the message, loud and clear. As you drop hundreds of feet through space, you notice other inhabitants milling about on the landing platform below. Being a friendly sort, you approach them. Big mistake: They open fire. Reflexively, fearfully, you begin to shoot back. Heads and arms start exploding. In this magical environment, only one form of social exchange is permitted—kill or be killed. The images this astonishing new technology is most often called upon to render so lovingly are rivers of blood and chunks of torn flesh." *Reflexively* and *fearfully*—note that there is no time for reflection. If they play enough games like this over and over again, kids will be less tempted to assume the best of strangers they meet. It will be "smarter" to assume hostile intent in the behavior of their classmates who are not in their own circle of caring.

A popular game with teen boys, *Grand Theft Auto III*, invites kids to kill police, blow up their cars with a bazooka, then machine-gun others and hear them scream. In this virtual reality, kids can go on to pick up a pair of prostitutes, spend time with them in a car, and then kick and beat them to the sidewalk—all these actions earning the player extra points. Such are the tales Plato wrote about "which may be devised by casual persons, and to receive into [our children's] minds ideas for the most part the very opposite of those which we should wish them to have when they are grown up."

Kids who are regularly exposed to media violence are apt to become *intimidated*. Believing the world is an unsafe and violent place, they become fearful and distrusting of others, overreacting to slights and minor incidents. The intimidation they feel can lead to depression—yes, bullies as well as their targets can become seriously depressed.

If your child is bullying others, chances are he will be more vulnerable to the effects of violent media. In an extensive quantitative review of the literature concerning television, researchers George Comstock and Haejung Paik concluded, "The strongest association between exposure to television violence and antisocial and aggressive behavior is the amount of exposure both to television violence and to aggressive and antisocial behavior." This conclusion has implications for both the bully and a child who is relentlessly bullied and has retreated to violent media as an escape from negative peer interactions.

What can you do as a parent?

- Be aware of television shows, movies, videos, music, and computer games your children are exposed to on a daily basis. Become knowledgeable about them. Offer to watch, listen, and play them with your children so you know what ideas are "received into their minds."
- Keep the television, video, and computer in a family area, and your teen's cell phone charging in your bedroom at night.
- Limit the amount of time for media exposure.
- Teach critical thinking skills to assess the various media messages, intentions, and manipulative tools.
- Expose your children to television shows, movies, plays, books, and games that teach values and virtues you would like them to learn.

- Be alert to the four danger signs of overexposure to "uncivilizing" media: desensitization to violence, numbing, imitation, and intimidation.
- Encourage kids to get involved with their peers in activities that promote creative, responsible, prosocial, and civil behaviors.

6. Engage in more constructive, entertaining, and energizing activities.

Your child can attack a rock-climbing wall with the same fervor he once used to attack his brother. This time, he will achieve a goal without "taking anyone out" in the process; he will feel a sense of accomplishment; and he can "do good" by teaching his brother to climb the same wall. He can "cruise" the river looking for great rapids to conquer rather than "cruise" the school hallways looking for weaker kids to bully out of their lunch money. He can throw a basketball through a hoop with the same energy and accuracy he had used to throw a punch at a peer. The more constructive, entertaining, and energizing activities your child engages in, the less time he will have to bully anyone else; the less he will need to use antisocial acts to get his needs met; the less likely he will be to even want to be antisocial. His poor social skills will be replaced with prosocial habits that reaffirm his own worth and abilities. He will be ready to take the next step in assuming a new role in his relationship with his peers—willing good.

7. Teach your child to "will good."

The real test of your child's ability to throw off the old role of bully and assume a new role of decent, caring, responsible human being will be when he is faced with a bully or a bunch of bullies who are taunting a peer. In his book *Integrity*, Stephen L. Carter writes of teaching children the concept of "willing good"—that is, speaking and doing what is right, "even when the burden is heavy." It involves helping children develop an inner moral voice (personal code) that guides them to do or say what is right, often in spite of external consequences and never merely because of them. This inner voice gives kids the strength to act with integrity when confronted with difficult situations, such as peer pressure intended to cause harm. Willing good involves three steps:

1. *Discerning what is right and what is wrong.* We can teach children the difference between right and wrong, but if they behave merely because they've been told to do so, or because they fear punishment, feel obligated, or are dependent on external approval, what we are trying to teach them will never become their personal code. If it never becomes their personal code, their conscience will be available for sale to the highest bidder. ("I was only doing what I was told to do." "She made me do it." "She deserved to be teased." "Everyone else was doing it." "They told me I could join the group if I taunted him.") By being good and doing good, your child has begun to develop his own inner moral voice. He can begin to engage in self-talk about what his ideals are, what he stands for, and the kind of person he is trying to be. He has practiced taking on another's perspective and feeling empathy toward that person. He will need courage to move to the next step.

2. *Act on what is right, even at a personal cost.* "Hey, guys, back off, leave him alone." At this point, your child is choosing doing good over looking good to his friends. He is willing

to take the sneers and jeers of his peers. ("Are you chicken?" "You just like him?" "Look at the do-gooder.") Willing good involves both taking a stand and taking an action. It is not enough for your child to feel the other child's pain. He must be willing to do something to alleviate it, even at the expense of alienating his friends. In his book *Can We Be Good Without God?* Dr. Robert Buckman asks the question "Why should I behave decently?" His answer: "Because it will be a better world for the human race if we all do."

3. *Say openly that you are acting on your understanding of right and wrong.* "I'm not going to be a party to any of this, and I'll do whatever it takes to get this taunting to stop."

When your son chooses to will good, "even when the burden is heavy," he is reminding his peers that he is not ashamed of doing what he has discerned is right, even at great cost to himself. Your son has come full circle—from bullying another child to being a brave-hearted witness for that child. He will find with practice that this new role suits him fine and serves him well.

Know Thyself

Teaching your children to become assertive, not aggressive, to get their needs met in responsible, constructive ways, and to "be good," "do good," and "will good" takes time and effort on your part. It involves all of the steps above as well as taking stock of the way you get your own needs met, the way you handle minor and major conflicts in your own life, and the way you respond to your children's mistakes, mischief, and mayhem. But the time and effort are well worth it. There will be no more bullies in the house.

Children learn to care by experiencing good care. They come to know the blessings of gentleness, of sympathy, of patience and kindness, of support and backing, first through the way in which they themselves are treated.

—**James L. Hymes Jr.,**
Teaching the Child Under Six

chapter ten

Is There a Bullied Kid in the House?

The fundamental law of human beings is interdependence. A person is a person through other persons.
—**Archbishop Desmond Tutu**

As horrible as it is to find out that your child is bullying someone else, it is heartbreaking to suspect that your son or daughter is being bullied. As I mentioned in chapter 3, don't count on your child telling you outright. Your daughter has good reasons for not walking in the door and declaring that her life is being made miserable by the bullies who refused to let her sit at their table in the lunchroom, pushed her off the swing, wrote ugly things about her on the bathroom mirror, and taunted her as she waited for the bus. Your son has just as many good reasons for remaining mum about being shoved into his locker, forced to hand over his jacket, called names in the hallway, tripped in PE class, and threatened with bodily harm if he didn't give up his lunch money. If you find out via the grapevine or through the telltale clues your kids are leaving, before you even think of confronting them with "Why didn't you tell me?" reflect on the reasons they may have kept the information from you:

- **They are ashamed of being bullied.** Most kids who are bullied are decent, caring human beings who would not target

220

another human being. They find it difficult to understand why someone would attack them for no reason—because there is no valid reason. Bullies bully because they can, and their methods of attack are intended to wound and diminish the targeted peer, often targeting attributes or characteristics the targeted peer has no control over.

- **They are afraid of retaliation if they tell an adult.** Bullies threaten and have every intention of acting on the threats, and your child knows it.
- **They don't think anyone can help them.** They feel helpless. They reported bullying before and nothing constructive happened; in fact, telling made it worse.
- **They don't think anyone will help them.** They feel hopeless. When they reported it, just like we told them to, they were told: "Walk down another hallway," "Avoid the bully," "Eat somewhere else if you don't like what's happening in the lunchroom," or "Ignore them."
- **They have bought into the lie that bullying is a necessary part of growing up.** We taught them the lies: "Boys will be boys," "Girls are just mean," and "It's part of growing up."
- **They may believe that adults are part of the lie.** They bully the child, too, and minimalize the bullying.
- **They have learned that "ratting" on a peer is bad, not cool, and "juvenile."**

As I mentioned previously, a deadly combination is a bully who gets what he wants from his target, a target who is afraid to tell, bystanders who either watch, participate, or look away, and adults who see bullying as teasing, as a necessary part of growing up, as "girl drama," as "boys will be boys." Add to this combination the helplessness and hopelessness felt by the bullied child and the injunctions about "ratting," and there is a good chance that as a parent you could well be kept in the dark about the pain your child is experiencing every day at the hands of her peers or even at the hands of adults you have entrusted with your child.

The Clues Revisited

If your children know that they can come to you with the good, the bad, and the ugly, and that you will actively listen and offer your support, guidance, and wisdom, there is a chance they might tell you they are being bullied. Even if they don't come right out and tell you, if you take the time to have a dialogue with them about their everyday activities and if you are involved in their lives and know their friends, you are more apt to be tuned in to the clues that something is wrong. When you see these warning signs or clues that your child is being bullied, listen beyond the words and look beyond the actions:

1. Shows an abrupt lack of interest in school or a refusal to go to school.
2. Takes an unusual route to school.
3. Suffers a drop in grades.
4. Withdraws from family and school activities, wanting to be left alone.
5. Is hungry after school, saying he lost his lunch money or wasn't hungry at school.
6. Is taking parents' money and making lame excuses for where it went.
7. Makes a beeline for the bathroom when she gets home.
8. Is sad, sullen, angry, or scared after receiving a phone call or an e-mail.

9. Does something out of character.
10. Uses derogatory or demeaning language when talking about peers.
11. Stops talking about peers and everyday activities.
12. Has dishevelled, torn, or missing clothing.
13. Has physical injuries not consistent with explanation.
14. Has stomachaches, headaches, panic attacks, is unable to sleep, sleeps too much, and is exhausted.
15. Creates art that depicts severe emotional distress, inner turmoil, or outright violence.

As well as dialoguing with your children about everyday events and looking for warning signs, you can ask outright:

- Are there any kids in your class who do mean or cruel things?
- If so, what kinds of things do they do or say?
- Are there any kids these kids tend to pick on?
- Do they ever say or do mean things to you?

No matter how you learn of the bullying, your first step is to respond to your child's expressed fears or signs of being bullied with encouragement, support, and love. She needs to know that nothing is too silly or too serious to talk about and that you are there as a caring adult to support and empower her.

A Few Do's and Don'ts

If you teach your kids to like themselves, to think for themselves, and to approach difficulties as problems to be solved, they are more likely to ask for your help, knowing from past experience that your help will be instructive and constructive—and not make the situation worse. They will also know that they can count on the following messages from you:

1. **I hear you; I am here for you; I believe you; you are not alone in this.** No matter what your child has to say or how he is saying it, a good line for you is "Tell me about it," then be quiet and listen. Asking your child to talk about the bullying without asking a lot of questions up front to frame his answers will give you insight into your child's perceptions, concerns, and anxieties. You may be able to get at reasons why the attack might have cut to the core of your child's sense of dignity and self-worth. (Is your child beating himself up for being beaten up by a bully? Is he ashamed of the way he responded or didn't respond to the bully? Was he humiliated by the peers who supported the bully and abandoned or shunned him?)

   After your child has talked about his own hurt and pain, you can begin to gather the facts of who, where, and when. To jump immediately to the facts is to miss the most important part of the incident—what it has done to your child's sense of well-being.

2. **It is not your fault.** The blame belongs on the bully. No one deserves to be bullied. There may be behaviors that your child is engaging in that aggravate or annoy the bully (more on that later). But those behaviors never justify the contemptuous behavior of the bully. This is no time for "If you would have . . . " "If you didn't . . . " "If you weren't so . . . " Remember, the bully has already demeaned your child: "You are not worthy of respect; you can't protect yourself; you have no control over what happens to you at school; and nobody likes you." Your child needs your help to counteract these ugly injunctions.

3. **There are things you can do.** "How can I help? You are not helpless and hopeless. And you don't need to do it alone. Together we can come up with an effective plan." You can help your child figure out ways to assertively stand up to the bullying, steer clear of dangerous situations, take her power back, and more fully develop the gifts and skills she has. She will need your help to explore options, analyze choices, and eliminate those that would make the situation worse or would put her in more danger or provoke more violence. "How will that be helpful?" "What else can you do?" Once those are eliminated, she can act assertively on a constructive option.

4. **Report the bullying to school personnel.** Your child's teachers need to know about the bullying your child is experiencing. They need the facts—the date, time, place, kids involved, and specifics of the incidents—and the impact the bullying has had on your child. Follow up on the follow-through to make sure the adults are actively involved in protecting your child and any other child who is being bullied, and that the bully is not being punished or rescued but is in fact being disciplined. Older kids will not want you to be the one to approach the school—they fear your involvement will only make matters worse. And know that it could if the school community is not committed to dealing with bullying as the serious problem that it really is. (More on this in chapter 13, "Caring Schools, Involved Communities.")

There are five things you don't want to do:

1. **Don't minimize, rationalize, or explain away the bully's behavior.** Bullying hurts a lot. No, the bully wasn't just teasing or flirting or having a conflict; and yes, the bully intended harm. By minimizing, rationalizing, or trying to explain away

the behavior of the bully, you are inadvertently telling your child that she really is in this all alone. It won't take her long to figure out it's best to suffer in silence.

2. **Don't rush in to solve the problem for your child.** Unless your child is in serious physical danger, your *taking over* the situation will convey to your child that he is even more helpless than he thought, convey to the bully that your kid really is a vulnerable target, and convey to his peers that the bully had it right—your son is a "wimp" or, worse, a "mama's boy." That said, we can't put all the responsibility on children to stop the bullying. We can give them tools to fend off and to stand up to a bully, but it is also our job as adults to create an environment that is not conducive to bullying and to confront bullying when we see it or hear about it. This is not the same as rushing in to take care of the bullying situation and rendering even more powerless the target. A bully learned to bully. She needs to learn how not to bully, and part of that teaching needs to be done by an adult. Since the majority of bystanders in some way support the bully, it is a *system* that has to be changed. All of the children playing out their own scripts are going to need support, instruction, and guidance to change the theme of their play.

3. **Don't tell your child to avoid or ignore the bully.** You are inadvertently telling him to keep running and hiding, remaining in fear of the bully. Bullies can "smell" that fear. Your son will begin to act like an ever-weakening target and in turn signal to any and all bullies in the schoolyard that he is an available target. It is okay to avoid the bully to avoid immediate and present danger, but it is not a long-term solution to the bullying. A sixteen-year-old complained to the principal of his high school that a group of kids were taunt-

ing him with ugly religious slurs and slamming him into lockers as he tried to get to class. The principal suggested he walk down another hallway, not just today until the problem could be addressed, but for the rest of the term. It is lousy when the onus is put on the target, not on the bullies.

To avoid is hard; to ignore is almost impossible. In attempting to ignore the relentless taunting and attacks, your child is likely to begin to internalize the messages of those who are targeting her, "I am dumb, I am stupid, I'm no good."

4. **Don't tell your child to fight back.** Do you really want to teach your child that fighting is the answer? It isn't and, besides, the bully probably picked on your son because he saw him as a less than equal match. After your child loses, there will be bigger bullies waiting for him. Defend himself, yes. Be assertive, yes. But being assertive more often than not will involve your child using his head and his feet—in that order. "This is a dumb place to be. I'm out of here." He heads out not because he is chicken, but because he is smart. Kids who respond assertively to the bully are more likely to successfully counteract the bullying than kids who try to fight back.

5. **Don't confront the bully or the bully's parents alone.** The bully learned to bully somewhere, and it might just be from his parents. They may be defensive and uncooperative and quick to blame the target. When the mother of a bully was confronted with the fact that her seven-year-old daughter had enlisted the help of several classmates to circle another classmate and call the targeted girl "brown and ugly," the mother insisted that her daughter wouldn't do such a thing, and that even if she did, the other little girl must have asked for it.

If at all possible, enlist the help of a school counselor to confer with you and your child and then with the bully and the bully's parents. (More on this in chapter 13, "Caring Schools, Involved Communities.")

Telling and Tattling—Discerning the Difference

Children need to know that they can and should tell an adult about the bullying, *even if they were able to stop the bullying themselves.* If not confronted, the bully will find another child to harass—one who may not be as capable of fending off the bully. A target who tells an adult in order to prevent someone else from sharing the same fate is playing the all-important role of witness.

In the *Sesame Street* episode "The Good Bird's Club," after Big Bird is relentlessly bullied by another bird in the neighborhood, Abby tells Elmo that they need to tell an adult about the bullying. Elmo replies, "I don't want to tattle." Abby responds, "It's not tattling; it's helping." Just like the bullying Big Bird was enduring, most bullying done by children is done under the radar of adults, and just like Elmo, children are hesitant to report it. We have to convince our children that we can be trusted, are powerful allies, and will act—if only they would tell us. That requires that we teach them what Abby already knows—to discern the difference between telling and tattling.

From the time our children begin telling tales on their siblings and peers, we admonish them, "Don't tattle, don't snitch." Then, when kids keep potentially lethal information from us, we ask, "Why didn't you tell me?" Even the words we use—*tattle, snitch, rat, squeal, fink*—have a harshness that communicates to our kids that it's not a good thing to ever tell on anybody. These words entrench children in the deeply embedded code of silence. What is lost in this code is the immorality of that silence in the face of malice.

228

Just as we can teach our kids the difference between teasing and taunting, flirting and harassing, and fighting and bullying, we can teach them the difference between telling and tattling. I use a simple formula:

> Telling: If it will get you or another child *out* of trouble, tell me.
> Tattling: If it will only get another child *in* trouble, don't tell me.
> If it is *both*, I need to know.

This formula does not tell kids what to report to an adult. It is a tool to help them *discern* what and when to tell, no matter what kind of situation they are facing.

Using everyday events as opportunities to practice, you can start teaching four-year-olds the difference between telling and tattling. "James is sucking his thumb again." (Telling me is an attempt to get him in trouble; don't tell.) "James's front tooth fell out, and his mouth is all bloody." (Telling me can get him out of a mess; tell.) "James's front tooth fell out when he was sucking his thumb, and his mouth is a bloody mess." (It's both. I need to know.) By the time kids are six, they can be taught the difference between teasing and taunting and sibling rivalry and bullying. If Johnny isn't sharing the swing, telling me will only get him in trouble, so don't tell me. Use the skills that I've taught you to negotiate with him. Remember, he controls 50 percent of the relationship—and at this point 100 percent of the swing. You control 50 percent of the relationship; you both can influence 100 percent of the relationship; and "No" is a complete sentence. If Johnny knocked Jeff off the swing and called him an ugly name, tell me, I need to know. If Susie is telling all the girls in grade six to exclude the new girl to see if she has what it takes to survive three weeks of being shunned, tell me, I need to know.

If this distinction is taught to children when they are young, it can pay off in the teen years. Adolescents will understand that it is not tattling, snitching, ratting, or squealing to tell you that their friend who has been tormented by peers is giving his possessions away and saying subtle good-byes to classmates. Telling may help get him out of the mess he is in; not telling could be life-threatening. Your daughter's girlfriend who is five months' pregnant and is binding herself up in an attempt to hide her pregnancy has sworn your daughter to secrecy about the baby. Telling might get her in trouble with some people, but it will certainly get her and her baby out of trouble. Your daughter has the tools to discern what to do. Will she do it? We don't know, but having the tools will help. There is going to be a fight after school, and an arsenal of weapons has been hidden in the lockers of rival teens; telling will get kids in trouble in the short term but out of big trouble and serious regret in the long term.

Julie's telling her mom about Meridith challenging Meghan to pull her pants down on the playground or risk being permanently ostracized from the group (chapter 3) was a matter of getting someone in trouble and someone out of trouble. Julie knew she could talk to her mom and that her mom would believe her and do something about the situation. In the end, all three girls benefited from her telling.

As well as practicing with everyday situations, keep the lines of communication open by being truly present and listening to what your kids are saying—or trying to say—with their fumbled words, body language, and actions. Kids won't say a word if they think their telling will be met with judgmental statements, disbelief, or threats: "Don't say such crazy things." "Don't tattle." "He wouldn't kill himself." "If I ever catch you doing something as stupid as he did, you'll be grounded." What teen would want to hear that his friend wouldn't be stupid enough to kill himself, that her pregnant friend is a slut, that fights like that don't happen in this part of town? Imagine what might have happened if Julie's mom had insisted that nobody would make a girl do that on the playground, or said that Julie must be mistaken or that it was not her problem?

That is what happened to Andy's friends. On March 4, 2001, in Santee, California, fifteen-year-old Andy boasted at a weekend sleepover of his plan to kill kids at his school. An adult, overhearing the plan, told the boy that if he ever said things like that again, the adult would turn him in to the police. To that threat, Andy responded, "I was just kidding." The next day, Andy killed two people and wounded thirteen more at his school. He wasn't kidding; he was trying to speak of unspeakable torment and hurt that had turned to rage.

Some of Andy's friends had been concerned enough to tell their own parents about the threat. One parent laments the fact she dismissed her own son's concern with the comment "Don't be silly, he wouldn't do such a thing." These same friends were concerned enough to pat Andy down when he arrived at school that day, but they missed the loaded handgun in his backpack. "We didn't think he was serious." "If we'd told, it would have gotten him in trouble." "He was teased a lot, picked on every day."

One can only wonder what would have happened had an adult been aware of Andy's pain, taken the boy aside, and offered a "Talk to me about it," alerted the boy's parent, asked the parent about the child's access to a weapon, and notified someone at the school of the rage this boy was expressing; if his friends had reported the plan to adults who had taken them seriously; if taunting a boy were not considered an okay thing to do; if . . .

That same week, an eight-year-old girl reported that a classmate had threatened to kill her. She was listened to and taken seriously; the loaded gun was confiscated from the eight-year-old boy's backpack. Yes, the boy is in serious trouble, but a lot less trouble than he'd be in if he had shot the girl. And the girl is alive to tell how she learned when to tell and whom to tell.

Young people who spend time in online communities need to learn the same lesson that the eight-year-old had figured out and that Andy's friends learned too late. On the night when twenty-two-year-old college student Elliot went on a shooting rampage in Isla Vista, California, killing six people before killing himself, several members of his online community quickly figured out that the man they had been "jousting with online" was the young man responsible for the killings. The *New York Times* recounted part of their conversation:

> "Could someone tip off the police just in case?" one wrote, even as six people had already died at Elliot's hand. "Why?" another asked. "Don't," someone else posted. "Whatever happens. We didn't do anything so just let it happen if it does."

And it did happen and will happen again. The signs will be there, the messages known to be "red flags" will show up. And when they do, will any kid tell, and will we listen?

Four Antidotes to Bullying

The four most powerful antidotes to bullying are a strong sense of self, being a friend, having at least one good friend who is there for you through thick and thin, and being able to successfully get into a group (and know when to get out). A bully will try to sabotage all of these, first by harassing your child, chipping away at his sense of dignity and worth; second by effectively isolating him so that he is unable to develop critical relationship skills with his peers; and third by enlisting peers to join in or at least not stop the bullying—

further shutting your child off from any positive peer relationships and critical friendships. Being bullied can lead to further rejection by peers. At a time when he is most in need of support from them, he is least likely to receive it. It seems nobody likes him no matter how hard he tries to fit in and be accepted. Your child begins to see school as a threatening, lonely place where he can't count on anyone to help him out. The more he is bullied without any relief or intervention, the more he will have to change what he does, where he goes, and whom he can hope to socialize with. The cycle of violence grinds on.

The cycle of violence is easier to break early on; but no matter when in the cycle you become aware of your child being bullied, you can help him strengthen his sense of self, show him how to be a good friend, teach him how to nurture strong, healthy friendships, and teach him how to introduce himself into a group. In a 1990 thesis, "The Behavioral Attributes of Victimized Children," doctoral student S. Pierce wrote about the five personality factors that seemed to protect kids from becoming increasingly victimized over the course of the school year: 1. friendliness, 2. willingness to share, 3. willingness to cooperate, 4. skill in joining the play of other children, and 5. possessing a sense of humor—all factors critical to the four antidotes to bullying.

Strong Sense of Self

If your kids see themselves as being capable, competent, cooperative, responsible, resourceful, and resilient, not only are they less likely to be cruel and combative bullies, they are more likely to be able to effectively fend off an attack by one. As you saw in "Scenes from a Tragedy" in chapter 1, the first response of bullied children is critical. When a bully comes along, who has contempt for a particular group and your children fit in that group, they may get targeted no matter how strong they stand, how secure they look, how quick with words they are. To tell kids that if they use their bully-proofing skills, a bully won't target them is a lie—a hopeful one, but a lie nevertheless. The reality is that the better your children feel about themselves, the less likely they are to *succumb* to the tactics of a bully should one be so foolish as to target them.

Children who use positive self-talk to develop confidence and respect for themselves are more likely to see the cause of the bullying as coming from the *outside* and, therefore, not something to beat themselves up over. The line I like to give children is, "I am a decent, caring, human being. I didn't ask for this. I don't deserve this. That kid is sure trying to get his needs met in a lousy way." Sometimes these lines are best spoken under their breath as they walk away from the taunting; sometimes the words are spoken directly to the bully. Either way, the targeted child affirms his own dignity and self-worth and begins to put the problem where it belongs—on the bully.

On the other hand, if your child lacks a strong sense of self, is praise-dependent, and tends to beat herself up for things that go wrong in her life, she will likely blame herself for being bullied. Kids who blame themselves for being bullied are more likely to succumb to the tactics of a bully and become vulnerable to more attacks. If they think the attacks are directed at something inherent in their makeup or character, they are more likely to get depressed and anxious (I am stupid, I am ugly, I am clumsy, I am friendless, I am inferior, I am crazy). When they ask the question "Why me?" they are right there bullying themselves to validate why the bully targeted them. These thoughts are self-defeating and reinforce their feelings of helplessness and hopelessness.

When kids practice the art of self-affirmation—positive self-talk—they tend to feel better about themselves. You can't just teach kids to mouth the self-affirming lines. Kids need people in their lives who offer them encouragement, feedback, and unconditional love. And they have to be guided to behave in ways that make them feel and act like decent, caring, and responsible people who like themselves, think for themselves, and know they are capable of solving problems. Looking back at the traits of the brick-wall family, jellyfish family, and backbone family (chapter 8), it is the backbone family that provides the structure for kids to flesh out the strong sense of self that is needed to rebuff the bully. Kids in a backbone family can freely express their feelings, make mistakes, grow from those mistakes, and know that they can act in their own best interest, stand up for themselves, and exercise their rights while respecting the rights and legitimate needs of others.

Sometimes self-affirmation is not enough. Your kids will need comeback lines—assertive retorts to the bullying. It is important that these one-liners be assertive, not aggressive or passive.

Aggression—be it verbal, physical, or relational—only begets more aggression. Kids who respond aggressively to an attack, angrily striking at the bully, usually end up losing the struggle. The bully was no fool and now has a target who is distressed, frustrated, and defeated.

In my research for this book, I came across some disturbing, aggressive one-liners a psychologist recommended targets use against the bully. I think these would probably agitate a bully even more and make a first-class bully out of your child as well.

These are lines I suggest you *not* give your child:

- Respond with a comment like "It takes one to know one."
- Reverse the teasing. Give the bully the same put-down.
- Call the bully by name and ask, "What did you say?" and "Could you say that again?" The bully may repeat what he or she said two or three times. Then you, in a condescending

manner, say something like "Good boy, Sam! You said that three times."

- Make the bully look foolish when he or she says something obvious. Example: "He noticed that I don't have any hair. Wow!"
- Make fun of the bully for repeating taunts: "You keep saying the same thing over and over. Can you say it in a different way, or even sing it?"

Why would anyone recommend that you teach your child to ridicule, taunt, make condescending comments, or make fun of another person—even if that person is a bully? We can begin to break the cycle of violence by confronting that kind of speech when we hear it and eliminating it from our own vocabulary. There is a Buddhist aphorism that states: "Believe nothing merely because you have been told it. . . . But whatsoever, after due examination and analysis, you find to be kind, conducive to the good, the benefit, the welfare of all beings—that doctrine believe and cling to and take as your guide." None of those one-liners is kind, conducive to the good, or to the benefit and welfare of anybody.

Passivity invites further aggression. Kids who respond passively to an attack—slumping over, begging, pleading, or quickly submitting to a bully's demands—only encourage the bully to keep up the bullying. Lines that a child might say to a friend who has inadvertently hurt him can backfire when said to a bully. "Hey, that hurts." "Don't do that. I don't like it." "Please leave me alone. I don't like what you're doing." To the ears of a bully, they are invitations to keep bullying. To cry in front of a bully or to let him know you don't like what he is doing is letting him know he has accomplished his goal. He'll crank up the volume and intensity of his contemptuous behavior. And each time he does so, his innate ability to feel any empathy is stifled or corrupted, his sense of shame is diminished, his callousness grows thicker.

Assertive lines and actions have the potential to dissipate the aggression of the offending party, and they will most certainly leave intact the dignity and self-worth of the person speaking the lines. "Yikes! I'm not up for this. I'm out of here." "Wow, man, you poured that on thick. I don't need this. I'm gone." "That was a gross thing to do. It's beneath both of us." These lines can be spoken out loud or said as self-talk. Either way, they affirm the targeted child's power to control how he acts and what he does with what the bully is throwing at him. In her book, *Tongue Fu!*, Sam Horn explains why assertive lines have a chance at stopping a bully. "Bullies push, push, push as a way of taking your measure. They test people to see what they're made of. In a perverse way, they admire only the ones who say, 'You're not getting away with that here.'"

The Gormans of the World

Michael McManus, a Canadian television producer, shared with me the story of his being bullied and the assertive one-liner his father gave him.

> Every day just before noon, Gorman, a big boy who sat directly behind me, placed his fist in my face and demanded, "You owe me!" I would run home for lunch and steal money out of my mother's purse to turn over to Gorman in the afternoon. After weeks of stealing money, my guilty feelings overrode the fear I had of Gorman. I told my father what I had done and why I did it. My dad said, "Michael, you are going to run

into Gormans all your life. You need to stand up to him and let him know it's over, the game's up, that you won't be intimidated by the likes of his kind."

I walked to school the next day practicing what I would say to the bully. When the fist came, I turned around in my seat, sat tall, and spoke the words my dad had given me the night before: "It's over, Gorman. There will be no more money." At that point, Gorman looked much smaller to me and I felt much bigger and stronger. I never saw that fist in my face again.

Will standing strong, walking confidently and with purpose, and speaking assertively always do the trick? No, but it is one more valuable tool your child will have. The key is to have several well-rehearsed scripts and a few actions readily available, with the ability to discern which one is the most appropriate for the given situation. Sometimes words spoken under your breath are best, sometimes words spoken out loud are, sometimes yelling for help is better, and there are times when you had best save your breath and start running. As Trevor Romain suggests in *Bullies Are a Pain in the Brain*, "You might look a bit foolish running down the street like a maniac, but you will look *alive*." And there are times when handing over money or a jacket is the wisest thing to do. Your children need to know that nothing they own is worth more than their safety.

A pre-emptive assertive action is to be friendly with a potential bully. In their 1998 study, S. K. Egan and D. G. Perry noted that children who are "agreeable" communicate to other children that they like them, and other children—even aggressive ones—are inclined to reciprocate the liking and thus avoid attacking them. I can attest to their findings from firsthand experience. In the summer of 1970, I was lifeguarding at a pool in north Denver. After weeks of failed negotiations with the powers-that-be in the Department of Parks and Recreation, in an attempt to get improvements to the swimming pool that would be equal to improvements at pools in the more affluent parts of Denver, a group of angry teens took matters into their own hands. They stormed the pool, wreaking havoc with the deteriorating diving boards, showers, and dressing rooms, as well as roughing up the guards. As four kids grabbed me, the leader of the "pool takeover" yelled at them to let me go. I quickly scrambled over the chain-link fence and ran home. Weeks later, after the pool had been repaired and upgraded, I ran into the young man whose command to his henchmen had spared me the roughing-up my fellow guards endured. I asked him why he had told the four to let me go. He shrugged and said, "Because you were kind to me once."

Three vital elements to a child responding assertively are a *belief* that no one can strip her of her own sense of dignity and worth, an *understanding* that she can control how she responds to a bully, and a *refusal* to get down in the mud with a bully and bully back.

Buddies, Friends, and Other Former Strangers

Stopping bullying is harder than preventing it in the first place. Having older kids as buddies, being a friend, and knowing how to hang around with potential friends can radically reduce bullying incidents your child might encounter.

Buddies

If your child is at risk of being bullied on the way to school, on the bus, on the playground, in the lunchroom, or in the hallways, it is helpful to find an older child to be your child's buddy. And since any child could possibly be at risk, an ideal plan is to "buddy" kids up early in the school year. The buddy program can serve a dual purpose: The younger child is less likely to be targeted by a peer when he has a bigger kid right next to him who is in a sense "protecting" him; and older kids who are buddies to younger children are less likely to bully any younger children. These older kids are too busy "being good," "doing good," and "willing good" to have the time or inclination to target someone smaller. The four essentials for successful peer relationships—empathy, sympathy, compassion, and perspective taking—are nurtured and strengthened. Some of the best buddies are reformed bullies. Their leadership skills and power that were inappropriately used to wreak havoc in the past can be great assets to them in their new role.

Friends

Just as being a friend can be good for a bully who is trying to turn his life around, it is equally good for a child who could be a target. Friendship skills play an important role in preventing bullying, buffering kids from the harmful effects of bullying, and helping kids cope after a bullying episode.

Children need to be taught to make friends wisely, to keep friendships growing, and to walk away from friendships that are harmful. "The Top Ten Ways to Keep Your Friends," listed on pages 210–211, works for bullied kids as well as for bullies. In his book, *Nurturing Good Children Now*, Dr. Ron Taffel writes about what he sees as the single most important factor in the development of these basic friendship skills—the way children are treated at home. "If we are accepting or critical, inclusive or exclusive, demanding or giving, relaxed or anxious, if we encourage siblings to be loving or allow them to mistreat one another at home—all of these behaviors can affect the kinds of friends our children choose." The way we interact at home also influences the way our children develop their social skills that help them make and keep friends. Your children need the opportunity to develop their abilities to listen, exchange ideas, and work with others toward a common goal. They need to be able to control their own behavior and anticipate the consequences of words they speak and actions they take. Kids bring to school the attitudes and behaviors they learned at home.

Kids who annoy or irritate their peers are at great risk not only of being the target of a bully, but of becoming increasingly isolated from even caring and compassionate peers. The more isolated they become, the higher their risk of being vulnerable targets, with bullies and not-so-innocent bystanders joining forces against them. In turn, they are likely to become seriously depressed or enraged. If your child is unwittingly contributing to rejection by his peers, he will need your help to find a solution to his problem. Be aware of how he behaves in his social circle. He may be resorting to inappropriate social tactics either because he does not know better or because he has run out of appropriate options in his repertoire of friendship skills.

It is important that your child know how to accurately read social cues—words, actions, and body language. Kids help teach one another about social behaviors—what works and what doesn't; what is acceptable and what is not; what's funny and what is hurtful humor. Your child needs to notice how others are reacting to her behavior and recognize the *cues* her peers are giving her that are *clues* to what is working and what is not. "Tell me what happened when you grabbed the toy." "Did everyone walk away when you started to act silly?" "Did your classmate frown when you commented on his outfit?" "Did everyone laugh at the joke?" "Did the target of the joke give any signals that he was hurt by what was said?" "What can you do when your behavior is annoying someone?" "One of your friends is crying. What can you say and do?"

If your child has a serious handicap or learning disability, he has a risk factor for putting him on the radar screen of the bully, but he will be at far greater risk if he lacks necessary friendship skills. In fact, friendship skills can mitigate a handicap or disability. A word of caution is due here. As much as you have taught your child who has a disability to be kind, caring, and accepting, you must also teach him to be wary, skeptical, and willing to be rude if necessary to protect himself from unscrupulous peers who "buddy" up to him in order to glean enough information to be used against him. Jeremy, a boy with a lisp, was asked by a group of ten-year-old boys to read aloud the poem he had written. He happily read the poem, only to have one boy repeat it—lisp and all—as the other boys laughed. Your child needs real friends who can help him see when someone is trying to "use" him, friends who can clue him in and stand by him.

The quality of your child's friendships matter. If your bullied daughter is hanging around exclusively with another child who has been bullied, the two of them are more likely to spend their time commiserating with each other and making each other feel even more miserable. Misery loves company. But neither girl will have the strength to support each other or stand up for each other. If your bullied son is hanging around with another bullied boy, the two of them are more likely to fuel each other's rage and spend time concocting ways to seek revenge on their nemesis and anyone else who failed to come to their aid. All four bullied kids need support and guidance to either turn these friendships into strong, helpful ones or to move beyond them into more positive friendships.

The former may actually be easier than the latter. Inviting either twosome to join you in challenging activities that require cooperation, strategizing, and supporting each other in order to accomplish a common goal can build both kids up and create a friendship devoid of the negative energies that brought the two together in the first place. Encouraging them to get involved in "doing good" in the community also enables them to get "outside" of themselves. It's hard to be miserable and giving at the same time.

Other Former Strangers

Just as being a friend and having friends are antidotes to bullying, so is a child's ability to introduce herself into a group. Kids who find themselves alone on the playground, unwilling or unable to join in a game or other social activity, are prime targets for bullies. If your daughter looks like a shrinking violet against the school wall or your son appears to be playing hide-and-seek, with him hiding and only bullies seeking him out, they both need to learn useful and effective ways to introduce themselves into a group and how to conduct themselves once they join—for example, observe, ask a question or say something positive about the group, ask to play or join, cooperate, play fair, share, and resolve conflicts non-violently. You can help them role-play various situations where they ask to join and are welcomed, rejected, or ignored. How they handle all three of these situations will increase or decrease their chances of being a part of any group in school.

They also need to be able to evaluate the various groups and recognize that some groups are better to be a part of than others. Some groups help them learn to get along with others and help them develop close friendships with people who enjoy doing the same things they like to do. Some groups help them feel good by doing good deeds in the community. Some groups thrive on having a scapegoat and might welcome your daughter to play the part. Others find their pleasure by regularly excluding selected targets. Your empathic son may struggle with the conflicted feelings of belonging to a group and hurting someone in a way he knows only too well. If your child finds himself in a group that purposely excludes other kids, makes other kids feel unwelcome, is mean to kids in the group or to a select few outside of the group, or requires that he conform to standards with which he is uncomfortable or do things he doesn't really want to do, it's time for him to find a new group of real friends who care about themselves, one another, and others outside of their group. The question your child needs to ask himself to determine if the group is a good one to join is "Can I be good (and true to myself), do good, and will good in this group?"

Negotiation and Conflict Resolution Skills

Kids who spend a lot of time together are guaranteed to have squabbles and get into fights. It is important that your child learn to solve problems and resolve conflicts peacefully. Both of these require that your child be able to be understanding of a friend's wishes and needs and assertive about her own. They also involve the ability to reach cooperative solutions centered on kindness and fairness. In *kids are worth it!: Raising Resilient, Responsible, Compassionate Kids*, I covered these topics in detail. The following is a summary of the essentials.

Problem Solving

No matter what the problem, solving it usually involves these six steps:

1. Identify and define the problem.
2. List viable options for solving the problem.
3. Evaluate the options—explore the pros and cons of each option.
4. Choose one option.
5. Make a plan and implement it.

6. Evaluate the problem and your solution: What brought it about? Could a similar problem be prevented in the future? How was the present problem solved?

When kids present their own ideas, listen to each other's reasoning, and work cooperatively to arrive at a solution, they learn that there is not always a definite right or wrong; there is no one correct way to solve most problems. The give-and-take, openness, and cooperation on the part of both children help them bond with each other. Kids who have solved problems successfully together are more likely to come to each other's aid when either is being bullied.

Resolving Conflicts Peacefully

The same is true if these friends have been able to peacefully resolve the conflicts they will inevitably encounter. Example is a powerful way to teach. If we see conflict as a contest, we will probably fight physically or verbally with our "opponents" until one of us has won and one is soundly defeated. We can run from conflict, showing our children how to run as well. We can also model resolving conflict assertively, without aggression or passivity. We can teach our kids constructive alternatives to the instincts to fight, flee, or freeze. We can teach them through example, guidance, and instruction that violence is an immature, irresponsible, and unproductive technique for resolving conflict and that using non-violent tools to resolve conflict is a mature and courageous act. This involves teaching kids to listen to all sides of the story, to use their heads before using their mouths, and to come up with a plan both kids can accept.

Sharing their feelings will help them learn to be less quick to judge and more able to be compassionate. Here's a simple format kids can learn:

When I heard (or saw) . . . **not** When you said (or did) . . .
I felt . . . **not** You made me angry.
Because I . . . **not** I couldn't help it.
I need (or want) . . . **not** You'd better, or else.

It takes time to teach kids to handle their feelings assertively, but in doing so, you teach them that their own feelings are important, that they can be trusted to handle those feelings, and that they can count on you for support and guidance when they have handled them poorly.

After both children have shared their feelings, they can move on to examining the five ingredients necessary for the peaceful resolution to the conflict:

1. Identify the issues that underlie the incident.
2. Figure out how each person contributed to causing the dispute.
3. Think about what they are willing to do to bring about a resolution.
4. Be prepared to both make concessions.
5. Ask themselves, "What do we want to have come out of this?"

Then together they can come up with a solution both can accept. It will be a solution formed with a greater understanding of each other's wants, needs, feelings, and perceptions.

Children need to be assured and reminded that in attempting to resolve any conflict, it is okay to

1. **Call time out.** ("We are both too angry to talk right now. Let's talk about this later." "I'm too upset to work through this right now. I need to take a break.") If either child is too angry

246

or too upset to speak calmly and responsibly, it is important to call time out and come back to the process later.

2. **Refuse to take abuse.** ("It hurts when you say those things about me." "You can be angry at me, but you can't hit me.") If one child becomes verbally, physically, or emotionally abusive, the other child has a right to refuse to take the abuse.

3. **Insist on fair treatment.** ("I won't borrow your pen without asking you first, and I want you to ask me first if you can borrow mine." "It's not fair for you to always be the one to get the ball at recess just because you can run faster than the rest of us. We've got to come up with a better solution.") Fair treatment is not always equal or identical treatment, but it is *honest*, *adequate*, and *just*.

Through our own example, resolving family disputes, and playing out "what if" scenarios with our children about their social situations, we can help them learn to recognize when it is necessary to call time out and that they have the right to be treated with respect, dignity, and fairness. They also have the responsibility not to let their feelings take over the situation; to see that they do not physically, verbally, or emotionally abuse another person; and to treat other people with the same dignity and regard they themselves hope for. Resolving conflicts peacefully enables kids to use their feelings as a positive energy source to establish and maintain productive relationships with each other.

We can impart to our children the wisdom of the peacemakers: Peace is not the absence of conflict. It is the embracing of conflict as a challenge and an opportunity to grow.

Unmasking Anger, Calming Rage

In 2000, Holocaust survivor Elie Wiesel was asked by a writer from *O Magazine* about his memoir, *Night*, in which he wrote about the Hungarian soldiers that drove him and his family from their home. "'It was from that moment that I began to hate them, and that hate is still the only link between us today,'" he responded. "I wrote that, but I didn't hate. I just felt terribly angry and humiliated. . . . I was terribly disappointed. I used the word *hate* because that was the strongest feeling I could imagine having. But when I think about it now, there was no hate in me. I grew up learning that hate destroys the hater as much as its victims."

Anger, humiliation, and disappointment—if your child has been bullied, he is probably feeling all of these emotions. The way he may express them is by saying he *hates* the bully, all those who joined in, laughed, stood idly by, or turned away, and the adults who did nothing to stop the bullying. What Elie Wiesel understood was that the word *hate* was really concealing more fundamental responses to the horrific indignities and inhumane treatment he witnessed and endured during the war. When the word *hate* was stripped away, anger, humiliation, and disappointment were still there. They needed to be acknowledged and accepted if Elie Wiesel was to resist being consumed or crippled by them.

Your child will need to do the same with his feelings. But first your child needs to know it is all right to feel. Feelings are not good or bad per se. It's what your child does with his feelings that makes all the difference. Feelings are motivators for growth or warning signs that something needs to change. Trying to cover up the grief will not serve your child. ("Come on, cheer up, just get over it; he won't hurt you again.") He needs to mourn any loss, be it loss of security, belongings, sense of well-being, academic progress, or social interactions. To make light of the incidents will only help the bullied child bury the pain deeper into himself—and it will stay there to fester. To shrug off his own feelings is to dismiss the important messages his legitimate feelings are sending. ("It wasn't much. It doesn't matter, really. I'll be okay. Let's drop it.")

To tell a child he can't or shouldn't be angry is to deny him a way to heal from his hurt and the opportunity to move on from the bullying. It also locks your child into viewing himself as a helpless victim and the bully in the one-dimensional role as oppressor. Your child could spend his days vengefully scheming ways to punish the bully. To heal and move on, he must be able to tell his story and be believed, have his pain acknowledged and express his anger. After he is able to say, "I am angry," you can help him unmask the anger and calm his rage. Anger is unmasked by helping your child answer the following questions:

- Where did it come from? ("From inside myself. The bully did not make me angry.")
- Is it masking another feeling? ("I am hurt, scared the bully will hurt me again, humiliated by what happened to me, disappointed in how my peers acted, and disillusioned by the adults who wouldn't listen.")
- Can I feel all of those feelings and still have anger? ("Yes. Denying anger, stuffing it down, or striking out won't get rid of the anger.")
- Why be angry, anyway? ("Because I care. If I didn't care, I wouldn't be angry. I can't be angry about something I don't care about.")

In *Yoga and the Quest for the True Self*, psychotherapist and senior Kripalu yoga teacher Stephen Cope writes of anger "as an energy existing, like all emotions, halfway between physical and mental experience. Like heat or other energies, anger wanes naturally if we don't hold it back with psychological defenses. . . .

Anger tends to arise in a very visceral wave. It arises, crests, and then passes away." The five sequential steps for the techniques he calls "riding the wave" can help your child stay with the raw feeling of anger without acting on it "until you're really clear."

1. *Breathe deeply.* This breathing will help your child take his mind off the physical tension in his body, the incidents, and the feeling of anger.

2. *Relax.* As he relaxes his muscles, the energy of the anger is accepted, not fought or acted upon.

3. *Feel.* By focusing on what his body is feeling and where in the body he is feeling it, he can explore how he uniquely manifests anger. Does his stomach churn? Do his shoulders tense? Is he quick to react? Does he let it overwhelm him? Does his mind move quickly to revenge? Does he beat himself up with the anger?

4. *Watch.* If your child can observe the sensation he is feeling, he can "make discerning choices about how to respond to it rather than reacting to it."

5. *Allow.* Not resisting the anger, but accepting it and watching it go through the body, allows your child to calm down and clear his mind so that he can decide what he needs to do and what he needs from the bully.

Once your child is clear on what he needs from the bully, the two of them can come together. If your child can get the assurance of safety and adult and peer support during the time it takes him to move through the anger and honor his sadness, he will find himself ready to look for creative solutions to solving the problems that both he and the reformed bully face in order to be reconciled. As I mentioned in the last chapter, this is not the same as seeing bullying as a conflict. The problems that need to be solved relate to how the two can live together in the school community after the bullying has been stopped and after the bully has worked through the steps of discipline. The bullied child has the power of choice this time around.

Even if the reformed bully came to your son with a heartfelt apology and offer of restitution, your child might want more time to become stronger himself before he can reconcile. The intention behind asking for time is not to hurt the bully, to make him feel the same pain he inflicted, or to make him suffer as much as your child suffered. The time may be needed for your child to face the hurt, to identify and express his emotions, and to begin to release any grudges and destructive feelings, so that he not only reclaims his own peace of mind, his sense of security and safety and well-being, he can also begin to open his heart and his hands to reconciliation with the other boy. If they both use the time that leads up to the reconciliation constructively, the two children who come together for this step will not only interact differently than in past encounters, they will be very different kids from the bully and the bullied kid who had been caught in the cycle of violence.

Self-Defense

I am asked often if putting a child in a self-defense class will help him or her strike back effectively against a bully. Striking back is the wrong goal. We want our children to be able to defend themselves. All three of my children studied aikido, a martial art that by its nature is *defensive*, not *offensive*. If a bully tries to strike, the target "moves" with the hit and harnesses the energy, ideally becoming a partner with the aggressor but in a way that dissipates the aggressive energy of the bully. ("That was a gross thing to do. It's beneath both of us.") Practicing aikido (or any other defensive martial art) helps your children resist reacting out of fear, focus themselves, get in touch with their inner calm, and have clarity of mind. When involved in the study of such a martial art, your children will tend to present themselves physically in an assertive manner, standing strong, head up, confident in their stride and strong in their voice.

In their book, *Aikido and the Dynamic Sphere*, Adele Westbrook and Oscar Ratti write of the ethics of self-defense according to Master Uysehiba's method: "A man must sincerely desire to defend himself without hurting others." The authors explain four levels of interaction between two people. Translated into a bully and a bullied child's encounters, they involve the following:

1. A bully, without provocation and on his own initiative, attacks the target and harms him. This is the lowest of the four levels of ethical behavior—unprovoked aggression in the form of an attack.

2. A bully tries to provoke the target to attack him through "obvious provocation, such as an insulting remark or more subtle provocation of a contemptuous attitude." When the target is invited to attack and does so, once again the target is harmed—physically, emotionally, or, as was the case with Rangi from New Zealand, suspended from school for supposedly starting the fight that was actually provoked by the other boys in the classroom. There is only a "shade of difference ethically" between this level and the lowest one.

3. The target neither attacks nor provokes the bully to attack. But when attacked, "he defends himself in a subjective manner, i.e., he takes care of only 'number one.'" Either

the bully or the target is seriously harmed. Ethically this is a more defensible action than the other two. This is the tactic most commonly recommended by parents of boys—be tough, suppress emotions, and strike back. ("If he hits you, just hit him back harder, so he will never think of hitting you again.") A popular radio announcer in Toronto recalls running away from a bully as a child. When he ran home, his father pulled out a strap and told him to go back and fight the bully or face the strap at home. Girls are often taught to verbally abuse back. ("It takes one to know one.")

In all three of these encounters, someone can be seriously harmed, and most often it will be the target. Not true with the fourth level of defense:

4. Neither attacking nor provoking the attack, the target defends himself in such a way, and with such skill and control, that the attacker is not seriously harmed. The provoker may be on the ground if a physical move was used, yes, but will not be seriously harmed, as the target, once disempowering the bully, walks away from the confrontation. The chances of being targeted again are slim. This is the ultimate in ethical self-defense. It is a skill that can be taught to children as young as six or seven. Michael McManus's dad gave Michael the tools to strike back with an assertive verbal response to Gorman's fist.

At this fourth level, aikido involves both the *practical means* of self-defense and *ethical intention*. "The practice of the art of aikido then becomes a harmonious interaction between two or more people, fulfilling Master Uysehiba's intention via translation of the highest ethics of the East (and West as well) into vital and active modes of conduct." In other words, such harmonious interaction would benefit the bully, the bullied, and the not-so-innocent bystander. As the authors noted at the end of their book, "If the student has accepted and is in agreement with the underlying principles of the art (restoration, reconciliation, harmony), he will endeavor to act in accordance with these principles by trying to apply these techniques as a means of neutralizing aggressions, not aggressors. Thus he achieves simultaneously the dual purpose of self-defense and restoration of that tenuous, living balance threatened by another man's temporary moral unbalance." This restoration is what is needed for your child and the child who bullied him to break out of the cycle of violence.

> *It is the principle of the pure in heart never to injure others, even when they themselves have been hatefully injured. Hating others, even enemies who have harmed you unprovoked, assures incessant sorrow.*
>
> **—Ancient South Indian Scripture,**
> *Tirukkural* 32:312–13, sacred Tamil text

chapter eleven

From Bystander to Brave-Hearted

My doctrine is this, that if we see cruelty or wrong that we have the power to stop, and do nothing, we make ourselves sharers in the guilt.

—A man named Wright,
in Anna Sewell's *Black Beauty*

The one thing that doesn't abide by majority rule is a person's conscience.

—Harper Lee,
To Kill a Mockingbird

Chances are, if your son or daughter is not one of the two main characters—the bully or the bullied kid—he or she has been one of the supporting cast. Whom your child supported and how will affect not only the two main characters but your child as well.

Using the Bullying Circle on page 146 you can discuss with your children the roles they might have played, how they played them, and why. From there you can begin to teach them ways to move out of those roles, as well as counteract and prevent bullying in the future. Since much of the bullying goes on "under the radar" of adults, a potent force is kids themselves showing bullies that they will not be looked up to, nor will their cruel behavior be condoned or tolerated.

If your child was a henchman who took an active part but did not start the bullying, you can go through the same seven steps with him that you would with the child who was the bully (see page 197):

1. Intervene immediately with discipline.
2. Create opportunities to "do good."
3. Nurture empathy.
4. Teach friendship skills—assertive, respectful, and peaceful ways to relate to others.
5. Closely monitor your child's TV viewing, video game playing, computer activities, and music.
6. Engage in more constructive, entertaining, and energizing activities.
7. Teach your child to "will good."

To those steps you can add a dialogue with your child about ways to avoid being so easily led into doing the bidding of a more powerful peer. That involves two steps: figuring out how not to be so easily led, and hanging around kids who will not lead you down that path.

Ten-year-old David had joined in when a group of boys held down and took turns kicking nine-year-old Lewis. David's friend, Peter, tried unsuccessfully to pull him off the younger boy and then ran to get a teacher. David's mom was not only distressed by what her son had done but disturbed that he was not like Peter, who had refused to be a party to the abuse, had tried to keep his friend from getting involved, and had alerted a teacher. David said he just got caught up in the heat of the moment and even joined in calling Peter a "snitch," but he felt awful and wanted to get rid of the feeling. He had genuine remorse for his actions.

David's mom helped him go through the seven steps and explored his reasons and excuses for joining the bullying. As well, he apologized to Peter and thanked him for trying to stop him and for getting help. David invited both Lewis and Peter over for an evening of pizza and games. The two older boys agreed to buddy with the younger boy on the playground (see page 239 for more information on being a buddy).

She Hurt Her Through the Grapevine

Your daughter may not be happy about going through the three Rs—restitution, resolution, and reconciliation—if she was not the one to begin an ugly rumor. She merely repeated it. Nevertheless, she can

1. apologize to the child who was harmed by the rumor;
2. go to everyone she told it to and tell them it wasn't true;
3. ask them to stop spreading it;
4. ask them to let everyone they told know that she played a part in spreading the rumor and wants to correct the damage done;
5. to the best of her ability repair any harm done to the target by her act of spreading the rumor; and
6. heal with the child she harmed—invite the target of the rumor to join her for lunch, for a bike ride, to a sleepover.

You can encourage and support your daughter as she deals with the mixed responses from those with whom she shared the rumor. ("Thanks for telling me." "Wow, I spread it, too, what can I do?" "Look, you don't need to apologize for spreading a rumor—that kid is such a loser anyway." "Who is making you apologize?" "What are you doing? Trying to make the rest of us look bad?" "It was only a rumor. What's the big deal?" "You're no fun.") She will need your encouragement and support again as she faces the anger, hurt, and sadness that the targeted child will probably express. Throughout the whole process, your daughter will see not only the damage a rumor can cause, and how difficult—if not impossible—it is to repair, but also that she is capable of taking full responsibility for mistakes she has made.

Once she has gone through this process, you can talk with her about ways to effectively block a rumor in the future. The Sufis have a "wisdom saying" that our words must pass through three gates: *Is it true?* If it isn't, don't say it. If it is true, it must pass through two more gates before you speak it: *Is it necessary to say?* and *Is it kind?* If it is not necessary to say, don't speak it. If it is necessary, find a way to say it in a kind way. Kind does not mean candy-coating the truth; it means saying what needs to be said in a way that leaves the dignity and worth of all parties intact. ("Kim is such a wimpy dork" wouldn't make it through the first two gates. "Kim doesn't seem to know how to effectively stand up to those girls who are taunting her" passes through all three gates and opens the door for further discussion on how your daughter can be of help.)

By listening to the way your daughter speaks about the bully and her target, you might discern if she supported the bullying but did not take an active part, or if she liked the bullying but did not display open support at the time it occurred. ("Susan invited me to a sleepover. She didn't invite Kim. Everybody knows Kim is such a wimpy dork. Susan told everyone what a stupid thing Kim did at Jane's sleepover two weeks ago.") You can use this opportunity to talk to your daughter about the damage rumors can cause and encourage her to become a witness for Kim instead of a bystander. ("I'm uncomfortable talking about Kim behind her back. We don't have to like her; but we also don't have to spend our time ripping her apart.") Your daughter can also figure out ways to include Kim in social activities at school, such as inviting her to join her for lunch. In middle school, such an invitation may be a courageous act, as those who have selected Kim to be the target of their rumors and ostracism may shun your daughter. Talk to your daughter about enlisting one or two friends to join her in stopping the rumors and sitting with her at lunch. A bully may be more powerful than any one person but will not be more powerful than a committed group of witnesses.

There Are No Innocent Bystanders

If your son was a disengaged onlooker who watched a bunch of bullies rough up another boy and told you it was "none of my business; it happens all the time; I just ignore it," you can talk to him about the harm that silence can cause, not only to the targeted child but to him as well. Not to acknowledge bullying for what it is or to simply dismiss it is to still be complicit in the bullying. When Elie Wiesel was asked, "What is the most important commandment in the Bible?" he said, "'Thou shalt not stand idly by.' The opposite of love is not hate, but indifference; indifference helps creates evil. Hatred is evil itself. Indifference is what allows evil to be strong, what gives it power." Your son's act of omission, although different from acts of commission by the other kids, can be addressed by going through the seven steps the followers/henchmen need to do to move from their respective roles to that of witness.

From henchman to disengaged onlooker, bystanders will often use the nine excuses discussed in chapter 6 for refusing to stand up and speak out against the bullying:

1. The bully is my friend.
2. It's not my problem! This is not my fight!
3. She is not my friend.
4. He's a loser.

5. He deserved to be bullied, asked for it, had it coming, so why stop it? He didn't even stand up for himself, so why should anyone else stand up for him?
6. Bullying will toughen him up.
7. Who wants to be called a snitch or a rat, blamed for getting someone else in trouble?
8. It's better to be in the in-group than to defend the outcasts.
9. It's too big a pain in the brain.

A bystander can weigh the pros and cons of remaining faithful to the group versus siding with the targeted kid. You can explain to your children how these excuses contribute to the overall erosion of civility in their peer group and increase the likelihood that they too will assume the role of bully. The erosion of civility could also cause your children to become targets for the bunch of bullies that would thrive in such an environment. You can assure your children that you know they are capable of moving out of the role of the not-so-innocent bystander. Stifling a bully requires a simple ethical principle: to do the right thing on behalf of a targeted peer, regardless of the actions of other bystanders.

Moving in the Right Direction

If your son or daughter is a possible defender—dislikes the bullying and would like to help out but doesn't, you can explore the four reasons kids may not help:

1. Afraid of getting hurt.
2. Afraid of becoming a new target of the bully.
3. Afraid of doing something that will make the situation worse.
4. Do not know what to do.

If validated and talked about openly, these four reasons for remaining on the sidelines can be jumping-off points for helping kids become brave-hearted witnesses, resisters, and defenders—standing up for a peer, speaking out against an injustice, and taking responsibility for what happens among themselves. Talk with them about overestimating the comfort and safety of siding with the bully. Since the bully "uses" peers, your daughter could find herself on the wrong side of the bully for no reason other than the bully may decide to single her out next time, or your son could find himself in as much trouble as the bully when he becomes one of the "bunch of bullies."

You can discuss actions ranging from those that involve the least amount of risk on your children's part to those that require the greatest courage: from refusing to be a party to the bullying (moving away from the lunch table where kids are actively excluding others); to supporting the target privately ("That was a mean thing that he did to you. Do you want to walk with us?"); to talking to the bully publicly or privately if she is a friend ("Leave her alone. Let's go get something to eat"); to intervening on behalf of the target, as Scott Russell and the football player did in the stories that follow. It might be as small a gesture as not repeating a rumor; inviting an isolated classmate to a sleepover; not laughing at a derogatory joke; offering kindness and concern to the targeted peer; telling an adult about the bullying; doing something riskier, such as joining with others to stand up to a bully; or stepping in alone. Indeed, as shown in Pepler and Craig's 1995 Toronto study of the roles of peers in bullying episodes in urban school playgrounds, 13 percent of kids were willing to stand up and speak out. And they often did it in spite of the group, rather than within the safety of a group.

Willing Good

In chapter 9, I discussed how a bully could take on a new role by "willing good"—that is, speaking and doing what is right "even when the burden is heavy." Helping your children develop an inner moral voice (personal code) that guides them to do or say what is right, often in spite of external consequences and never merely because of them, can give your children the strength to act with integrity when confronted with a bullying situation.

A fourth-generation Japanese-American and a highly successful conflict resolution consultant, Derek Okubo, recalled an event that happened to him on the playground over thirty-five years ago. The only Japanese child in his class, he was surrounded by peers who beat him and called him names they had heard at home and in the classroom: "You little yellow Jap, go back where you came from." One boy, Scott Russell, came to his defense, took him away from the bunch of bullies, and invited Derek to join in a game. What Scott did at that moment demonstrated his own personal code. No slogans ("Celebrate diversity"), threats ("If you bully anyone, you will be suspended from school"), commands ("Don't call anyone else ugly names"), or even the Golden Rule ("Do unto others as you would have them do unto you") affected his decision so much as his own inner moral voice. Scott didn't come out of the womb knowing how to act with integrity. He had to learn it. He certainly didn't learn it on the playground.

Sad to say, he didn't learn it in the classroom, either. The incident on the playground came soon after Derek's teacher grabbed him by the shirt and yelled, "You get a 'U,' you little yellow Jap," as Derek struggled with a "heel-to-toe, toe-to-heel, heel-together" activity in physical education class. Derek stood there stunned as his classmates watched this big man bully him verbally and physically. It's no wonder some of the kids felt comfortable attacking him on the playground. What was a big wonder to Derek is that one boy would be willing to stand up and speak out. As Derek told me his story some thirty-five years later, he remarked that it had such an impact on his life that he could remember the activity he struggled with at the time, the words screamed at him both in the classroom and on the playground, and the full name of the boy who came to his aid.

Sharing, Caring, Helping, and Serving

In his book *Raising Your Child to Be a Mensch*, Neil Kurshan explains how kids like Scott learn to become witnesses: "Children do not magically learn morality, kindness, and decency any more than they learn math, English, or science. They mature into decent and responsible people by emulating adults who are examples and models for them, especially courageous parents with principles and values who stand up for what they believe." It's important that our children see us stepping in, speaking up, and taking a stand against injustices, be those injustices in the family room, the boardroom, the classroom, or the city streets. When we do more than give lip service to our beliefs, when we walk our talk, we model for our children ways to be that potent force in stopping the bullying.

Preben Munch-Nielsen, whom I wrote about in chapter 7, was willing to rescue Jews in Denmark because "[y]ou just did. That's the way you were brought up." The majority of people in his community were willing to intervene on behalf of their neighbors. But our children must see us willing to stand up even when the rest of our neighbors are not. On March 2, 2002, in Ahmadabad, India, Virsing Rathod took such a stand. Beth Duff-Brown of the Associated Press wrote of his heroism:

Horrified by the screams of his Muslim neighbors being beaten and burned alive, Virsing Rathod did what many other Hindus could not get up the courage to do.

The burly Hindu and his two sons jumped in a truck, rammed their way through frenzied Hindu rioters, and began pulling Muslims from the flames just before midnight Thursday.

He saved 25 Muslims that night and has since sheltered dozens in safe houses across Ahmadabad, which is engulfed by Hindu-Muslim violence that has claimed 544 lives. . . . He shrugged when asked whether he's a hero.

"I did it out of humanity, because in my heart I knew it was the right thing to do."

How important it is for our children to see us stand by what we say, be accountable for it, and be willing to act on it—to do what is "the right thing to do."

Beyond *modeling*, we can give our children chances to practice being a witness. Rather than merely tell kids what to do or not to do, we can explain the whys of sharing, caring, helping, and serving and give kids the opportunity to do all four. They need to know that we care as much about their intent as we do about their actions. We can teach them to reflect on the impact of their actions on other people and be able to see things from another person's point of view. Once they can do that, they can begin to feel for the other person and put themselves in the other person's shoes. The ability to take another's perspective is crucial for "willing good." Not only was Scott able to take Derek's perspective and feel empathy and sympathy for him, but Scott also had the compassion and courage to take the next step: "Hey, guys, back off, leave him alone." At this point Scott was choosing doing good over looking good to his classmates. Some kids may *want* to do something but are not able to withstand the peer pressure to conform. Scott was willing and able to withstand the sneers and jeers of his peers ("Jap lover") because he had a strong sense of self that had been nurtured by adults in his life.

Willing good involved taking a stand *and* taking an action. It was not enough for Scott to feel Derek's pain. He needed to do something to alleviate it, even at the expense of alienating his friends. When Scott chose to step in "even when the burden was heavy," his words and actions gave others an opportunity and a way to at least opt out of the bullying, even if they were not ready to actively engage in doing the right thing. He also was teaching Derek an important lesson in bigotry and intolerance. It was "white boys" who attacked him and a "white boy" who rescued him. The anger toward "white kids" that was beginning to boil inside Derek was cooled by the kindness and courage of one boy.

Taking a stand and taking action both require courage and moral independence. In their thought-provoking book, *Bringing Up a Moral Child*, psychologist Michael Schulman and school psychologist Eva Mekler write about the three principles that foster moral independence:

1. *Teach your child that he and only he is responsible for the consequences of his actions.* (Kids who accept responsibility for their own actions are more likely to live up to their own moral code—holding themselves accountable for their own behavior and not blaming someone else.)
2. *Build your child's confidence in his or her ability to make good decisions.* (Kids who have confidence in their own judgments are not easily manipulated by others. They are not afraid to think and act independently.)

3. *Teach your child how to evaluate reasons on his or her own.*
    (Kids who have confidence in their own ability to reason are
    more questioning and more resistant to passive acceptance of
    orders. They are able to evaluate whether or not an action is
    the right thing to do.)

The authors go on to mention the study "Altruistic Behavior
and the Parent-Child Relationship" by Dr. Martin Hoffman. Dr.
Hoffman found that "parents who stress such 'altruistic' values as
'showing consideration of other people's feelings' and 'going out
of one's way to help other people' were the ones most likely to have
children who 'care about how other kids feel and try not to hurt
their feelings,' and who 'stick up for some kid that the other kids are
making fun of or calling names.'"

Another Act of Kindness and Courage

Randy Binstock, a man who suffered through his school years with
undiagnosed dyslexia, shared with me his story about the time he
paid attention to the pain of a classmate and was willing to risk the
scorn and assault of his peers to keep another teen from experiencing the humiliation he knew only too well.

I was always picked on, from grade one till the end of high
school. My best years were in kindergarten and grades one
and two: they let us color, which was great because I didn't
have to speak. As I got older I was always made fun of because
I couldn't read, and when the teacher asked me a question,
I tried to turn myself into my favorite animal: the turtle. I
thought if I could put my head into my shoulders she would
never see me. Well, she did, and my classmates laughed at and
made fun of me.

One year at Dufferin Heights Secondary School, some boys (a bunch of bullies) were picking on a big boy, Martin, who had a high voice. When they started beating him up I couldn't stand it anymore and almost snapped. I told them they should stop beating him up and if they wanted they could beat me up instead. "Where the hell did that come from," I asked myself. I thought someone else had said it, but it was me. I got beat up. But you know, it was worth it because from that point on neither Martin nor I was ever beat up again. I got over the embarrassment of losing a fight and it didn't kill me.

I've always taught my kids to be tolerant of everyone no matter how smart, stupid, fat, skinny, ugly, or just not able to communicate [they are]. There are usually a few things these people are able to do better than anyone in the world. I taught my kids that this is how we show love and respect for one another.

Randy's actions help demolish the myth that kids who are targeted for taunting—as he was repeatedly—are losers, worthless, inferior, or undeserving of respect. The opposite is more likely to be true. Targeted kids are often caring, compassionate, sensitive, creative, and thoughtful individuals.

Just as Scott could not stand by and let Derek be humiliated, so Randy was willing to take a risk for Martin. Each boy benefited from the small but not insignificant courageous acts of these two.

Becoming a Witness and Saving a Life

A Holocaust survivor listed the three actions to change a bystander into a witness: "Pay attention, get involved, and never ever look away." On October 17, 1996, a high school football player did just that. For more than three months, members of a group known as

Skaters terrorized a freshman, Josh, at Powell High School in Powell, Tennessee. They mocked, taunted, and chased him, threatening to beat him to death with their chains and a baseball bat. Josh finally fought back, hitting one of the Skaters with a lunch tray, thinking that if he took on one of them, the bullying would stop. He was wrong. The two boys punched at each other, and Josh slipped and fell. As Josh lay on the floor unconscious, the other boy hit him in the head several times, shattering his skull. As other students looked on, a football player leapt over two tables and dragged Josh away, probably saving his life.

If your children have been courageous enough to stand up to the bully and defend the targeted kid, you can thank them for acting courageously and talk to them about what they did, how they think the bullied child felt, how they felt themselves when they acted, and what more they can do. You may be inclined to think that your children should be "rewarded" for their courage. I would caution you to step back and reflect on the courageous act itself and the strong sense of satisfaction they felt by relieving the suffering of another child. An external reward can in fact "cheapen" the courageous act. (See chapter 8 for discussion on bribes and rewards.)

If your children are comfortable talking with you about the good, the bad, and the ugly, they will probably share with you the conflicted feelings they might have had before they acted on behalf of a bullied child—empathy, fear, sadness, or anger—and the discomfort they may have felt in going against the group. You can assure them that these feelings are normal and only reaffirm how courageous it was for them to step in and help a peer who was being harmed.

Sometimes it is a conscious act of disobedience when a child steps back, as Peter did, running to get help as the bully is giving marching orders to his henchmen. Or when Julie defied the orders (threats) Meridith dished out to her grade two peers to go along with her story about Meghan pulling her pants down on the playground and told her mom what really happened. Mark Twain's Huckleberry Finn committed a similar act of conscious disobedience in order to save a life. Sitting with a copy of the letter he wrote in which he told of the whereabouts of Jim, the slave he helped to escape, Huckleberry Finn struggled with feeling sympathy and compassion for Jim, guilt over Jim's possible recapture thanks to the information in the letter, and fear of breaking the law and committing a grave sin—the state and the church having legal and moral injunctions against helping slaves escape. Tearing up the letter, Huckleberry says to himself, "All right then, I'll go to hell."

Taking the Risk of Telling an Adult

Even reporting a bullying incident to an adult can be a courageous act. The lesson about the differences between telling and tattling for a bullied kid is the same lesson you can teach your child (page 229). Once those ground rules—if it will get you or another child *out* of trouble, tell me; if it will only get another child *in* trouble, don't tell me; and if it's both, I need to know—are understood, you can remind your children periodically that they can come to you with their concerns and fears. "You've heard it from me before, and you'll probably hear it from me again. If you are being bullied or if you know that someone else is being bullied, you need to report it to an adult you trust."

In Steps to Respect, the award-winning bullying prevention program developed by the Committee for Children, the authors teach elementary school kids how to *recognize* bullying (Is it fair? How does it feel? Does it keep happening?); *refuse* bullying (reject or say no to bullying behaviors); and *report* bullying (any time bullying is recognized it *can* be reported, but it *should* always be reported to an adult when "someone is unsafe; someone is touching or showing private body parts; or refusing the bullying doesn't work"). Along with the ground rules of "in trouble, out of trouble, or both," young kids can easily remember these three "should report" bullying situations. As a parent, you can play the "what if" game with your kids and help them role-play the witness—practicing recognizing, refusing, and reporting. You are not only teaching your kids virtues you hold dear, you are helping them with the lines and actions for this all-important role. Aristotle summed up in four words the basics of teaching virtues to children: "Virtue is a habit."

Kids need to know you will treat the information seriously and confidentially (not disclose to the bully the source of your information) if necessary—but that you won't keep it a secret. Bullying thrives on secrecy. Kids have to trust that telling an adult will make a positive difference. Once they have shared the information with you, talk with them about what they can do and what you are going to do. If your son begs you not to get involved, hear him out and then share with him your concerns about the possible consequences of not acting and the possible actions you both can take—inaction is never an option when bullying is involved.

Younger children are more likely to tell an adult because they still believe an adult can and will do something that will make the bullying stop—not so with preteens and teenagers. Aside from the fact that they often believe adults will do nothing or that if they do, it will only make matters worse, adolescents are trying to find their own way in the world, without the interference of grown-ups. But the bullying experienced in high school often has far more devastating consequences for all parties involved, and appropriate adult intervention is usually necessary for serious bullying to be stopped. In the next chapter, we will look at how you and your children can work effectively with the school and the community to "recognize, refuse, report"—and respond.

A Pledge

Days after the shooting at Columbine High School in Littleton, Colorado, a group of Nashville, Tennessee, students created a website: www.IWillPledge.Nashville.com. They invited other students throughout the world to sign the following pledge:

As part of my community and my school, I WILL:

- pledge to be a part of the solution.
- eliminate taunting from my own behavior.
- encourage others to do the same.
- do my part to make my community a safe place by being more sensitive to others.
- set the example of a caring individual.
- eliminate profanity toward others from my language.
- not let my words or actions hurt others . . .

. . . and if others won't become a part of the solution, I WILL.

These kids were willing to take a leadership role, knowing that if they took a stand, others might follow. They also recognized that even if no one else followed in their footsteps, they would do what they knew was right.

Since this was created, many schools and organizations throughout the world have created their own pledges. (For a mind-boggling display of pages of pledges, just Google "anti-bullying pledges worldwide.") Caution: don't let it be just a poster on the wall, a placard in the lunchroom, a sign on the door, a pledge in a handbook, a band on a wrist. It needs to be an honest and sincere commitment to take a stand.

Cowardice asks the question: is it safe?
Expediency asks the question: is it politic?
Vanity asks the question: is it popular?
But conscience asks the question: is it right? And there
comes a time when one must take the position that is nei-
ther safe, nor politic, nor popular—but one must take it
because it's right.

—Martin Luther King Jr.

The power of choosing between good and evil is within the
reach of all.

—Origen (c. 184–254)

chapter twelve

Keeping Young People Involved, Connected, and Safe in the Net Neighborhood

As savvy as children and teens may be about the Internet, there are still many things they do not know about life and making safe and responsible choices. Sometimes they take risks. Your child already is, or can be expected to become, a "technology expert." But as a parent, you are still the "life experiences" and "risk management" expert. An effective parent-child partnership to address Internet issues is essential.

—Nancy Willard,
Raising Cyber Savvy Kids: Empowering Children and Teens to Make Safe and Responsible Choices When Using the Internet

Since I wrote the first edition of this book, there has been a rapid development and expansion of high-tech tools that are influencing the very fabric of our lives. A recent study of more than two thousand eight- to-eighteen-year-olds by the Henry J. Kaiser Family Foundation found that children are doubling up on their media exposure—watching TV while plugged into the Internet, text messaging while listening to music and researching a paper online—and packing as much as 8.5 hours of media exposure into a day, seven days a week. Kids are plugged in, turned on, and tuned out for the equivalent of a forty-five-hour workweek, every week. Media technology has the power to help define reality for our kids; it also has a tremendous influence on who our kids become and what kind of world they actually inhabit. Media technology has become so powerful that we cannot afford to be laissez-faire about its consequences for our kids.

Connecting to the Internet is like opening the door to a new and vast city. Some parents look at the ugly and absolutely scary stuff out there and refuse to let the Internet be a part of their family life at all. Some rigidly control their child's access to the computer and his or her time spent on the Net, regardless of the child's age, ability, sensitivities, and needs.

Some parents are so ill informed and have so little desire to be computer literate that they allow their children to roam any and all streets, back alleys, and freeways of the Internet. And there are parents who know how ignorant they are and make an effort to learn at least as much as their young children know, and more—especially about cyber savvy (smarts), cyber civility, and cyber safety. They realize the Net is here to stay and that teaching children to use it to their advantage, to get the most out of it, and to be savvy, civil, and safe requires the same tools that communication and relationship skills require in offline neighborhoods. (For a sensible overview of all of these basic tools translated for the digital world, a good website is www.StopCyberbullying.org, created by Internet security and privacy lawyer, Parry Aftab, who believes that digital technology can change our children's lives for the better.)

If you are reading this book, you are probably among the parents who want to make the most of the Internet for themselves and their children. The first step is to get all of the up-to-date information you can. There are many good books on taking your kids online, protecting them in cyberspace, and navigating the Net. I recommend you browse your local bookstore, talk to other parents, and to educators. And explore the Net for resources. Take advantage of the skills of your computer-savvy kids. Ask them to help you learn the language and the culture of these new neighborhoods. When your child acquires a screen name and password to use IM and enter chat rooms and gaming sites, many new neighborhoods open to them. Do you know them?

Immigrants, Natives, and Masters

Some of us did not have a computer in our homes—or in our schools—when we were growing up. "On line" was a clothesline and "party line" was six families sharing one phone line. And who needed the Internet? The phone operator knew everyone's business and could spread a rumor faster than the next generation could speed dial. We are *immigrants* to this new Net community. We don't know the language, the idioms, the landmarks, the road signs, the customs, or the culture.

Some of you are *natives* of the Internet. You grew up with a computer in the family room and in the classroom. You knew the language and could read the road maps. You grew up as the Internet was coming of age. You acted as the interpreter for us immigrants, translating the language, interpreting the idioms, explaining the acronyms, and absorbing the customs and culture as easily as you breathed the air.

And we immigrants' grandchildren and you natives' young children are *masters*—the third generation. Many of these children were introduced to social media in the birthing room as their parents tweeted, texted, and shared photos minutes after the birth. These children wonder why a circle in a book doesn't respond to their touch and animate the character on the page, or why the pages don't slide or grow bigger or smaller at the command of their fingers.

My daughter asked me why I gave my four-year-old grandson the password to my iPhone. I assured her I hadn't. I asked Chance how he had figured it out. He said, "I just watched you, Grandma." Who knew covering the iPhone screen when unlocking it in the presence of a four-year-old was as necessary as covering the touch pad at the ATM? With no effort, Chance could unlock the phone, swipe to Netflix, and pull up *Dinosaur Train*, season one, episode six—and he can't read yet.

These young masters may intuitively know the workings of the tech tools and use them with ease, but they still need to learn to be savvy, civil, and safe:

1. **Cyber Savvy**—being smart about the cyber world, and smart about how to behave in it—like, don't fight (flaming); don't steal; don't talk to, give to, or accept anything from a stranger; knowing how to use but not be abused by the Internet and social media, and how to make them a part of a whole life—not the whole of their life.

2. **Cyber Civil**—being kind and courteous; being able to dialogue, argue, and debate in an assertive way; being willing to stand up for another person and to speak out against an injustice; being able to refuse to participate in acts of cruelty.

3. **Cyber Safe**—knowing how to "surf defensively," i.e., how to avoid dangerous cyber situations; how to report abuse and possible cybercrimes; knowing when and how to use the four steps to staying safe when targeted—Stop, Copy, Block, and Tell; knowing how not to download malware or open spyware;

and, as Parry Aftab suggests, "keeping an eye on your devices; creating good passwords—easy to remember, hard to guess; and having proper privacy settings—not sharing too much with the wrong people."

This is where your parenting skills come in. Just as you introduce new responsibilities and decision-making opportunities in other parts of your child's life, and decrease limits and boundaries as they demonstrate the ability, confidence, and competence to be responsible, resourceful, and resilient people who know how to act with integrity, civility, and compassion, so, too, do you teach your children to live in the Net neighborhood and to navigate its roads. You want to know their friends offline, and you need to also know their friends online. You want them to be honest offline, and you need them to be honest online. You want them to treat others with dignity and regard offline, and you expect them to treat others online with the same regard.

In the early years of exploring the Internet, just as with exploring their own neighborhood, young children should be supervised, with you giving advice, suggestions, and tools for dealing with unexpected intrusions or cyberbullying. As kids get older, they can increasingly be trusted to handle the Net appropriately, as you continue to teach them such skills as how to deal with someone who "flames" them (sends an inflammatory e-mail or text that is intended to anger or hurt), and what to do if they ever feel uncomfortable in a chat room. You can teach them to think twice before they hit send once, and to refuse to participate in cyberbullying.

It is important that you stay close, both physically and relationally, as your children learn to explore the Internet. As they grow older, remain close in terms of being aware of what they are doing on the computer and other social media tools, including their cell phones, and the amount of time they are spending on them. Trust but verify! Get familiar with their Web friends and buddies, as you would with their school friends. Find ways to keep the lines of communication open, and opportunities to talk together about life in general and about their friendships in particular. If your children can share the good, the bad, and the ugly with you, and you've taught them how to navigate the Net neighborhoods, and what to do if things go haywire, they will be far better equipped to handle any situation that might come up, or if they can't figure something out, to come to us for help and advice. Our children benefit more from a proactive involvement than prohibitive don'ts. Children whose parents are involved in their lives, who keep talking with them, who know where they are, what they are doing, and who they are doing it with are less likely to get in trouble in their own neighborhoods, at school, or on the Net.

Stopping the Cyberbullying

Whether the cyberbullying is done via the cell phone or any other electronic tool—or a combination of tools—the response should begin with the loss of privileges related to the use of these tools. Parents and educators can use the same seven steps discussed on page 197 to hold cyberbullies accountable and help turn them around.

1. Intervene immediately with discipline.
2. Create opportunities to "do good."
3. Nurture empathy
4. Teach friendship skills—assertive, respectful, and peaceful ways to relate to others.
5. Closely monitor your child's TV viewing, video game playing, computer activities, and music.

6.   Engage in more constructive, entertaining, and energizing activities.
7.   Teach your child to "will good."

The discipline involved is a constructive and compassionate response to cyberbullying that takes into consideration the intent, the severity of the cyberbullying, and the restorative steps needed to help the cyberbully take on a more prosocial role in face-to-face encounters with peers and in the virtual neighborhood.

Helping the Cyberbullied

As the stories at the beginning of the book demonstrate, being targeted in cyberspace can have devastating and sometimes deadly consequences. The warning signs that kids exhibit when being cyberbullied are similar to those exhibited if they are bullied in any other way, but the spiral down into depression, illness, and academic failure is usually accelerated when cyberbullying is involved. This is because the target of cyberbullying gets no relief or respite from the bully. With low-tech bullying, the targeted child can escape by going home and/or staying home from school. Cyberbullying can and does happen any time and anywhere. All of the reasons for not telling about being the target of low-tech bullying are the same for cyberbullying:

1.   They are ashamed of being bullied.
2.   They are afraid of retaliation if they tell an adult.
3.   They don't think anyone can help them.
4.   They don't think anyone will help them.
5.   They have bought into the lie that bullying is a necessary part of growing up.

6. They may believe that adults are part of the lie, since it is not only kids who are bullying them.

7. They have learned that "ratting" on a peer is bad, not cool, "juvenile"—even if that peer is bullying them.

8. They fear that parents and educators will take the bully's word over theirs.

With cyberbullying, there is the added fear that if the child reports being targeted, their parents will take away their cell phones and restrict their computer access. Assure them in advance that you will not do that.

It is important to teach children how to respond to a cyberbully before they are cyberbullied. The situation is often made worse by responding to the cyberbully, whether that response is passive, aggressive, or even assertive. An assertive response to a face-to-face bullying scenario often stops the bullying. Not so with cyberbullying. You can teach your children to SCBT (Stop, Copy, Block, and Tell a trusted adult).

- *Stop*. Don't respond to the cyberbully. Chances are the target will respond out of anger or hurt and the response will only fuel the cyberbullying. Any response could be used to convince the authorities that the target was the provocateur (see discussion of cyberbullying by proxy in the next section of this chapter), or be altered by cutting and pasting to "put words in the target's mouth."

- *Copy*. Make copies of all messages and pictures, and save cell phone text and voice messages. (For a quick study in how to save all types of cyber messages, see *Internet Awareness for Parents: A Practical Guide for Safeguarding Your Family* by Robert Borys and John Salata; check online help for products

you are using; or go to www.Cyberbullying.org for illustrated instructions.)
- *Block* or filter communications through IM contact list or e-mail.
- *Tell* a trusted adult.

If the cyberbullying is threatening or vicious, you may need to do the following as well:

1. Change e-mail address, account, username, phone number, and/or SIM (subscriber identity module) card for cell phone users.
2. File a detailed complaint with the school (see page 225).
3. File a complaint with the website (through the "contact us" e-mail address on the site's home page), Internet service provider (through the "contact us" or support e-mail address on the ISP site), or cell phone company (trace the number and contact the phone company).
4. Contact the police if the cyberbullying appears to be criminal. Under the Criminal Code of Canada, it is a crime to communicate with someone if the communication causes targets to fear for their own safety or the safety of others. It is also a crime to publish a "defamatory libel," writing something that is intended to insult targets or harm their reputation by exposing them to hatred, contempt, or ridicule. If a bully spreads hate or discrimination based on race, national or ethnic origin, skin color, religion, age, gender, sexual orientation, marital status, family status, or disability, the cyberbully may be violating the Canadian Human Rights Act. Threats of violence, obscene text messages, stalking, racial-bias bullying, sexual bullying (including "revenge porn"),

creating or sending sexually explicit pictures, or taking pictures of someone where privacy is expected (locker room, bathroom, bedroom) could be a crime.

5. If the cyberbullying is revenge porn, i.e., nonconsensual pornography posted and distributed online, you can contact the Cyber Civil Rights Legal Project (www.CyberRightsProject.com) for legal assistance on a pro bono basis worldwide. Created by two attorneys, David Bateman and Elisa D'Amico of the law firm K&L Gates, to provide global legal resources for people who have been targets of revenge porn, it is a "civil rights pro bono project that aims to rectify serious cyber civils rights violations." Another resource is the Cyber Civil Rights Initiative (CCRI) Crisis help line: 844-878-CCRI (2274). For additional information, go to www.cybercivil-rights.org. At the time of this book's publication, the help line can provide assistance only to callers from the United States. Revenge porn is a crime in many jurisdictions today.

6. For other types of cyberbullying you can contact an attorney in your own community. It is possible to seek financial damages from the cyberbully and his or her own parents, as the family from Trois-Rivières, Quebec, was able to do. Think carefully before you take this step. It may be the appropriate one, but know that it can be costly and time consuming. It may involve months or years of litigation.

Most bullying is done "under the radar" of adults, and young people are hesitant to report it. Cyberbullying happens not only under the radar of adults but so thoroughly invades a child's life space that he or she feels overwhelmingly isolated and violated. We have to convince our kids that we can be trusted, are powerful allies, and will act—if they will only tell us. But first they must know that we know something about cyberbullying, can imagine the awfulness of it, and know ways to stop it.

Bystanders

Just as bystanders can play the various roles of henchmen, active supporters, passive supporters, disengaged onlookers, or scared potential witnesses in face-to-face bullying, so too can they be willing or unwitting accomplices to cyberbullies. Bystanders can cheer on the bully, help spread rumors, set up websites to further spread the cruelty, get pleasure from the target's pain and humiliation, stand by and watch it happen, or be afraid to step in, fearing they may be the next target.

Cyberbullies can use bystanders to do what is known as "cyberbullying by proxy." The cyberbully gets others to send provocative or humiliating messages to the target, or provokes the bystanders with a false rumor or accusation. The bystanders, in turn, attack the target. The cyberbully lets others do the actual bullying and can claim innocence when the bystanders get caught. Sometimes the proxy is not a bystander but an Internet service provider (ISP), such as AOL, MSN, or Google Mail. StopCyberbullying (www.StopCyberbullying.org) details this form of cyberbullying by proxy:

> "Warning" or "Notify Wars" are an example of cyberbullying by proxy. Kids click on the warning or notify buttons on their IM screen or e-mail or chat screens, and alert the ISP or service provider that the targeted kid has done something that violates their rules. If the target receives enough warnings or notifications, they can lose their account. The service providers are aware of this abuse, and often check to see if the warnings were justified. But all the cyberbully has to do

is make the target angry enough to say something rude or hateful back. Then, BINGO! they warn them, making it look like the target had started it. In this case, the ISP or service provider is the innocent accomplice of the cyberbully.

Bullies can also use the target's parents or school personnel as their proxy by simply taunting the target and forwarding the target's response to the parents or school personnel. Adults are thereby led to think that the target is actually the bully.

A more devastating—and at times deadly—form of proxy bullying is posting a target's cell phone number, screen name, and address in hate group or sex solicitation chat rooms and on their message boards. (If your child has been targeted in this way, law enforcement must be contacted immediately as there is a high risk of your child being reached online or offline by members of these groups.)

From Bystander to Witness

It is never easy to stand up to a bully or defend a target. But just as there are ways to act courageously in the offline world, there are ways to stand up, speak out, and defend a target in the online world. As a parent or educator you can teach young people the following tactics:

- Don't contribute to a blog or Web poll that denigrates or humiliates someone. Sign off or click "end" instead.
- Don't forward or copy-and-paste derogatory, harmful, or hurtful e-mails, text messages, or pictures to another site.
- Save, copy, and print out such examples of cyberbullying and give them to the person being targeted so he or she can

be aware of what is happening. Sharing such information in a caring and supportive way will help your peer feel less isolated and alone.

- Tell a caring adult you trust who will keep your identity confidential, who will act to support the targeted peer, and who will make sure the cyberbully is held to account.
- Tell the cyberbully that you are not comfortable getting involved in the cyberbullying.

Kids have to trust that telling an adult will make a positive difference. Once they have shared the information with you, talk with them about what they can do and what you are going to do. If your son or daughter begs you not to get involved, hear them out, and then share your concerns about the possible consequences of not acting and the possible actions you both can take. Inaction is never an option where cyberbullying is concerned.

Three Ps: Policy, Procedures, and Programs

Even though most cyberbullying occurs outside of school, it negatively impacts students and the school environment. It has already led to violence—including murder and suicide—in schools throughout the world. If your school already has a bullying prevention policy, procedures in place for the bully, the bullied, and the not-so-innocent bystanders, and programs that help break the cycle of violence and create a more deeply caring, more inclusive environment, it is important that a digital component be added to all three Ps:

- Policies at school must include sanctions against cyberbullying as well as all other kinds of bullying. Students and their parents need to be informed that cyberbullying, in all its forms, will not be tolerated.

- Procedures for restorative justice must be tailored to the unique problems and possible solutions required to repair the damage done through cyberbullying—especially the very *public* and potentially *permanent* and *pernicious* aspects of it. (On the Internet, it's forever and never forgotten.)
- Programs must address what cyberbullying is; how it impacts students; what students need to do if they are targeted, or if they are aware of another student being targeted; and ways to use cyberspace in a creative, constructive, responsible, and respectful manner.

What is needed is a comprehensive school-led community-based approach. The adult community must be educated not only about the dangers of low-tech and high-tech bullying, but also about the world of high tech in general as both an environment and a tool for socializing that the younger generation has fully embraced.

Red Hood Project

Parents, educators, and young people cannot stop cyberbullying alone. Nor is cyberbullying the only issue when it comes to dangers in the digital world. Before her bullycide at fifteen, Amanda Todd was targeted by peers who bullied her viciously and relentlessly through social media. The abuse and humiliation began when a thirty-five-year-old sexual predator posed as a teen on a social media site and preyed on, blackmailed, and stalked Amanda—as well as hundreds of other young people—before being arrested in the Netherlands in 2014. It is next to impossible for parents, educators, and young people to completely block sexual predators and cyberbullies from accessing kids on the various social media platforms. We must also look to the technology industry for much needed help. Raffi Cavoukian—a renowned singer, children's champion, ecology advocate, and recipient of the Order of Canada—has written a powerful critique of the Internet, our children's connection to it, and the potential disconnects resulting from an unquestioning and uncritical embrace of social media. In his 2013 book, *#Lightwebdarkweb: Three Reasons to Reform Social Media Be4 It Re-Forms Us*, Raffi describes the present dangers of the digital world and how all of us can help to make it safer and more secure, inspirational, and helpful to our kids. He and community activist and lawyer Sandy Garossino are cofounders of the Red Hood Project, a movement that looks for solutions to cyber-abuse issues from the source—the tech industry itself. In a letter to me, Sandy Garossino wrote:

> Companies like Facebook and Google are extremely highly resourced and have the finest computer engineers on the planet. These companies are much larger than the entire U.S. auto sector, and the public should expect the same level of commitment to safety and security of online child users that we expect from car manufacturers. We need them to step up and provide some answers.

The Red Hood Project (www.RedHoodProject.com) calls for solutions like user ID verification for all platforms accessible to children, much stronger site monitoring and management, and liability for damages resulting from anonymous or fake account abuse. The Red Hood Project advocates for a systemic change, beginning with these four proposed minimum standards:

1. Age verification and enhanced site supervision for children under sixteen.
2. Disabled location and Web browser tracking so that children cannot be physically located by anyone online.
3. Default privacy settings for children and youth that prevent public disclosure of kids' identity information.
4. Firewall protection for children's data online, so that children "can be protected from unwelcome monitoring, surveillance, and communication from strangers."

Change won't happen until we all work together. It isn't just a matter of stopping cyberbullying; it's about affirming, nurturing, and protecting the well-being of all our children.

> *The first reason to reform social media is safety. The second reason, intelligence, is directly related to the first. If the young of our species cannot be safe to develop their intelligence using the most popular and seductive technological invention, then we should certainly rethink its value and its place in our lives. Let us now consider the intelligence at play in and impacting the digital world.*
>
> **—Raffi Cavoukian @Raffi_RC,**
> *#Lightwebdarkweb: Three Reasons to Reform Social Media Be4 It Re-Forms Us*

Decoding the Code

Kids use shorthand to quickly send text messages to one another. A few of the common terms used are:

- HHOJ: Ha, ha, only joking (Or JJ: Just joking. Both are used to absolve cyberbullies of any responsibility for their taunts.)
- LOL: Laughing out loud.
- BRB: Be right back.
- 182: I hate you.
- 20: Location.
- YRDM: You are dead meat.
- YBS: You'll be sorry.
- ASL: Age/sex/location.
- LMIRL: Let's meet in real life.
- F2F: Face to face.
- SOHF: Sense of humor failure
- ?^: Hook up.
- GAL: Get a life.
- PA: Parent alert (also P911).
- WTGP: Want to go private?
- RUIND?: Are you in the dark?

RUIND? If you think POS means Parent Over Shoulder, think again. Or better yet, ask your teen. Check out websites such as www.NetLingo.com for the latest shorthand and acronyms, backronyms, leetspeak, and textonyms. Ask your kids to teach some of this lingo for when you're texting with them. It is important that you know and make the effort to keep up with the lingo your kids are using.

Some Basic Terminology

There is a virtual dictionary of terms associated with the online world—and it behooves us as parents and educators to be able to speak the language so that we can help our kids navigate the online world in a smart, civil, and safe way.

Blog: Shorthand for "weblog," an online journal that is frequently updated and intended for the general public. Some kids have two or more blogs, one "nice" and the other more menacing or provocative. Some kids use these to damage a peer's reputation, invade their privacy, or threaten them. Some kids set up blogs pretending to be their target and say things to humiliate them.

Buddy List: A list of friends' screen names that a user can communicate with via instant messaging or e-mail.

Chat Room: A virtual meeting place where friends can have typewritten conversations.

DSO: Dangerous stranger online. Sexual predators, child pornographers, hate-group recruiters, terrorist organizers, and others who do not have young people's well-being at heart lurk in the various Net neighborhoods and are skilled at manipulating vulnerable kids.

File-Sharing: Peer-to-peer technology that enables kids to search for and copy files, such as digital music files (MP3s), directly from one another's computers.

Flaming: Sending an e-mail or text message that is intended to inflame a situation or enrage a target.

ICT: Information and Communication Technologies.

ISP: Internet service provider, such as Rogers, Bell, Earthlink, AT&T, or XFINITY.

Instant Messaging (IM'ing): Users can see who on their buddy list is online and send messages and images instantaneously. (Cyberbullies often engage a target in IM'ing in order to get the target to reveal sensitive personal information, and then forward that information to others in order to hurt or humiliate the target.)

Internet Gaming: Games played on gaming devices (such as the Xbox 360, Sony PlayStation, and Wii U) or on cell phones, computers, and PADs that allow players from around the world to play with or against one another.

Internet Polling: Using the Net to poll peers on the ranking of kids. (Can be used to bully with such demeaning questions as: "Whose the biggest slut in your school?" "Who is the ugliest classmate?" "Who should die?")

Message Board: Online virtual place where people "chat" about a common interest.

Proxy Bullying: Using accomplices to spread ugly rumors, or harmful, hurtful, or hate-filled messages directed at a target.

Social Networking Websites: A complex web of friends and buddies connected online by common interests. Facebook is one of the fastest growing and most popular of these sites. Some kids post other kids' personal information and pictures, putting these kids at greater risk of being contacted by predators. Some kids create webpages specifically to torment or insult other kids.

SN: Screen name

Spam: Junk mail. (Being spammed is to be inundated with spam that has been ordered up by the bully to be sent to the target. Cyberbullies sign up their target for offensive, pornographic, IM, and e-mail marketing lists.

Text Messaging: Using a cell phone keypad to type short messages that are instantly sent to other cell phone users.

Web Bugging: Sending viruses, spyware, hacking programs, or Trojan Horse programs to a target's computer in order to destroy the computer, erase the hard drive, control the computer, or otherwise wreck havoc with the computer.

Weblog: Online diary, personal, public, permanent—certainly not private.

This is only a bit of basic vocabulary to get you started. Additional terms can be found in Appendix 2, "Internet and Social Media Terms."

> *A lot of people get the genre wrong when they talk about*
> *bullying.*
> *People who see it from the outside think that it's about*
> *drama.*
> *People who live it understand that it's horror.*
> *We're all just trying to outrun the monster.*

—Shane Koyczan,
Stickboy: A Novel in Verse

chapter thirteen

Caring Schools, Involved Communities

Bully/victim problems in school really concern some of our basic values and principles. For a long time, I have argued that it is a fundamental democratic right for a child to feel safe in school and to be spared the oppression and repeated, intentional humiliation implied in bullying. No student should be afraid of going to school for fear of being harassed or degraded, and no parent should need to worry about such things happening to his or her child.

—**Dr. Dan Olweus,**
in "Sweden," *The Nature of School Bullying:*
A Cross-National Perspective

Since most instances of bullying occur in school-related settings, as a parent you will want to know what your child's school community is doing to make sure all students feel safe at school. Over the years, I have looked at many anti-bullying programs. I am as disillusioned with some of them as the researchers who have studied the effectiveness of dropping such programs into schools and considering the problem solved, the mandate met, the legal requirements covered. We need to look at a more comprehensive plan to create conditions in our homes, schools, and communities that will strengthen inhibitions against violence and nurture the bonds that connect us to one another. We can use those bonds to nourish a deep passion to alleviate others' pain and sorrow. That does not mean that we don't use well-developed bullying prevention materials as *part of* a more comprehensive initiative. Kids need to know what bullying is and what it isn't; about the "trap of comradeship"; the difference between teasing and taunting, flirting and sexual bullying; and what it means to be brave-hearted. But these concepts are best taught by integrating them into the whole of a school's ethos— not as something just dropped in.

Dan Olweus (Olweus@psych.uib.no), one of the leading international authorities on bullying, developed a highly successful intervention initiative in Bergen, Norway, that has proven to significantly reduce bullying in the schools that have adopted it correctly, seeing it not just as an *anti-bullying program* but as part of a comprehensive plan to create the *antithesis of bullying*, i.e., a more deeply caring community. His program is built on a set of four key principles: to create a school (and ideally also a home) environment characterized by

1. warmth, positive interest, and involvement from adults;
2. firm limits as to unacceptable behavior of all kinds;
3. in case of violations of limits and rules, consistent application of non-hostile, non-physical sanctions (discipline as opposed to punishment); and
4. behavior by adults at home and at school that creates an authoritative (not authoritarian) adult-child interaction or child-rearing model (backbone as opposed to brick-wall structure).

These four principles translate into actions on an individual level, whole-class level, and school-wide level in any number of ways.

Three Ps

Check to see if your school has the three Ps necessary for a good bully prevention structure.

1. **Policy**

    This policy must be clearly articulated, consistently enforced, and broadly communicated. It should include a clear definition of what bullying is, the types of bullying, and the overlays that often increase the cruelty and impact of the bullying.

    Sample: "Bullying is a conscious, willful, deliberate activity intended to harm, in which the perpetrator(s) get pleasure from the targeted child's pain/and or misery. It can be verbal, physical, and/or relational; have as its overlay race, ethnicity, religion, gender (including sexual orientation and sexual identification), or physical or mental ability; and includes all forms of hazing and cyberbullying. It can be and often is continual and repeated over time, but does not have to be. Once is enough to constitute bullying."

    Included in the policy should be a statement of responsibility of those who witness the bullying to try to stop it by intervening, helping the targeted student escape, and/or telling a caring adult.

    (Check your federal, provincial, or state laws, and school district rules and guidelines for the policy applicable to your school. Most provinces and states have reconsidered the statement found in earlier laws that mean and cruel events had to be continual and repeated over time to constitute bullying, and they now recognize that a one-time attack can constitute bullying.)

2. **Procedures**

Clearly outline the consequences for the bully—and any henchmen or other not-so-innocent bystanders who played an active supporting role in the bullying.

These procedures should include disciplinary measures that will be taken to hold the students accountable for their actions. I recommend some form of restorative justice, i.e., restitution, resolution, and, if possible, an attempt at reconciliation at the targeted student's behest.

Procedures for restorative justice are tailored to the unique problems in a given situation and possible solutions to repair the damage done.

It is helpful to incorporate into the plan the six other ways to reform the perpetrator(s). Parents of both the bully and the bullied are notified of the bullying and asked to take measures at home that will help in the restorative justice process.

Clearly outline what measures will be taken to keep the targeted student safe at school, give him or her the tools to stand up to the perpetrators, and offer support to keep the targeted student from succumbing to the bullying.

Identify a person or persons to whom the student can safely report any further bullying incidences.

Notify parent(s) of the incident and the school's plan.

Give parent(s) a protocol to follow to report any further targeting of their child. (See how to report, page 225.)

3. **Programs**

Develop programs that back up and reinforce the policy and help to create a safe, caring, and welcoming environment for all students.

Ask for a copy of your child's school's bullying prevention policy. Check to see that it has Olweus's four principles and the three Ps necessary for an effective policy. In the end, you want to know that your child's school has a strong bullying prevention policy that is *clearly articulated, consistently enforced,* and *broadly communicated.* It is one thing to have a policy; it is wholly another to make sure the policy is not just placards on the school wall or an inspirational piece of writing at the beginning of the student handbook. It is the school culture and social environment that these policies, procedures, and programs create as well as reflect.

One project that includes all three—policy, procedures, and program—is the previously mentioned critically acclaimed Steps to Respect developed by the Committee for Children (www.CFChildren.org). Steps to Respect is used in elementary schools throughout the world. Developed as an integrative program, it includes bullying prevention as part of the whole of the curriculum. Designed not just to decrease bullying, it also helps students build more supportive relationships with one another. It teaches skills for coping with bullying, including recognizing bullying, using assertive behaviors to refuse bullying, and reporting bullying to adults. It is one of the few programs that addresses the negative roles of not-so-innocent bystanders and helps kids to become witnesses, resisters, and defenders. Steps to Respect emphasizes the responsibility of all members of the school community to create a more deeply caring community. Lessons in the various units teach empathy for targets of bullying and specific helpful ways children can respond when they witness bullying. The program also emphasizes the adults' crucial role: "Bullying can be a seriously destructive element in relationships among children at school, among adults in the workplace, and within families. The school setting provides educators with the opportunity to teach children that bullying is wrong—and that there are positive ways of influencing others. Through the lessons they teach in class and their actions on the playground, adults can demonstrate the power of caring, respectful, and responsible citizenry." Steps to Respect recommends for optimal intervention the following school-wide components:

1. *Gathering information about bullying at school directly from students.* This would involve first increasing awareness among students, educators, and parents about the definition of bullying, the four ways and three means of bullying, and the roles students can and do play (see the Bullying Circle on page 146). Second, it entails surveying anonymously students, educators, and parents about the nature and quality of peer relations at the school. Don't be surprised if students report more incidents of bullying than parents or educators suspect. Third, it is necessary to ask kids what they need from adults in order to feel safe.

2. *Establishing clear school-wide and classroom rules about bullying.* Kids need to know what the rules are, that they will be enforced, and how they will be enforced. It is important that the constructive consequences require that those partaking in the bullying go through the three Rs: restitution, resolution, and reconciliation. There also needs to be a plan of action if the intervention does not work and the bully does not change his or her behavior. This plan can include removal from a class or school and a referral to another program such as an alternative school, a mental health agency, or the police. Along with the rules, the school needs to create strong social norms against bullying, with programs to prevent, identify, and combat bullying.

3. *Training all adults in the school to respond sensitively and consistently to bullying.* Bullied kids want to know that

they will be supported and protected and that adults will take responsibility for the safety of all students. Educators should teach diversity awareness and model positive, respectful, and supportive behaviors. No longer will "kids will be kids," "it's his own fault, he was asking for it," or "they were just teasing" work as excuses by educators for not intervening.

4. *Providing adequate adult supervision, particularly in less structured areas, such as on the playground and in the lunchroom.* Students want a greater adult presence in all areas of the school as well as on the school bus. One of the most effective strategies to make a school safe is the physical presence of responsible adults.

5. *Improving parental awareness of and involvement in working on the problem.* You as a parent can model positive, respectful, and supportive behaviors; help your children develop a strong sense of self; teach them how to make friends; and teach them how to become a part of a group. You can teach them to relate to others in a positive and respectful way, to be assertive, and to stand up and speak out against injustices.

You can volunteer to help create a greater presence of caring adults in the school, work with educators to make sure policies are implemented, and serve as an advocate for your child.

You can lobby your school board or board of trustees for adequate funding for additional staff needed for supervision, for support services, and for programs that can back up the strong policies and rules and consequences that states and provinces are mandating. Severe cutbacks in funding in both the United States and Canada have undermined the safety of students. Boards have eliminated supervisory functions teachers used to perform; hall monitors are almost non-existent; there are few, if any, lunchroom monitors left, fewer educational assistants and guidance counselors—all critical elements for the safety and well-being of students.

Find out what kind of communication will be forthcoming from the school if your child is bullying or being bullied—phone, letter, note—and what procedures you can follow if you are concerned about a bullying situation that school personnel may not know about yet.

Kids can't stop the bullying they experience or witness all by themselves. They need adults at home, in the school, and in community programs committed to breaking this cycle of violence wherever they see it and whenever they hear about it.

Positive Programs

The following are two programs for middle and high schools that address teen-violence prevention and have proven track records in schools that have implemented them as part of a larger school initiative.

1. *Safe Teen: A Life-Skills and Violence Prevention Program* (www.safeteen.ca) by Anita Roberts of Vancouver, British Columbia, offers an in-depth look at issues and skills such as

   • how to access inner strength and form healthy relationships;
   • the importance of building and respecting boundaries;
   • how to deal with bullying and sexual harassment;
   • the importance of embracing differences and understanding the roots of racism, sexism, and homophobia; and
   • how to make wise choices about personal safety, drugs, and alcohol.

300

Anita Roberts has also written a book, *Safe Teen: Powerful Alternatives to Violence,* which both teens and their parents can read to learn ways teens can deal with peer pressure, de-escalate violence, and develop a strong sense of self.

2. *Personal and Social Responsibility* and *Mastering Anger/ Resolving Conflict* is a two-part curriculum series for middle and high school students (www.IASD.com) developed by Constance Dembrowsky of the Institute for Affective Skills Development of La Luz, New Mexico. These courses address

   - developing self-discipline;
   - identifying consequences before taking action;
   - recognizing the impact of the student's actions on others;
   - getting what the student wants in ways that maintain dignity and respect for himself and others;
   - mastering anger, not surrendering to it; and
   - resolving conflicts peacefully.

These two courses can be taught sequentially or can stand alone. The *Personal and Social Responsibility* curriculum includes materials for optional parent training sessions. The activities in both courses include discussion and experiential learning opportunities that connect the activities to what is going on in the lives of the students; myths and legends engage the students and help to illustrate the concepts being taught.

Dembrowsky writes about the two critical elements that are essential to help students move from being a target to their own best witness, resister, and defender:

1. *Hope* is the wellspring that empowers kids to validate their uniqueness, inherent dignity, and worth. Being hopeful, they feel more confidence in their ability to respond effectively to a bullying situation; they are energized to generate multiple solutions to address the bullying problem so they're not stuck if the first solution doesn't work; and they are able to take positive actions on their own behalf, instead of feeling helpless, overwhelmed, defeated, isolated, and alone.

2. *Resilience* is needed to get through being targeted and not succumbing to the attack. Instead of feeling helpless, overwhelmed, and defeated, students learn that they have the power to change their own vocabulary and self-talk, which in turn allows them to change their attitude and feelings. This then lets them take different actions in both their verbal responses and physical responses. Resilient kids engage in multiple-choice thinking as opposed to no-choice thinking.

Giving teens the tools to develop self-discipline, to act respectfully and responsibly, to master their anger and resolve conflicts peacefully, to develop strong friendships, to know how to successfully engage in constructive group activities, and to know when and how to remove themselves from a group if necessary in order to stand up and speak out, are not just bullying prevention skills—they are life skills.

A website worth looking at is www.GirlsRespectGroups.com. Lorna Blumen from Toronto, Ontario, has created several programs that involve high school girls helping middle school girls "press the reset button on respect." Working together, both sets of young girls learn to make choices grounded in respect for themselves and others, and to explore ways they can choose healthy relationships with other girls and with boys. Blumen asks, "What's up with girls' friendship these days? . . . And why are we letting our kids learn their relationship skills from *The Real Housewives of Atlanta*?" Used in eighty countries worldwide, these programs can either stand alone or be integrated into pre-existing girls' programs.

Regular blogs on the website address issues related to "boys' respect" as well as "girls' respect," and cover such topics as "Celebrities Behaving Badly—Double Standards for Kids?" and "Self Respect: Crucial Life Skill For Kids, Teens and Adults."

Dynamix Adventures Inc., founded by Corey Szwarcok and Mitch Zeltzer of Montreal, Quebec, offers a proactive approach to overcoming bullying in schools. At the core of its powerful programs are team-building experiences that use a relationship-based approach to build community, promote kindness, and *prevent* bullying. Through hands-on activities and exercises, Dynamix empowers children and teens with the right tools to think independently and act responsibly toward themselves and others. The team's learning-by-doing approach engages children by putting words into action, which boosts both a strong sense of self and a strong sense of community. Learn more about their programs at www.TeamMakers.com.

As a parent or educator you may want to be involved with your school's research into these and other programs that can help create a school climate that supports creative, constructive, respectful and responsible activities and work toward reducing all forms of violence, including bullying. Just buying a packaged product or holding an anti-bullying day event sounds so much easier and it is—and far less effective.

Bullying happens in every school. You want to be sure that your child's school is proactive and deals with the four ways (one-time event, continual and repeated, hazing, and cyber) and three means of bullying (physical, verbal, and relational) promptly, firmly, and consistently. Educators need to be vigilant in addressing all incidents of bullying. If your child's school does not have a bullying prevention policy with procedures and programs to back up the policy, you may find yourself in the same spot Hoss's mom found herself in when her son's teacher saw the bullying as the bullied kid's problem.

Nicknamed Hoss by his family when he was a toddler, five-year-old Howard was subjected to unmerciful taunting by a small group of boys on the playground. His teacher called his mom and suggested that in order to eliminate their favorite taunt, "Hossy Bossy," Hoss should start going by his given name of Howard. Not seeing how changing his name would stop the taunting, Hoss's mom retorted, "Why? So they can call him Howard the Coward instead?" A more satisfactory solution would have been to deal with the tormentors directly. But it is not uncommon that the situation is viewed as the target's problem to solve alone. Targets of bullies often elicit little empathy from classmates and adults. You may have to be persistent in your insistence that bullying be addressed at its source—the bully. There will be times when you may have to help your bullied child work on behaviors that get in the way of healthy relationships with peers, but nobody ever deserves to be bullied. If you are concerned about the teacher's proposed solution or lack of response, know that you can go to that teacher's supervisor or to the principal, as Sophie's mother did.

Twelve-year-old Sophie, who had a hearing impairment, was being taunted by her classmates out of sight and earshot of her teacher. When the taunting became unbearable, Sophie told her mom. Mom and daughter had a meeting with the teacher— Sophie's mom being there as a support while Sophie talked about the incidents. The teacher expressed sympathy, then shrugged and said, "That's just how girls this age behave." Worse, she began to list all the things she thought Sophie was doing that brought on the ugly name-calling and suggested that if she weren't such a wimp, this wouldn't be happening. Fortunately for Sophie, her mom didn't stop with this one meeting. She informed the teacher that she felt the bullying was not normal, nor should her daughter or any other child have to tolerate such meanness. The next step was a meeting with the principal and this teacher. The principal agreed with Sophie's mom, promptly dealt with the bully and her followers, supported Sophie, and required the teacher to attend a workshop entitled "Dealing Effectively with Bullying."

Beware: Zero Tolerance Can Equal Zero Thinking

At the opposite end of the continuum, all fifty states and most Canadian provinces, as well as the three Canadian territories, have instituted zero-tolerance policies against bullying and other forms of violence as well as against possession of weapons and use of drugs. The intent of these policies is laudable, but the singular procedure—one size fits all (that is, mandatory suspension or expulsion)—that many school districts have implemented is inflexible, harsh, and lacking in common sense. It requires an "all or nothing" approach that gives administrators the message "You have no choice" and has resulted in a reckless and punitive approach that has an overtone of vindictiveness and has also brought increased lawsuits against schools regarding unfairness and inequities.

In December 2013, two ten-year-old students from Fawn Grove, Pennsylvania, were suspended under the school district's zero-tolerance policy against weapons when one pretended to shoot his friend with an imaginary bow and arrow, and the other pretended to shoot back using only a hand signal intended to imitate a gun. These students are not the only ones to have been suspended as a result of such "zero thinking." Other examples of zero-tolerance policies equaling zero thinking:

- A first grader suspended for three days for pointing a breaded chicken finger at a friend as if it were a gun.
- Two eight-year-olds arrested and charged with "making terrorist threats" for wielding a paper gun in class.
- A thirteen-year-old boy expelled for making a list of his enemies, which a classmate found in the trash and showed to a teacher.
- An eleven-year-old arrested for having a plastic knife to cut the chicken in her lunchbox.
- A ten-year-old expelled for "possession of a lethal weapon" after she voluntarily turned in a small knife she found in her lunch bag. The girl had inadvertently taken her mom's lunch bag instead of her own. The small knife was to cut an apple. The teacher thanked the girl for doing the right thing; the principal promptly suspended the girl because there was "no leeway in the law."
- A six-year-old accused of "sexual harassment" for running out of the bath in his own home to tell the school-bus driver to wait for him.
- A sixteen-year-old expelled after he turned in an English assignment in which he wrote about his thoughts of getting revenge on those students who had taunted and physically harassed him daily.

In March 2001, the American Bar Association released a statement opposing such zero-tolerance procedures, calling them a "one size fits all solution to all the problems that schools confront. It redefined students as criminals, with unfortunate consequences."

A bullying prevention policy that has zero tolerance for bullying is a good thing. No one wants his child bullied at school. What is needed are procedures to support that policy that provide opportunities for administrators to exercise fairness, common sense, and sound discretion. All bullying should have some sanction. It doesn't mean you apply the maximum sanction for every offense.

At San Marcos High School in San Marcos, California, a student drew up a list of his tormentors on the back of a class handout. Parents of some of the students on the list insisted that the principal do something. Principal Frans Weits did what they demanded, but not in the way they expected. He ordered an investigation. Students were asked what they had done to their classmate that would merit getting their name on his list. He then called to account everyone involved in the incident—bullies, henchmen, active supporters to disengaged onlooker, and the bullied boy who wrote the list. The principal was quoted in the *San Diego Union-Tribune*: "In light of what's happened in neighboring districts, San Marcos High now has a zero-tolerance policy toward bullying. And everyone—faculty, staff, students and parents—is on notice that students will be held accountable for everything from verbal harassment to physical aggression." San Marcos had a policy, procedures, and a committed administrator who was willing to follow through in order to create a safe school community for all of the students. The zero-tolerance policy in that district was accompanied by procedures that allowed for the exercise of fairness and common sense as well as sound discretion and judgment on the part of the administrator. Each student had to take responsibility for his or her own behavior and go through disciplinary procedures that were, as Dan Olweus suggests, "non-hostile, non-physical sanctions."

One of the neighboring districts the principal referred to was Sante, California, where weeks before, a boy whose cries went unheard, whose pain was ignored, and whose oppression went unabated and unrelieved struck back with a vengeance, killing two schoolmates and wounding thirteen more, as well as several adults. In other districts across both Canada and the United States, kids, feeling they have no other way out of the pain and torture heaped on them by their tormentors, no one to turn to, and no one to tell, kill themselves. In their book, *Bullycide*, Neil Marr and Tim Field point an accusing finger at those who do not do what principal Frans Weits saw as critical: "Each bullycide is an unpalatable fact that a child has died as a result of the deliberate actions of another in an environment where the responsible adults have failed to provide a mechanism for reporting, intervening, and dealing with physical and psychological violence. The excuses of 'we didn't know' or 'we didn't understand' are no longer valid."

School Climate and Culture

Along with a bullying prevention policy and procedures, check to see that your child's school has programs that actually work toward changing the climate and culture of a school.

Most educators want "to do the right thing" and stop hurtful behavior, says Arthur Coleman, deputy assistant secretary in the U.S. Department of Education's Office for Civil Rights. Coleman was part of a team that created "Protecting Students from Harassment and Hate Crime: A Guide for Schools." (The full text is available online at www.ed.gov/pubs/Harassment.) The guide emphasizes that schools take a comprehensive approach such as developing written policies that prohibit harassment and instituting a formal complaint policy. In an interview for ASCD (Association for Supervision and Curriculum Development) Curriculum Update Fall 1999, the authors of the guide explain, "We want to help educators look for ways to be proactive and strategic on the front end to avoid heartbreak on the back end." They also note, "[W]ritten anti-harassment policies and complaint procedures will not stop or prevent harassment." In the same update, Terrence Deal, Irving R. Melbo Professor of Education, University of California, agreed: "In and of themselves, policies and procedures, rules and regulations, often serve as substitutes for values—they hang on the wall and not in people's heads and hearts. What schools need is that shared sense of 'this is the way we do things here.'"

Written by Steve Seskin and Allen Shamblin and made famous by Peter, Paul and Mary, the song "Don't Laugh at Me" (chapter 5) serves as the theme for the critically acclaimed project Operation Respect: Don't Laugh at Me (www.DontLaugh.org). Founder and director Peter Yarrow developed this program, available free to schools that want to create "safe and caring climates in which children learn to treat each other with respect." In the fact sheet accompanying the program, Peter Yarrow reiterates the need for that shared sense of "This is the way we do things here": "Let's not wait to fix our children after the fact anymore. Let's not wait for the good-spirited, open, malleable clay of young children to become hardened. Though we must address the needs of all children with equal passion, let's not just focus on those who have become troubled and potentially dangerous to themselves and to others. Let us work proactively together to help evolve a next generation of whole, caring, confident, and productive citizens."

In their book *Peacemakers*, Roger and David Johnson write of the importance of the education of the whole child, of tending to children's social and emotional development as well as to their academic growth: "While schools teach math, reading, social studies, and science, perhaps the most important thing for students to learn is how to interact effectively and peacefully with each other and the world at large." Whether your child is the bully, the one bullied, the not-so-innocent bystander, or the brave-hearted witness, resister, or defender, your active participation in the school community can help assure that there is a shared sense of "This is the way we do things here"—at home, in school, and in the community—that the needs of all children are addressed with "equal passion," and that your child and her classmates learn to "interact effectively and peacefully." Your involvement can range from volunteering in the classroom or helping supervise open areas of the school (high school included) to participating in the parent-student-teacher organization active in your child's school or assisting in club activities. Once again, the key to dealing effectively with bullying is to "pay attention, get involved, and never ever look away."

Planned intervention in our schools can greatly reduce bullying and its subsequent negative impact on individual children, the school community, and the entire community. Research has shown that bullying can be reduced if educators, students, and parents work together to create a climate in which there is an esprit de corps—the spirit of devotion and enthusiasm among members of a group for one another, their group, and their purpose—and in which all kids believe they have worth, are capable human beings, are expected to serve, and can resolve conflicts non-violently. In middle schools and high schools, however, there is a major cultural obstacle to this esprit de corps—cliques.

Cliques

In the movie *The Breakfast Club*, five students at a high school with a rigid social system were assigned to Saturday suspension for a variety of "crimes" they had committed. Each student had to compose an essay telling who they thought they were. Instead they spent the day in a series of adventures that allowed them to go beyond their facades, their pretenses, and their roles and come to know one another as human beings—more alike than different and more caring than "cool." The final essay, composed as a letter and read by one of the teenagers, but submitted to the vice principal on behalf of all five, railed against the rigid social system that was artificially created and followed blindly until that fateful Saturday:

Dear Mr. Bernard,

We accept the fact we had to sacrifice a whole Saturday in detention for whatever it was that we did wrong. What we did was wrong. But we think you're crazy to make us write an essay telling you who we think we are. What do you care? You see us as you want to, in the simplest terms and the most convenient definitions. You see us as a brain, an athlete, a basket case, a princess, and a criminal, correct? That's the way we saw each other at seven o'clock this morning. We were brainwashed. But what we found out is that each one of us is a brain, an athlete, a basket case, princess, and criminal. Does that answer your question?

Sincerely yours,
The Breakfast Club

   In his book *Nobody Left to Hate: Teaching Compassion After Columbine,* Elliot Aronson wrote about this poisonous atmosphere in middle and senior high school, which he saw as one of the root causes of violence:

It's the cliquish atmosphere of rejection and humiliation that makes a very significant minority of students; I would say 30 to 40 percent of them, very, very unhappy. If kids at the top of the pyramid start calling a kid a nerd, then the kids in the second tier of cliques tease him because that's one way of identifying with the powerful group. The next thing you know, everybody's teasing him. Everybody in school knows what group everybody belongs to. They know whom they can get away with taunting.

It is reasonably clear that one of the root causes of the recent school shootings is a school atmosphere that ignores, or implicitly condones, the taunting, the rejection, and verbal abuse to which a great many students are subjected. A school that ignores the values of empathy, sympathy, and compassion—or, worse still, pays lip service to these values while doing nothing concrete and effective to promote these values—creates an atmosphere that is not only unpleasant for the "losers," but one that shortchanges the "winners" as well.

Eric Harris and Dylan Klebold wrote about the resentment they had for the caste system, where popular athletes were accorded star status at their school. After the shootings at Columbine, other students voiced similar concerns about the hierarchy of cliques perpetuated by students and tolerated by administrators. Evan Ramsey, at the bottom of the rigid social system of his small high school in Alaska, was the target of abuse for years. Alexandra Shea wrote of the "junior capos who run the social underground." The kids from the Breakfast Club found a way for kids from various backgrounds to begin to accept one another not as the same, but as uniquely different, each with gifts and talents and foibles to bring to the table—and to projects (granted, some of the projects the Breakfast Club engaged in would not be ones you want to encourage, but it was the working and sharing and being human in front of one another that began to break down the prejudices, stereotypes, and bigotry they originally held).

The more opportunities students from diverse backgrounds and interests have to work and play together, the less likely they will be to form cliques that have as their hallmark exclusion and derision of those "beneath" them. The more administrators and other adults in the school as well as in the community refuse to elevate one group over all the others—with all the accompanying privileges—the less likely it will be that these groups will have the notion that they can bully someone who is not a part of their "elite" group. No small task, I know, to dismantle the social caste systems in our middle schools and high schools, but I agree with Elliot Aronson that to tackle bullying, we must tackle its root causes—and a rigid social system of cliques is one of those causes. To establish a bullying prevention policy and at the same time condone a poisonous social environment that implicitly supports social stratification and social privilege, which in turn results in injustice, oppression, subjugation, and humiliation, is to be silently complicit in fueling the rage of those at the bottom of the heap.

Been Bullied

Whether your child tells you about being bullied, your child's best friend's parent breaks the news to you, or you find a note dropped in the backseat of the car detailing the ugly incidents, after you have talked with your child (chapter 8), you will want to let her teachers know about the bullying she is experiencing at school. There are five steps to take:

1. Arrange a meeting for you and your child with the appropriate person at the school. If your school has a bullying prevention policy and procedures in place, there may be a specific person in the building assigned and trained to intervene

effectively. It is important that your son or daughter who was bullied be an important part of finding a solution to the problem of the bullying. If all the adults get together to talk about a solution without the child being actively involved, the child is even further disempowered. If your child is a teenager, she can take the lead at this initial meeting, with you as her support.

2. Bring to the meeting the facts in writing—the date, time, place, kids involved, and the specifics of the incidents—and the impact the bullying has had on your child as well as what your child has done to try to stop the bullying that didn't work. (Putting everything in writing beforehand will help you and your child effectively present the facts that could be forgotten if you both rely on memory in what could be an emotionally charged meeting.)

3. Work with your child and school personnel on a plan that addresses what your child needs right now in order to feel safe, what she can do to avoid being bullied or to stand up to any future bullying, and to whom she can go for help. The plan will also include what the adults are going to do to keep her and other potential targets safe and stop further bullying.

4. Find out what procedures the bully will be going through and what kind of support the school is expecting from the parents of the bully. At this point, you can discuss the possibility of your child and the bully meeting *at a later date* for the third step in the discipline process—reconciliation. No one is likely to see this as an option right now, but let the school know that you feel it is important that the healing take place if possible *after* the bully (or bullies) has gone through the other steps. Set a time to review the plan with the appropriate school personnel.

5.   If you feel the problem is not being adequately addressed by the school, know that you can express your concerns and let the teacher and/or administrator know that you will take the next step to the school district board office and if necessary—especially in cases of serious abuse or racist or sexist bullying—to the police (in the United States, you can contact the U.S. Department of Education Office for Civil Rights [OCR], which can often initiate legal action against the bully or the school board). Schools are responsible for protecting students and are culpable when they don't.

To Change or Not to Change

Your child has a right to be educated in an environment that is free of fear and harassment. Your child is likely to need a lot of support if he has been bullied for a length of time. Know that he may be in shock, physically and emotionally harmed, fearful that the bullying will happen again, incredibly sad, and just plain unwilling to trust the kid (or bunch of kids) who bullied him. His thoughts may have turned to revenge, his feelings to rage. To help him begin to heal, you will need to create for him an atmosphere of compassion, kindness, gentleness, and patience and provide a safe and secure environment. Ideally, that environment would include your child's school, where the adults treat bullying as a serious matter and respond sensitively and effectively to your child's report; where the bully is required to go through the process of reconciliatory justice, and where peers are respectful and friendly toward your child.

I am not a strong proponent of moving the target of bullying to another classroom or school to get away from the bullying. Two things can happen. The bullying continues at the first school, and the target—without proper support and intervention—will be in a weakened state and an even more vulnerable target at the new school. But sometimes a move, with support and intervention, may be the best solution for your child. It was for Rachel, the girl mentioned in chapter 5, who, after suffering five and a half years of bullying, moved to a new school and thrived as she was "treated like a human again." I agree with Judith Rich Harris, author of *The Nurture Assumption*, who wrote, "If my kid were at the very bottom of the local totem pole, and if all the higher-ups were beating on him, I would want to get him out of there. Victims are victimized partly because they get a reputation for being victimizable, and it is extremely difficult to change the peer group's mind about things like that. Usually moving is a disadvantage for a kid because he loses his peer group and whatever status he had in it. But if the peer group is making his life miserable and his status is zero, he doesn't have much to lose."

The decision to change or not change a child's classroom or school is not a simple or easy one. Dan Olweus's four principles along with the three Ps and the five school-wide components listed in Steps to Respect can help you identify a school in which your child can thrive. These elements and components, combined with your knowledge of your child, as well as his own input, can help you choose the best option. Running away is not a solution, but sometimes moving to a more caring classroom or school is the best one.

A Bully on the Home Front

If it is your child who is doing the bullying, be he the main character or a henchman of the bully, the phone call from the school may leave you sad, angry, frustrated, and disappointed. It is important that you listen and not try to justify, rationalize, minimize, or make excuses for your child's bullying. ("The other boy must have asked for it." "Everyone calls everyone else names like that. Why are you picking on my son?" "He was just teasing." "His father and I are getting a divorce. It's not his fault that he is acting that way.") To get the most constructive outcome, Ted Feinburg of the National Association of School Psychologists recommends:

1. Strive to be non-defensive. You want to hear the school's concerns.
2. Ask exactly what happened. Try not to react emotionally.
3. Ask what the school has done to remedy the problem.
4. Ask your child what happened. (See chapter 9, "Is There a Bully in the House?")
5. If a meeting is scheduled to deal with the problem, make sure you understand the agenda. Write down any concerns you have about how the school is dealing with your child.
6. If your child acts differently at home, or if there are discipline strategies that have worked for you, tell the school official.
7. Work with the school to solve the problem. Make clear that you're an ally here and that you trust the school will act as an ally.

If you try to rescue your son or blame your son's target, you run the risk of shutting down any constructive communication and inviting defensiveness on the part of school personnel. As well, you are sending your son the message that you sanction his bullying. If the school uses punishment (suspension) instead of discipline, you can act as an advocate for both your son and for the child your son bullied by suggesting a plan that incorporates the seven steps discussed in chapter 9:

1. Intervene immediately with discipline.
2. Create opportunities to "do good."

3. Nurture empathy.
4. Teach friendship skills—assertive, respectful, and peaceful ways to relate to others.
5. Closely monitor your child's TV viewing, video game playing, computer activities, and music.
6. Engage in more constructive, entertaining, and energizing activities.
7. Teach your child to "will good."

Your son may still be suspended, but the suspension can be used constructively to fix what he did (restitution), figure out how he is going to keep it from happening again (resolution), and come up with a plan to heal with the child he has harmed (reconciliation). As an educator, I always welcomed ideas from parents who wanted to be a part of the solution, were willing to listen, and were open to suggestions from those of us who were with their children five hours a day.

You can discuss ways you will help your son do the seven steps and suggest how the educators working with your son can help. For instance, your son may be able to "do good" by reading to second graders or helping out in the library.

When Bullying Becomes a Crime

If your teenager's bullying has caused serious injury, irrevocable harm, or death (or if it was your child who was seriously harmed), you may want to read the chapter entitled "Mistakes, Mischief, and Mayhem" in my book *Parenting Through Crisis*. In that chapter, I address how families and communities around the world have used reconciliatory justice in the aftermath of such violence. Reconciliatory justice is a visible expression of forgiveness and the act of healing in a community. It is perhaps the one tool that can begin to cut through the chains of violence. It does not excuse the violence, and it does not deny the dignity and worth of the targeted person or the humanity of the bully. It does justice to the suffering without perpetuating the hatred. It is a triumph of mindfulness and compassion over vengeance and retribution. Reconciliatory justice is not about punishment; it's about maintaining human connections.

During the process, we hold out two hands to the bully—one of restraint, the other of compassion. The first hand keeps the bully from causing more harm to himself or to others; the second hand offers compassion to the bully, allows time for reflection, and invites reconciliation. As our two hands reach out, there is at once an attempt to bring about balance and a tension created that keeps both parties actively engaged in the reconciliatory process, as we strive to heal the rift created. We are attempting to restore community. The end goal is an embrace in which the bully takes responsibility as is warranted, is willing to make restitution, resolves to keep the bullying from happening again, and commits to once again becoming an active participant in the community. In that embrace, we are ready and willing to have him as a participating member of our community.

In April of 2002, the teenager who was convicted of threatening and harassing fourteen-year-old Dawn-Marie before she committed suicide agreed to participate in an aboriginal healing circle with Dawn-Marie's family. The dead girl's mother suggested that the healing circle be used because she was frustrated with the traditional justice system that didn't allow the families of the offender and the victims to communicate. Any sentence imposed by the healing circle would include actions that would invite healing and restoration. First Nations elder and author Ovide Mercredi writes in the book *In the Rapids*, "We use elders to deal with the source of the problems, not just the symptoms, and to correct the imbalance in the community by healing both the victims and the offenders. The focus is on healing and restoration, not the adversarial process and punishment . . . decisions would be rendered from the perspective of healing, compensation, and reconciliation as opposed to . . . punishment, deterrence, and imprisonment."

In *No Future Without Forgiveness*, Archbishop Desmond Tutu wrote about this same kind of justice, "We contend that there is another kind of justice, restorative justice, which is characteristic of traditional African jurisprudence. Here the central concern is not retribution or punishment. In the spirit of ubuntu the central concern is the healing of breaches, the redressing of imbalances, the restoration of broken relationships."

If creating more caring, more compassionate, less alienating, less violent communities is a goal, we must give up our desire for swift revenge and retribution, stronger punishments and stiffer sentences. When the main goal is to make children "pay dearly" for what they have done and serve as examples for others who might think of doing the same, hate and bitterness find rich soil in which to grow. How bullies are treated will influence what kind of people they will grow up to be and what kinds of lives the rest of us will live. If we don't help them reconcile with the community, we could well condemn ourselves to a lifetime of fear, distrust, and mayhem.

When an entire community is committed to reconciliatory justice, bullies are invited to rise above their misdeeds and violent acts. The goal is to mend and restore rather than isolate and punish. The search is not for vengeance, but for ways to heal people and relationships.

A Community Incident That Involved the School

Five peers at a sleepover at a classmate's home attacked a thirteen-year-old boy. He was taunted, then jumped on and slammed into furniture. He ended up with cuts and severe bruises that would be documented by a doctor and police the next day. In the meantime, too afraid to call home, he stayed the night and participated the next day in the school activity the boys were supposedly preparing for at the sleepover. During that day, he tried desperately not to call attention to himself. It was only when his mom picked him up from school that he broke down and told her about what his classmates had done the night before.

The school administrators decided to mount their own investigation side by side with the police and said that they were appalled that such a violent incident could occur among classmates at a private religious school. Their comment: "We will take steps to see that if it did occur, it won't again. The safety and well-being of our students is our top priority." It may have been a top priority—good policy—but there were no procedures in place to protect the bullied child. He returned to school after taking one day off. But the boys who beat him were now bragging about the attack and said they would "do worse if he didn't shut up about the incident." The thirteen-year-old then stayed home the rest of the week. (When procedures are not in place to immediately provide safety for the target and put some kind of restraint on the bullies—be it closer supervision, alterations to their schedule, or temporary exclusion—it is the bullied child who suffers once again by missing school out of fear of further bullying.)

Many of the older kids called the bullied boy and offered support and protection—true brave-hearted witnesses, resisters, and defenders instead of not-so-innocent bystanders.

His parents sent out letters to all of the parents in their son's class. None of the families of the bullies responded or apologized after receiving the letters. Frustrated by the lack of response from the parents of the bullies, the parents of the bullied child filed charges against the bullies, hoping the charges would convince them and their parents of the seriousness of the incident.

Once it moves into legal territory, an adversarial situation will probably develop whereby neither side will be able to talk with the other or reach any kind of reconciliation. This was the same frustration that Dawn-Marie's mother experienced as sides were drawn up and animosity grew. Consider the contrast if all of the parties agreed to some kind of healing circle. In the healing circle, each boy would be able to admit his own part in the incident and develop a plan for fixing what he did, figuring out how to keep it from happening again, and healing with the boy who was bullied. In such a setting, the main bully would have a different problem and thus a different plan and follow-up than the boy who joined in willingly, or the one who joined reluctantly but joined nevertheless, or the one who hung back, too scared to do anything but watch.

Such a circle can involve school personnel at all stages of the healing process, assessing meaningful consequences for each boy, following up on their plans to keep the bullying from happening again, and—as overseers of the social setting where the boys spend the most time—encouraging school activities that heal the rift and thus heal the school community.

A Bully in the Backyard

What do you do when the bully is right in your backyard, terrorizing your children and their peers who gather in your yard to play? It is important that you distinguish between the usual hassles, disagreements, and conflicts all kids engage in with one another and actual bullying. Kids themselves can handle most squabbles, and they should be encouraged to do so. But if it is bullying, you will want to intervene. It is helpful to both the bully and the bullied child if you can use the same steps you would have used if it was one of your children twisting your other child's arm behind his back (page 199). You can also appeal to the better side of the child's nature and invite her to do something helpful. "You are so strong, can you help me move this planter away from the sandbox?" As she is helping you, you can tell her how she is misusing her leadership skills and how she can use those skills in a better way. And make it a point to hang around within view and earshot of the group as they continue to play. As with schools, one of the easiest ways to ensure safety for kids is the physical presence of responsible adults.

If it is serious bullying and you are unable to get the bully to see the error of her ways, you may have to ask her to go home. If the situation happened at school, I recommend that you not call the parents directly but let the school act as an intermediary. In this case and other situations in your neighborhood, however, you may have to go it alone. When you call the bully's parent, just as you appealed to the better side of the bully's nature, you can appeal to her parent's better side as well. "I would like very much for your daughter and mine to play together. Today, an incident happened that I know you will want to know about. Can we get together and talk about it with both of the girls? It is important to me that our girls be able to play together."

The parent may still try to justify, rationalize, minimize, or make excuses for her daughter's behavior. Remember, just as you taught your children, you control only 50 percent of this relationship—you can't make the other parent help her daughter accept responsibility for her bullying behaviors. But the way you handle it will greatly influence her response to you. You are not attacking her child, you are attacking a problem, and you would like to offer her some solutions that worked for you with your children. At the end of the meeting, you will have a better idea of what you will need to do next. Ideally, it will involve giving the girl another opportunity to play at your house. But if there is no resolution, you may have to insist that for a while she will not be able to play in your yard. This is the least desirable outcome, but sometimes it is a necessary one. You can let the parent know that you would like to make this work for everyone and that you will check in at a later date to see if it can be worked out. Often, time and distance will make a difference in the way the parent views the situation and the way the daughter decides to play—especially if other parents approach the bully's parent with the same complaint.

Sometimes, it is helpful if a group of parents express the same concern together and do it in a way that is respectful and assertive. It will help no one if you gang up on the bully's parent and launch into a tirade about how awful her child is. But by standing up together, you can help your children be safe and help a bully come around to playing a new, more productive role in the neighborhood. During the time all of these interactions may take, it is important that you talk with your children about how to stand up for themselves, how to report any dangerous situations—and how to treat even this bully in a respectful way. When we respond with a generous spirit, wisdom, discernment, abundant kindness, and mercy, when we help alleviate the suffering of others and offer them our compassion and empathy, we create caring communities and safe harbors for all of our children.

Rewriting the Script

The bully, the bullied, and the not-so-innocent bystander—I hope you now have a clearer understanding of these roles and how the interactions involved in such role-playing, though commonplace in our culture, are not healthy, not normal, certainly not necessary, and, in fact, are devastating to the young people playing them. We as parents and educators can rewrite the script and create for our children alternative, healthier roles that require no pretense and no violence. A daunting task, but a necessary one. When farm workers organizing in the United States faced what appeared to be insurmountable obstacles in their fight for recognition of their dignity and worth as human beings, for decent wages, and for decent living conditions, human rights activist César Chávez challenged them to say "*Sí, se puede*" (Yes, it is possible). Breaking the cycle of violence and creating deeply caring communities: yes, it is possible.

> *Never doubt that a small group of thoughtful committed citizens can change the world. Indeed, it is the only thing that ever has.*

—**Margaret Mead**

appendix 1

Responding to Cyberbullying

Below is a quick guide to the escalating levels of response to a cyberbullying incident, adopted from the website www.StopCyber-bullying.org.

Talk to Your Child

Caution them about responding "in kind." This is not a time for them to lash out or start a cyber war themselves. See if they think they know the identity of the cyberbully or cyberbullies. See if this is related to an offline bullying situation, and deal with that quickly. And don't confuse the language most kids use online with cyber-bullying. It may be shocking to us, but unless it is shocking to your child, it's not cyberbullying.

Leave It Alone and Let It Go

A one-time, seemingly unthreatening act, like a prank or mild taunting, should probably be left alone, with the targeted kid "let-ting it go," recognizing it's the bully's problem, not your child's. This may be enough to convince the bully that it's not worth the effort to try to torment your child. (If it's a threat, you must report it.) At the same time, you may want to consider using some preventive measures, such as the ones that follow.

Restrict the People Who Can Send You Communications

Consider restricting all incoming communications to pre-approved senders, such as those on your child's buddy list. (If the cyberbully is someone on their buddy list, though, this method won't help. In that case the cyberbully will have to be removed from the buddy list and/or blocked.)

Restrict Others from Being Able to Add Your Child to Their Buddy List

Cyberbullies track when your child is online by using buddy lists and similar tracking programs. These programs will let them know when one of their "buddies" is online, when they are inactive and, in some cases, where they are. This is like adding a tracking device to your child's online ankle, allowing their cyberbullies to find them more easily and target them more effectively. This feature is usually found in the privacy settings or parental controls of a communications program.

Google Your Child

Make sure that the cyberbully isn't posting attacks online. When you get an early warning of a cyberbullying campaign, it is essential that you keep an eye on your child's screen name, nicknames, full name, address, telephone and cell numbers, and websites. You can also set up an "alert" on Google to notify you whenever anything about your child is posted online. To learn more about "Googling" yourself or your child, visit www.StopCyberbullying.org.

Block the Sender

Someone who seems aggressive or makes you or your child uncomfortable and does not respond to verbal pleas or formal warnings should be blocked. This way, they will not be able to know when your child is online or be able to contact them through instant messaging. Even if the communications are not particularly aggressive or threatening, if they are annoying, block the sender. (Most ISPs and instant messaging programs have a blocking feature to allow you to prevent the sender from getting through.)

"Warn" the Sender

If the cyberbully uses another screen name to avoid the block, otherwise manages to get through or around the block or communicates through others, "warn" them, or "notify" the ISP. (This is usually a button on the IM application.) This creates a record of the incident for later review, and if the person is warned enough, they can lose their ISP or instant messaging account. (Unfortunately, many cyberbullies use "warning wars" or "notify wars" to harass their victims, by making it appear the victim is really the cyberbully. This is a method of cyberbullying by proxy, getting the ISP to be an unwitting accomplice to the cyberbullying.)

Report to ISP

Most cyberbullying and harassment incidents violate the ISP's terms of service. These are typically called a "TOS violation" (for a "terms of service" violation) and can have serious consequences for the account holder. Many ISPs will close a cyberbully's account (which will also close their parents' household account in most cases.) You should report this to the sender's ISP, not yours. (If you use monitoring software, like Spectorsoft, this is much easier.)

If your child's account has been hacked or their password compromised, or if someone is posing as your child, you should make a formal report to *your* ISP as well. You can call them or send an e-mail to their security department (NOT their terms of service report line). But before changing your password, you should scan your computer for any hacking programs or spyware, such as a Trojan horse. If one is on your computer, the cyberbully may be able to access the new password. Most good anti-virus programs can find and remove a hacking program. All spyware applications can. We recommend SpyBot Search and Destroy (a freeware) or Ad-Aware (by Lavasoft; they have a free "lite" program).

Report to School

Most cases of cyberbullying occur off school grounds and outside of school hours. In the United States, often the school has no legal authority to take action relating to an off-premises and off-hours activity, even if it has an impact on the welfare of their students. The laws are tricky, and vary jurisdiction by jurisdiction. So while you should notify the school (especially if your child suspects who is behind the attacks), they may not be able to take disciplinary action. They can keep an eye on the situation in school, however. And since many cyberbullying incidents are combined with offline bullying incidents, your child may be safer because of the report.

Also, while the school may have limited authority over disciplining the cyberbully, they can call the parents in and try and address the situation. They can also institute an educational and awareness program to help stop further cyberbullying by students, and to help educate parents about the problem.

Report to Police

Someone who threatens you physically, who is posting details about your or your child's offline contact information or instigating a cyberbullying by proxy campaign should be reported to the police. (Although you should err on the side of caution and report anything that worries you.) Using a monitoring program, such as Spectorsoft, can facilitate the investigation and any eventual prosecution by collecting and preserving electronic evidence. (Printouts, while helpful in explaining the situation, are generally not admissible evidence.) If you feel like your child, you, or someone you know is in danger, contact the police immediately and cut off contact with this person or user, staying offline if need be until you are otherwise instructed. Do not install any programs, or remove any programs or take other remedial action on your computer or communication device during this process. It may adversely affect the investigation and any eventual prosecution.

Take Legal Action

Many cases of cyberbullying (like their adult cyber-harassment equivalent) are not criminal. Someone may come close to violating the law but may not cross the line. Most of the time, the threat of closing their ISP or instant messaging account is enough to make things stop. But sometimes, either because the parents want to make an example of the cyberbully or because it isn't stopping, lawyers need to be brought in. It may also be the only way you can find out who is behind the attacks.

Think carefully before you decide to take this kind of action. Even if you win in the end, it may take you two or three years to get there and cost you tens of thousands of dollars. You may be angry enough to start it, but make sure that you have something more than anger to sustain the long months and years of litigation.

appendix 2

Internet and Social Media Terms

Third Parent: Protective Parenting for the Digital World (www. ThirdParent.com) is a valuable resource for parents and educators to help young people navigate the digital world. They have developed material for parents of kids under thirteen, parents of teens, and professionals. Third Parent has listed some common and uncommon Internet and social media terms and their definitions. They encourage you to e-mail them at info@ThirdParent.com if there is something you can't find or don't understand.

Adware—a program that delivers targeted advertising content to users often by gathering information from a user's computer about what that person does online and which websites are visited.

Android—mobile operation system for cell phones designed by Google.

App—a specialized computer program typically downloaded to mobile devices.

Capper—a social media user, usually in a video chat forum, who tries to trick others into exposing themselves.

Catfish—someone who uses social media or other online communication to impersonate another. Usually used to create a bogus romantic relationship either to extract money or to embarrass.

Checkin—convention which allows social media users to inform others of their location.

Cyberbullying—any bullying that uses electronic technology, including cell phones, computers, and tablets as well as communication tools such as social media sites, text messages, chat, and websites.

Doxing—the process of Internet users exposing the true identity of another user, even though that user has been posting anonymously.

DM—direct message—a message sent privately from one Twitter user to another. Two users must both follow each other to send a DM.

DoS—denial of service attack. In a DoS attack, the target's device or servers are flooded with so much Internet traffic that the legitimate users can't get through.

Geolocation—identification of the real-world geographic location of an object using radar, a computer, or a mobile device via the Internet.

Geotag—metadata added to pictures or other media that allows one to identify the location of said media.

Hack—the act of altering a computer program or the operating system of an electronic device to perform functions not intended by the original designer or manufacturer.

Hashtag (#)—a label used on Twitter, Google+, Instagram, and Facebook to make posts more easily searchable. Can also be added as a humor device.

iOS—mobile operation system (for cell phones) designed by Apple. Only available on Apple hardware.

IP Address—unique address that identifies where a computer connected to the Internet is located.

Jailbreak—a computer hack usually performed on a mobile device, which enables the user to run programs or apps that were not permitted by the device manufacturer or cell phone carrier.

Like—a feature on Facebook that allows a user to endorse other users or their content.

Malware—short for malicious software—any software installed on a device or website designed to steal money, extract personal information, or take over your device.

Metadata—data that provides information about other data, such as Internet content.

Neknomination—a social media/drinking/dare game favored by teens and young adults that has been linked to at least four deaths recently.

Phishing—an attempt, by e-mail, text, or other communication to install malware on your computer or device for the purposes of stealing money or extracting personal information.

Photo Sharing—enabling other users to view your photo or video content by transmission via text, e-mail, or app or by posting it to a social network or photo hosting site.

Pin—an element of content posted to the social media network Pinterest.

Privacy Policy—part of the terms of use of a social media network or app which states, among other things, how the network may collect and use your personal information.

Retweet—on Twitter, reposting a tweet posted by another user. Once the tweet is retweeted, if the original sender deletes the tweet, the tweet will remain online.

Revenge Porn—sometimes call involuntary porn—posting nude or sexually suggestive photos or videos of another person to the Internet without their permission.

Sexting—the act of sending someone sexually explicit messages, photographs or video, usually via cell phone.

Share—posting content to social media, usually so that it can be viewed by others.

Skype—Internet telephony software and services owned by Microsoft.

Social Media—websites or online platforms designed to allow users to communicate and share information.

Social Network—online community of people, often sharing a common interest.

Spyware—a software program that monitors your computer usage without your knowledge.

Subtweet—a Twitter message sent to or about another Twitter user, without specifically naming that Twitter user. Can be used for bullying or harassment.

Tag—in Facebook, tagging someone links your post to that friend's timeline. The tag may indicate that the friend was at an event or that you are trying to share your post with them.

Tor—a service that allows Internet users to browse the Web anonymously. Tor is often used by individuals engaged in illegal activity.

TOS—terms of service—the rules that users of social media sites or apps are subject to, and the list of rights and protections offered them by the platform.

Troll—a person who does or says something on the Internet or social media with the goal of getting a response (usually anger or frustration) or attention.

Tweet—a message sent on social network Twitter.

Vague Booking—posting a deliberately vague message on a social media network that is understood by your friends but not by parents, teachers, or other authority figures.

Virus—a malicious piece of computer code that can replicate itself.

appendix 3

Responding to Revenge Porn

The problem of nonconsensual distribution online of intimate images, i.e., "revenge porn" or "nonconsensual porn," is a growing concern for tweens, teens, and young adults—and their parents. The campaign "End Revenge Porn" (www.EndRevengePorn.org), organized by the Cyber Civil Rights Initiative, advocates for technological, social, and legal innovation to fight this menace and provides direct support and referrals for take-down services to young people who are targeted by former friends or lovers. ERP operates a Web support system for people who have been targeted throughout the world and a twenty-four-hour toll-free hotline (844-878-CCRI) for people needing such help in the United States.

Collaborating with law firms such as K&L Gates (www.Cyber-RightsProject.com) and private attorneys to provide pro bono legal services to young people who have been targeted, ERP works with major social media and tech companies to develop policies and procedures to prevent the proliferation of revenge porn. It also works with U.S. legislators on a local and federal level to draft legislation to prohibit this practice, which can destroy a young person's reputation and well-being in an instant.

To help young people make wise choices about photos they have in their possession, the Cyber Civil Rights Initiative created the following flowchart. Although the chart explains that you can post sexually explicit pictures of yourself online, this is true only if you are not underage. Tweens or young teens can get into legal trouble for creating and/or posting child pornography, even if the picture in question is of themselves. It is important to remember that new laws deal with more than nude photos. The Illinois revenge porn law recognizes that targeted young people "can be deeply harmed by non-consensually distributed sexual images regardless of nudity."

If in doubt, don't upload it, download it, share it, or store it.

FLOWCHART

FOR ANYONE IN POSSESSION OF NUDE PHOTOS

So, you have some nude photos and you're not sure what to do with them. Cyber Civil Rights Initiative has developed this easy-to-follow flow chart to help you out.

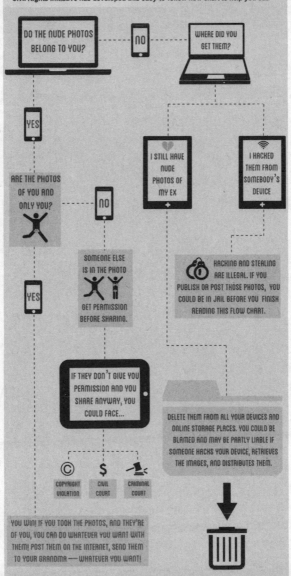

DO THE NUDE PHOTOS BELONG TO YOU?

NO

WHERE DID YOU GET THEM?

YES

ARE THE PHOTOS OF YOU AND ONLY YOU?

NO

I STILL HAVE NUDE PHOTOS OF MY EX

I HACKED THEM FROM SOMEBODY'S DEVICE

SOMEONE ELSE IS IN THE PHOTO GET PERMISSION BEFORE SHARING.

YES

HACKING AND STEALING ARE ILLEGAL. IF YOU PUBLISH OR POST THOSE PHOTOS, YOU COULD BE IN JAIL BEFORE YOU FINISH READING THIS FLOW CHART.

IF THEY DON'T GIVE YOU PERMISSION AND YOU SHARE ANYWAY, YOU COULD FACE...

DELETE THEM FROM ALL YOUR DEVICES AND ONLINE STORAGE PLACES. YOU COULD BE BLAMED AND MAY BE PARTLY LIABLE IF SOMEONE HACKS YOUR DEVICE, RETRIEVES THE IMAGES, AND DISTRIBUTES THEM.

COPYRIGHT VIOLATION

CIVIL COURT

CRIMINAL COURT

YOU WIN! IF YOU TOOK THE PHOTOS, AND THEY'RE OF YOU, YOU CAN DO WHATEVER YOU WANT WITH THEM! POST THEM ON THE INTERNET, SEND THEM TO YOUR GRANDMA — WHATEVER YOU WANT!

FOR MORE INFORMATION VISIT WWW.ENDREVENGEPORN.ORG

Acknowledgments

My heartfelt thanks to:

David Kent, president of HarperCollins Canada—the one who asked me to write the book and trusted that I could—for being there to listen, question, and put the energy and resources into making this book possible.

Toni Sciarra, senior editor at HarperCollins (US) for your keen eye, probing questions, and ability as taskmaster. I am grateful for your patience, support, and friendship through all of my writing projects.

Brad Wilson, my editor at HarperCollins Canada, for hanging in there with me through the good, the bad, and the ugly. I appreciate your support, keen insight into the topic of bullying, and the calm you bring to my chaotic writing.

Iris Tupholme, publisher of HarperCollins Canada, for your encouragement, support, and willingness to listen to my arguments for early publication in spite of my tardiness with the completed manuscript—and doing whatever it took to make it happen. You are amazing.

Patrick Crean, my literary agent, for listening to me rant about never, ever writing another book and then being there with your wisdom, knowledge, and humor every step of the way through this writing adventure.

Nicole Langlois, for orchestrating the production of the first edition of this book, bringing together such talented people as copy editor Sona Vogel, typesetter Roy Nicol, and proofreader Carolyn Black—wow!

Noelle Zitzer, senior managing editor at HarperCollins Canada, for bringing all of the necessary people together to make this thoroughly updated edition possible.

Copy editor Natalie Meditsky, for your keen eye and thoughtful questions. You not only caught my grammatical errors but challenged me to be more succinct and accurate.

Proofreader Deborah Viets, for catching what I missed.

Ruth Pincoe, for creating an index that goes beyond the usual topics and pages, and connects terms, themes, and authors for easy reference.

Alan Jones, for creating a new cover that tied the two editions together yet is unique and distinct.

Lisa Bettencourt, for meticulously typesetting the manuscript.

Ian Murray, with a deadline looming and me at my wit's end, for your invaluable assistance in cutting through the red tape to finalize the many permission requests.

Martha Watson, director of publicity, Sara James, senior publicist, and Lisa Zaritzky, publicist, for your creativity and talent for getting the word out and your willingness to create a book tour for the first edition that was more than a book tour.

Publicist Julia Barrett, who studied my work in university and who, with passion and skill, helped create a fascinating book tour for this latest edition.

Julie Hauck, for giving freely of your time, phenomenal research skills, and graphic design talent, but most of all for dialoguing with me as I explored the concept of contempt as it related to bullying. I am grateful for your insight and wisdom.

Satomi Morii Okubo, for keeping our office running and my

schedule in some semblance of order, for your insight into the cultural difference between bullying in the United States and your homeland, Japan, but most of all for your friendship.

Parry Aftab, for your insights and humor, and for freely sharing your expertise and advice in the realm of cyberbullying.

Sandy Garossino, for introducing me to the works of the phenomenal Shane Koyczan, and for sharing your passion and commitment for the Red Hood Project. Your passion is contagious.

Raffi Cavoukian, for reaching out to me and introducing me to your insightful and thought-provoking book, *#Lightwebdarkweb*, and to the Red Hood Project. I thank you for welcoming me into the discussion about both the light and dark of the Web and so powerfully demonstrating to me how we can't optimize the benefits of the Web for our children unless we act to reduce its social, ecological, and health hazards.

My friends and colleagues, Linda Ingram, Sally Hauck, Dee Jaehrling, Michael McManus, Derek Okubo, Dianne Reeves, Nancy Samalin, Randy Binstock, Christine Moore, Carol Jonas, Frank Gaskill, and Carol Todd for sharing your stories, your research, your expertise and suggestions.

Barry McCammon, a science educator and author, and Donna Wilson, an educator, counselor, and family mediator, for reading the entire manuscript from an educational perspective and offering your thoughtful criticisms and suggestions.

The authors I have quoted throughout this book, whose writings have greatly influenced my work.

My three grown children, Anna, Maria, and Joseph, for your love, encouragement, and daily presence through phone calls, e-mails, and quick visits.

Anna and Maria, for once again pitching in to find facts, search for obscure books, and share childhood stories, and for inviting me on journeys away from my desk—even if one of those journeys included rolling a sea kayak.

Joseph, for capturing in your sketches the contempt, pain, and complicity played out in the Bullying Circle.

Adriana, Chance, and Dominic, for making grandmotherhood such a joy and for giving me a reason to update this book so that you can be free to be . . .

Don, for not only keeping both our home books and our office books in the black while I buried myself in the research for this book, but for laughing, crying, and celebrating with me as we watched our three kids embark on their own journeys away from home and begin to build their own families.

—Barbara Coloroso, July 2002; February 2015

Sources

Excerpt from the motion picture *The Breakfast Club*. Copyright © 2003 by Universal Studios. Courtesy of Universal Studios Publishing Rights, a Division of Universal Studios Licensing, Inc. All rights reserved. Excerpt from the motion picture *Chocolat*. Reprinted courtesy of Miramax Films. Excerpt from Janna Juvonen and Sandra Graham, *Peer Harassment in School*. Reprinted courtesy of Guildford Press. Excerpt from Dr. Phillip McGraw, "We're in Crisis," in *O Magazine* (June 2001). Reprinted courtesy of the author. *Lost Boys: Why Our Sons Turn Violent and How We Can Save Them* by James Garbarino. Copyright © 1999 by James Garbarino. Reprinted with permission of The Free Press, an imprint of Simon & Schuster Trade Publishing Group. *The Nurture Assumption: Why Children Turn Out the Way They Do* by Judith Rich Harris. Copyright © 1998 by Judith Rich Harris. Reprinted with permission of the Free Press, an imprint of Simon & Schuster Trade Publishing Group. Excerpt from Neil Kurshan, *Raising Your Child to Be a Mensch*. Reprinted with the permission of Scribner, an imprint of Simon & Schuster Adult Publishing Group. Copyright © 1987 Neil Kurshan. Excerpt from Tim Field, *Bullycide, Death at Playtime: An Expose of Child Suicide Caused by Bullying*. Reprinted courtesy of the author. See his website for more information at www.SuccessUnlimited.co.uk. Excerpt from Professor Lewis P. Lipsitt's article in *Children & Adolescent Behavior Letter* (May 1995). Reprinted courtesy of Manisses Communications Group, Inc. Excerpt from Carl Upchurch, *Convicted in the Womb*. Reprinted courtesy of Bantam Books, a division of Random House Inc. Excerpt from Chuck Green, "Jocks Still Hold Sway at School," in the *Denver Post* (May 23, 1999). Reprinted courtesy of the *Denver Post*. Excerpt from Keith Sullivan, *The Anti-Bullying Handbook*. Reproduced by permission of Oxford University Press Australia. Copyright © Oxford University Press, www.OUP.com.au. Excerpt from "Don't Laugh at Me," Copyright © 1998 Sony/ATV Tunes L.L.C., David Aaron Music and Built on Rock Music. All rights on behalf of Sony/ATV Tunes L.L.C. and David Aaron Music administered by Sony/ATV Music Publishing, 8 Music Square West, Nashville, TN, 372032. All rights reserved. Used by permission. Excerpt from *Protecting the Gift* by Gavin de Becker. Copyright © 1999 by Gavin de Becker. Used by permission of The Dial Press/Dell Publishing, a division of Random House, Inc. Excerpt from Alexandra Shea, "What I Didn't Do at Summer Camp," in the *Globe and Mail* (May 28, 2001). Reprinted courtesy of the author. Excerpt from John Betjeman, *Summoned by Bells*. Reprinted courtesy of John Murray (Publishers) Ltd. Excerpt from Dr. Dan Olweus, *Olweus' Core Program Against Bullying and Antisocial Behavior: A Teacher Handbook*. Reprinted courtesy of the author. Excerpt from Archbishop Desmond Tutu, *No Future Without Forgiveness*. Reprinted courtesy of Doubleday, an imprint of Random House Inc. Excerpt from John W. Gardner, "National Renewal," a speech given to the National Civic League. Reprinted courtesy of the author. Excerpt from Michele Borba, *Building Moral Intelligence*. Copyright © 2001 by the author. Reprinted by permission of John Wiley & Sons, Inc. Excerpt from *Cliques, Phonies & Other Baloney* by Trevor Romain © 1988. Used with permission from Free Spirit Publishing Inc., Minneapolis, MN; 1-800-735-7323; www.FreeSpirit.com. All rights reserved. Excerpt from Paul Keegan, "Culture Quake," in *Mother Jones* (November/December 1999). Copyright © 1999 by the Foundation for National Progress. Reprinted courtesy of the publisher. Excerpt from *Teaching the Child Under Six* by James L. Hymes. Copyright © by the author. Reprinted by permission of Pearson Education, Inc., Upper Saddle River, NJ. Excerpt from A. Westbrook and O. Ratti, *Aikido and the Dynamic Sphere*. Published by Charles E. Tuttle Co. Inc., of Boston, Massachusetts and Tokyo, Japan. Chapter Eight epigraph from *To Kill a Mockingbird* by Harper Lee. Copyright © 1960 by Harper Lee. Copyright Renewed © 1988 by HarperLee. Reprinted by permission of HarperCollins Publishers Inc. For additional territory contact Eugene Winick, McIntosh & Otis, 353 Lexington Avenue, Flr. 15, New York, NY 10016. Excerpt from Beth Duff-Brown's article reprinted with permission of the Associated Press. Excerpt from "Chapter 1: Sweden," by Dan Olweus, in P. K. Smith et al., *Bullying: A Cross National Perspective*. Reprinted courtesy of Thomson Publishing Services. Excerpt from *Nobody Left to Hate: Teaching Compassion after Columbine*, © 2001 by Elliot Aronson. Reprinted by permission of Henry Holt and Company, LLC. Excerpt from "Our Estrangement from God," by Rabbi Michael Lerner, from *From the Ashes: A Spiritual Response to the Attack on America*, © 2001 by Rodale, Inc. and Beliefnet, Inc. Reprinted courtesy of Rodale Inc. Excerpt from *Family Politics* by Letty Cottin Pogrebin. Copyright © 1993 by Letty Cottin Pogrebin. Originally published by McGraw-Hill Book Company. No part of this material may be reproduced in whole or in part without the express written permission of the author or her agent. Excerpt from Martin Luther King Jr.'s speech reproduced with permission of his estate. Excerpt from Dr. Howard Spivak, "Bullying Behaviors Among U.S. Youth," in the *Journal of the American Medical Association* (265:16). Reprinted by permission of the United States Federal Government. Excerpt from Dianne S. Reeve's letter to the author is reproduced with her kind permission. Michael McManus's story is reproduced here with his kind permission. Hoss's story is reproduced here with Christine Moore's kind permission. Randy Binstock's story is reproduced here with his kind permission. Quick guide to the escalating levels of response to cyberbullying from the website www.StopCyberbullying.org. Used with permission. Internet and Social Media Terms by Third Parent: Protective Parenting for the Digital World, used with permission. See www.ThirdParent.com. Flowchart in Appendix 3 reprinted by permission of Cyber Civil Rights Initiative.

Index

Page references in *italics* indicate an illustration.

Index

283, 307; fears of, 147–48; as henchmen, 19, 143, *146,* 239, 256, 283, 307; impact of bullying on, 2–3, 140–42; intervention skills for, 147–48; as passive supporters, 143, *146,* 283; as potential defenders of target, 143, *146,* 283; reasons for non-intervention, 147–50, 259–61; trap of comradeship for, 142, 144, 294; typecasting of, 14–15; witness/defender roles for, 79, 97, 258–60, 267–69, 284–85

calumny, 76
Can We Be Good Without God? (Buckman), 218
Canada: Canadian Human Rights Act, 281; Canadian Human Rights Commission, 92; Criminal Code of Canada, 281
capper, 333
caring: and empathy, 195–96, 207–208; and perspective, 207–8
Carney, Michael, 67
Carroll, Maxine, 155
Carter, Stephen L., 217
catfish, 333
Cavoukian, Raffi, 287, 288
cell phones: cell-phone bullying, 64–66; incidents recorded on, 56–57; used for gaming, 68, 291; used for texting, 291, 335; used in cyberbullying, 60, 63–64, 278, 280–82, 284
Central Kings Rural High School (Cambridge, Nova Scotia), 156
Chabris, Christopher, 105
Champion, Robert, 53
character actor, 13, 143
chat rooms, 290
Chávez, César, 325
checkin, 333
children: accountability in families, 185; artwork by, 128, 223; bullied by adults, 124, 262–63; code of silence, 59, 123, 149, 228–29; constructive activities for, 197, 216; criminalization with zero-tolerance policies, 306–7; education of the whole child, 309–10; Internet/cyber safety for, 274, 287–88; Internet mastery of, 275–76; listening to, 224, 230–31; negative influences on, 211–12; personality factors, 233; safety in schools, 293–94, 314, 315–16; social behaviors and skills, 241–42; talking about bullying with, 223–28; warning signs of bullying, 125–28, 222–23. *See also* schools
Children and Adolescent Behavior Letter (Lipsitt), 107
Children and Bullying (Rigby), 39

Children Now (advocacy group), 23
circle of caring, 18, 182, 188, 202, 214
civil rights movement, 159–60
civility: cyber civility, 274; elements of, 212; erosion of, 150, 260; fragility of, 106
cliques, 44, 79–82, 149, 210, 310–13
Cliques, Phonies, & Other Baloney (Romain), 210
Coalition of Immokalee Workers (CIW), 159–60
code of silence, 59, 123, 149, 228–29
coding, 64
Coleman, Arthur, 308
Coloroso, Barbara: *kids are worth it!,* 167, 168, 244; *Parenting Through Crisis,* 318
Coloroso, Joseph (Joey), 142, *146*
Columbine High School, 80–82, 149, 271, 311–12
compassion: bully's lack of, 193; corruption of, 141; definition and characteristics of, 40–41; link with empathy, 205; restraint combined with, 319
competition, 171–72, 188
computer games. *See* games and gaming
Comstock, George, 215
confident bully, 109
conflict: bullying distinguished from, 98, 100–101, 103, 198, 202; fight/flee/freeze reactions to, 245; harmonious interactions, 253–54; peace as an embracing of, 247
conflict resolution: in bullying prevention programs, 103–4; in family environment, 180, 184, 245–47; necessity of, 101; peaceful process for, 245–47; preceded by discipline process, 104, 106, 202–3; role of anger in, 246–47; skills for, 212, 244–47
conflict resolution workshops, 202
contempt: apathy linked with, 148; and indifference, 148; link with bullying, 42–46, 149, 202; psychological characteristics of, 43–44
continual and repeated acts of malice: legal recognition as bullying, 295; as marker of bullying, 18–19, 49, 50–51, 70, 84, 88; vertical vs horizontal, 70
Convicted in the Womb (Upchurch), 44–45
Cope, Stephen, 249–50
Cornell University, 129
corruption: of empathy or sympathy, 41–42; wrong players accused of, 78–79
Craig, Wendy M., 24, 145, 261
criminal bullying, 89–91, 101–3, 318–20
"Culture Quake" (Keegan), 214
Cyber Civil Rights Legal Project, 282
Cyber Civil Rights Initiative (CCRI), 282, 337, *339*

cyber civility, 274, 276, 284–85
cyber safety, 274, 276–77
cyber savvy, 274, 276
cyberbullying, 60–70, 273–92; defined, 334; anonymity of, 63–64, 66, 67, 70; and changing nature of childhood, 60, 273–76; and cyber civility, 276; cyber sexual bullying, 69–70; escalating levels of response to, 327–32; flowchart for nude photos, 337–38, *339*; illegality of, 281–82; parents' role in preventing, 37, 65; prevention policies, procedures, and programs for, 285–86; by proxy, 283–84, 291, 329; public, permanent, and pernicious aspects of, 286; and Red Hood Project, 286–88; reporting of, 279–80, 282–83, 284; responses to, 280–82; with rumors, 76; suicides resulting from, 60, 62–63; tactics for witnesses in, 284–85; vertical vs horizontal, 70; with weight-based targeting, 29. *See also* Internet
cycle of violence: broken by antidotes to bullying, 233; broken by brave-hearted witness, 144–45, 160; broken by caring communities, 165–66; broken by changing roles, 210; broken by changing vocabulary, 236; broken by community building, 325; broken by empowered children, 191, 233; broken by reconciliation, 251; broken by restoration of balance, 254; broken with a new rule, 76–77; replaced by circle of caring, 182, 202

Dacunha, Erika, 117–18
Dail, Danielle, 45–46
D'Amico, Elisa, 282
dangerous stranger online (DSO), 290
Darby, Joseph, 155–56
De Becker, Gavin, 116, 134–36
Deacon, Sister Florence, 94
Deal, Terrence, 309
decision-making. *See* discernment and decision-making
Defying Hitler (Haffner), 144
dehumanization: with racism, 43, 45; with sexual bullying, 92; of target by peers, 144; violence as, 192
Dembrowsky, Constance, 301–2
"The Demise of Guys" (Zimbardo), 213
democracy, 183–84, 293
denial of service (DoS) attack, 334
Denmark, 154, 165, 263
depression: in bullied bullies, 111; in bullies, 134; with cyberbullying, 279; and media violence, 215; in targets of bullying, 18–19, 20, 29, 130, 241; as a warning sign, 134, 137

desanctification, 192
difference(s): intolerance toward, 18, 64–65, 80–81, 97, 150, 193; targets singled out because of, 112, 114–15, 116, 118–19
DiGiacomo, David, 82
digital attacks. *See* cyberbullying
dignity and respect: of bully in discipline process, 198; in the cyber world, 277; in four-step discipline process for bullies, 198; and hope, 302; in I/Thou/We relationships, 40; of individual and group, 38; in peaceful conflict resolution, 247; in restorative (reconciliatory) justice, 318–20; and self-worth, 224, 233–37; with three gates for our words, 258; universal right to, 325
direct message (DM), 334
disabilities: autism, 157–59; children defined by, 14; disability-based targeting, 26, 91, 115, 242; dyslexia, 266–67; and friendships, 242; impulsive aggression against, 100; learning disabilities, 110, 242; neurological damage, 196; and proximity bias, 30
"Disarming the Rage" (Arias), 120
discernment and decision-making: for bystanders, 149–50; for cyber safety and civility, 277; for dealing with anger, 250; family background for, 174, 184, 189, 265; for teasing vs taunting, 85; for telling vs tattling, 228–32; for willing good, 217, 219; for witnesses, 166, 262
discipline: for cyberbullying, 278–79; defined, 197; in families, 178, 184–85; vs punishment, 198–99, 294, 317; in seven-step plan, 197–204, 251, 256–57
disengaged onlookers (of bullying), 143, *146*, 259, 283, 307
dissing, 64
DM. *See* direct message
doing good. *See* goodness and morality
"Don't Laugh at Me" (Seskin and Shamblin), 113, 309
DoS attack. *See* denial of service attack
doxing, 334
drug abuse. *See* substance abuse
DSO. *See* dangerous stranger online
Duckwitz, Georg, 154
Duff-Brown, Beth, 263–64
Dynamix Adventures Inc., 303
dyslexia, 266–67

Eddington, Arthur, 144
Education Support Professionals (ESPs), 25–26, 27
educators: as bullies, 29, 40, 87, 262; response to bullying reports, 78–79, 104, 299, 304–5; role in bullying prevention, 304, 308; as

Index

Stoppard, Tom, 142
substance abuse (drugs, alcohol, etc.): of
    bullied bullies, 111; of parents, 177;
    prevalence of, 23; as a warning sign, 134,
    137; zero-tolerance policies on, 305
subtweet, 336
Sufism: three gates for words, 258
suicide: of bullied victims, 3–9; bullycides,
    3, 41, 51, 129–33, 286, 308; linked to
    instant messaging, 62–63; linked to verbal
    bullying, 71–72; murder-suicides, 74; of
    transgendered youth, 34
Sullivan, Keith, 94–95
sympathy, 40–42; bully's lack of, 193;
    corruption or negation of, 41, 42, 141; and
    empathy, 40–41, 205
Szwarcok, Corey, 303

Taffel, Ron, 240
tags, 336
Take-Two Interactive, 68
Tarasewicz, Benjamin, 157–58
target consent, 54
targets (victims) of bullying, 113–39, 220–54;
    adults' knowledge of, 122–24; aggression
    or violent actions of, 120–21, 133–38,
    235–36, 307–8; anger or rage of, 18–19, 20;
    blamed for bullying incidents, 19, 90, 95,
    149, 227, 317; buddy programs for, 239–40;
    as bullied bullies, 110–11; bullies posing
    as, 284; bullycides of, 3, 41, 51, 129–33,
    286, 308; in bullying playscript/scenario,
    16–21; bullying prevention procedures
    for, 285–86, 321; as caring, creative, and
    thoughtful individuals, 267; characteristics
    of, 113–21; of cyberbullying, 279–83;
    dehumanization of, 43, 45, 72; depression
    of, 18–19, 20, 29, 130, 241; educators as,
    74–75, 87; friendships among, 242; hope
    and resilience for, 302; hopelessness and
    helplessness of, 122–23, 135, 220–22,
    225; myths and rationalizations about,
    115–16, 119; parents' steps for, 223–28,
    313–16, 323–24; personality factors of, 233;
    physical/mental disabilities of, 26, 91, 115,
    242; portrayed as "losers," 72, 115, 148,
    172, 257; potential defenders of, 143, 146,
    283; restorative justice for, 318–20, 322;
    safety for, 238, 293–94, 314, 315–16, 321;
    school changes for, 315–16; self-blame of,
    27, 234; self-harm by, 27–28; warning signs
    for, 125–28, 133–38, 222–23; weakening
    and victimization of, 119–21; weight-based
    victimization (WBV), 26; as witnesses or
    role models, 157–59, 301–2

tattling. See under telling
taunting: defined, 84–85; vs teasing, 78, 82–86
teachers. See educators
Teaching the Child Under Six (Hymes), 219
team-building programs, 303
teasing: defined, 83–84; vs taunting, 78, 82–86
technology-assisted bullying. See cyberbullying
"Teens and the Screen Study," 35
"A Teen's Story of Allergy Bullying—and
    Bravery" (Dacunha), 117–18
Teilhard de Chardin, Pierre, 192
television. See media (television, Internet)
telling (reporting a bully): and code of silence,
    59, 123, 149, 228; confidentiality promised
    with, 75, 270, 285; courage required for,
    269–70; for cyberbullying and cybercrimes,
    276–77, 279–80, 281, 285; ground rules
    for, 269–70; reasons for bystanders'
    silence, 269–70; reasons for targets' silence,
    122–23, 220–22, 279–80, 282–83; reporting
    to school authorities, 313–15; vs tattling or
    ratting, 124, 221, 222, 228–32, 269, 280
terms of service (TOS), 329, 336
text messaging, 291; shorthand codes for,
    288–89
Thomas, Marlo, 92–93
threats: used by bullies, 47–48, 52, 63, 77, 193;
    used by parents, 170–71, 178–79
Thurber, James, 139
Tirukkural (Tamil text), 254
To Kill a Mockingbird (Lee), 255
"To This Day" (Koyczan), 157
Todd, Amanda, 286
Tongue Fu! (Horn), 237
Tor (web browser), 336
TOS (terms of service), 329, 336
trap of comradeship, 142, 144, 294
Tread Softly (Fleming), 130–31
troll, 336
Trudel, Jonathan, 62
Truth (app), 66, 67
Tutu, Desmond, 45, 152, 220, 320
Twain, Mark, 269
tweet, 336
typecasting, 13, 14

ubuntu (concept), 45, 320
United Nations Entity for Gender Equality and
    the Empowerment of Women, 34–35
United States of America: Centers for Disease
    Control and Prevention, 130; Civil Rights
    Act (1964), 92; Civil Rights Movement,
    159; Department of Education Office for
    Civil Rights (OCR), 308, 315
University of Bergen (Norway), 142